THE DIARY OF THE REV. RALPH JOSSELIN

THE DIARY OF THE REV. RALPH JOSSELIN

1616-1683

Edited for the Royal Historical Society

By

E. HOCKLIFFE M.A.

KALPAZ

ISBN: 978-93-5128-755-1(HB)

First Published in 1908
Indian Reprint in 2017

Published by

Kalpaz Publications
C-30, Satyawati Nagar,
Delhi – 110052
E-mail: kalpaz@hotmail.com
Website: kalpazpublications.com
Ph.: +91-9212142040

Cataloging in Publication Data—DK
Courtesy: D.K. Agencies (P) Ltd. <docinfo@dkagencies.com>

Josselin, Ralph, 1617-1683, **author.**
The diary of the Rev. Ralph Josselin, 1616-1683 / edited for the Royal Historical Society by E. Hockliffe (M.A.).
pages cm. — (Camden third series ; vol. XV)
Reprint. Originally published: London : Offices of the Society, 1908.
ISBN 9789351287551

1. Josselin, Ralph, 1617-1683—Diaries. 2. Prices—Great Britain—History. 3. Great Britain—History—Stuarts, 1603-1714. 4. Great Britain—Social life and customs—17th century. I. Hockliffe, E. (Ernest), 1863- editor. II. Royal Historical Society (Great Britain) III. Title. IV. Series: Camden third series ; vol. XV.

DA375.J67 2017 DDC 941.06 23

PREFACE

The diary of Ralph Josselin, Vicar of Earles Colne from 1640 to 1683, consists of 185 pages about 8 inches by 5 written very closely on both sides of the page in a very fine and clear hand. It is bound in calf with the royal arms stamped on either cover with the letter G on the one side and the letter K on the other side of the shield; doubtless this cover belonged originally to some other book. In the year 1702 the diary was still in the possession of the family as on one of the pages are the words " John Spicer his book;" it will be seen that a Mr. Spicer married the Vicar's youngest daughter Rebekah. Its subsequent history is unknown, until it was discovered among the late Mrs. Oliphant's books after her death; how it came into her possession is uncertain.

Less than half the original diary is here published. There are many entries of no interest whatever—endless thanks to God for his goodness " to mee and mine, " prayers, notes about the weather or his sermons, innumerable references to his constant " rheums " and " poses, " trivial details of every day life, records of visits to his friends etc. etc. The aim of the present edition has been to extract so much personal detail as is required to give a picture of the actual life of the author, and to include everything that possesses any historical interest. The author's spelling has been carefully preserved.

The entries in the diary are frequent and are made almost daily in the earlier years, but from about 1665 onwards the vicar seems to have made usually only one entry a week.

Ralph Josselyn belonged to the ancient family of Josselyn whose name is supposed to be connected with the town of Josselin in Brittany, the head of the senior branch of which is the Earl of Roden. There was a Ralph Josselyn of Roxwell in Essex, yeoman, whose will was proved on May 4, 1632; he had seven sons of whom the eldest was John. John Josselyn was born about 1583 and died in 1636, and was the father of the author of the diary: he had six other brothers one of whom, Thomas, emigrated to New England in 1635; and in Dr. Shaw's "History of the English Church during the Civil Wars &c." will be found the names of other members of the same family. The following extract from the will of Ralph Josselyn of Roxwell (the grandfather of the author of the diary) will show that the family was clearly well to do. "Ralph Josselyn of Roxwell in the county of Essex yeoman. To wife Dorothy a yearly rent of £20 for life, she abiding with my sons Ralphe and Symon. I have given unto my eldest son John his full part of my estate amounting to £800. To my son Richard £200 for his portion. To my son Joseph Josselyn £160." It will be seen from the diary April 30, 1647, that the author after some difficulty with his uncles received "free and peaceable possession of those parcels of land given to Joseph; this land part of our ancient inheritance; now I have about £20 per annum in land."[1]

Ralph was born on January 26, 1616-17, though, judging from an entry in the diary under the date January 25, 1654-5, "rose this morning and I found my birthday was 26 not this day as I thought hitherto", he had up to that time reckoned the 25th as the day of his birth. The greater portion of his life was spent at Earles Colne of which he became Vicar in the year 1640.

It is an ancient town which owes its prefix Earles to the fact that the Earls of Oxford were the founders of the Priory which flourished till the Dissolution. Effigies of some of the family may still be seen at the Priory, a comparatively modern house near the site of the ancient monastery. "The 17th Earl of Oxford sold Earles Colne, with

[1] My thanks are due to John H. Josselyn Esq. of Ipswich for this information about the Josselyn family; also to Mr. Ralph Nevill, F.S.A., for his interest in the subject.

the tombs of his ancestors, to his steward Roger Harlakenden for £2,000 in Sept. 1583" and with the Harlakendens of his day our Vicar was very intimate. The church itself was built in 1532 and upon the tower may be seen the quarterings of John de Vere, 16th Earl of Oxford, supported by two reindeer with boar for crest. From it in the year 1641 "upon an order of the House of Commons to that purpose we took down all images and pictures and such like glasses." The Vicar had come there in 1640, stayed with Mr. R. Harlakenden, preached on the Lords Day and "upon their approbacon they desired mee I would come and live with them as yr minister." So after he had "passed all with the bishop", he took "peaceable possession" in March 1640 and remained there till his death in 1683.

In the "Valor Ecclesiasticus" the value of the living appears as £8. 10*s*. 8*d*. but from the diary under the year 1640 it will be seen that the actual value was £80, made up as follows.

Tithes	£40. 0. 0.
Mr. Rich. Harlakenden wood and money	20. 0. 0.
His tenants in contribucon	2. 0. 0.
Mr. Thomas Harlakenden	3. 0. 0.
The town contribucon.	15. 0. 0.

But the Vicar rarely gathered in the whole of this income.[1]

Ralph Josselyn appears to have begun to keep a full record of his life only in the year 1644. In that year he wrote "Many things I have omitted; but now henceforward I shall be more exact and particular," and from that time till the day of his death we have a full account of his life. Through all the chances and changes of that time he remains Vicar of Earles Colne. No sketch of his career need be given here; its details are plainly recorded in the following pages and a study of them will give a very graphic picture of the life of this pious and at the same time business-like clergyman of the 17th century. By legacies, by profits from his farm, by augmentations to his living, by his salary as schoolmaster or as

[1] Further information upon this with the text of the Harlakenden endowment in 1673 will be found in Morant's *Essex*, ii, 214.

Chaplain to Col. Harlakenden's regiment, he gradually amassed a fortune which enabled him to portion one of his daughters with "my house I dwell in and land belonging thereto worth £400, and an £100;" to another daughter about a month later he gave "£500 down and with my blessing sent her away." "Halfe I have gained" he writes at another time "hath not been from Colne but on other occasions." Clearly he enjoyed a greater measure of prosperity than many a clergyman of that day.

The price of land, food, cows and pigs, the wages of servants, the cost of a birthday entertainment, the salary of a schoolmaster, the excise duty on hops—such details as these will be found scattered over the various pages of the diary. We may see the books he reads, we may watch him at work upon his Reconciler, in which he attempts to reconcile passages of scripture apparently contradictory, or discussing the choice of elders with other ministers; we may hear him lamenting "the heavy burthen of the book of Common Prayer;" at another time he tells us how he administers the Sacrament upon Easter day 1665—"I believe its 22 or 23 years since received on that day or occasion;" he is appointed "an assistant in ejecting of ministers or schoolmasters for inefficiency," he grumbles vigorously at the Quakers, he is summoned to the Bishop's court in 1669 for not wearing the surplice, and returns "safe;" he remained obstinate upon the point apparently till 1680. Under May 17 of that year he writes "Rid to court; the matter is the surplice which I see no sin to use and shall endeavour to live as quietly as may be to the end of my race."

The picture in fact is full of interesting detail, and perhaps more than enough has already been said to describe the general character of the book. Such as Josselyn was, no doubt were many of his contemporaries; pious and devout, a preacher of long sermons, a devoted adherent of the Parliament, a hater of Laud—"that great enemy of the power of godliness" he writes, "that great stickler for all the outward pomp in the service of God left his head on Tower Hill" and in that simple entry there sounds a note of triumph such as doubtless thrilled many a Puritan of that day. But devoted as he was to the Parliamentary cause, he yet laments "the black providence of putting the king to death," and is evidently reconciled to the return of Charles II. He has all the curious egotism which is the mark of a certain type of religious mind; when in one week he has lost both a child and a "dear friend," though he laments their deaths, he seems at the same time to regard them chiefly as a warning, in fact a "great mercy" sent by God to himself. (*vide* June 4, 1650.)

Yet with all his piety, his continued "exercises" and "expoundings, his "profitable and spiritual discourses," he combined a strict attention to his interests as a farmer, and shrewd business calculations jostle cheek by jowl with fervid expressions of piety. We hear that "Huggins is undone," and in the same breath that Josselyn has taken care to seize his crop for rent.

A kindly if somewhat self-seeking figure he lives again in the pages of this diary, and when his story ceases abruptly on July 27, 1683, with a broken entry, we feel with real sorrow that we have parted from a friend.

NOTE.

From a paper on the Harlakenden family contributed to the Topographer by G. Steinman (Windsor Herald) it appears that Josselin's diary was in the year 1847 in the possession of the family of Carwardine which is descended from the Harlakendens. The diary also seems to have been at Colne Priory in the year 1765. This information, for which I am indebted to Capt. Geoffrey Probert, Equerry to H.R.H. Princess Louise, Duchess of Argyll, unluckily reached me too late for insertion in the first page of the Preface.

THE DIARY OF THE

Rev. RALPH JOSSELIN

1616-1683

A THANKFULL OBSERVACON

OF DIVINE PROVIDENCE & GOODNESS TOWARDS MEE & A SUMMARY VIEW OF MY LIFE:

BY ME RALPH JOSSELIN.

Jan: 26: 1616: I was borne to the great joy of ffather & mother being much desired as being their third child and as it pleased God their only sonne. I had this happiness in my birth to bee the seed of the righteous, both parents being in the judgment of man gratious persons: the place of my birth was Chalke-end my ffathers patrimony: I was the eldest sonne in our whole ffamily and yett possest not a foote of land, in which yett I praise God I have not felt inward discontent & grudging; God hath given mee himselfe, and he is all and will make up all other things unto me. An: Dni 1616.

My father, selling his inheritance, retired from Roxwell to Bishops Stortford in Hartfordshire, where my ffather, my mother being received up into Heaven, gave mee good educacon, by his owne instruction, example & in schooles as I was capeable, I having devoted my selfe to the worke of the Lord in the Ministery. 1618:

In my infancy I had a gratious eye of providence watching over mee, preserving me from dangers by fire, a remembrance I shall carry to my grave on my right thigh; by knives, being stabd in the forehead by my second sister, a wild child, but now I hope God hath tamed & sanctifyed her spirit; falls from horse, water & many casualtyes.

But y[t] which I have most cause to admire was the goodness of God to preserve mee from poysonous infections from servants, & bestowing his grace upon me to restrayne mee from lewdnes; though full of spirit, and of a nimble head & strong memory, preserved from many untowardnesses that young boys fall into. I hope I shall never forgett Gods fitting mee for a scholler, and giving mee a spirit for the same, from which nothing would divert mee; at last God putt it into my fathers heart to listen to mee;

I confessse my childhood was taken with ministers and I heard with delight & admiracon & desire to imitate them from my youth, & would be acting in corners. 2. I had a singular affection to the historyes in the bible, being acquainted with all those historyes in very yong dayes, & so with divers historyes prophane & civill, upon which I emulated other languages that I might see what historyes were in those tongues. 3. My father was a widdowe, and my corrupt heart feared a mother in law & undoing by her & truly so it proved in respect of estate as will appeare : & y^r^ fore I desird to bee a scholler ; so should I make ye better shift if from home, & bee able to live of my selfe by Gods blessing.

My father, moved by God, yielded to my desires & placed mee with Mr Leigh, a painfull man to me, whom I have cause to love & blesse God for his labours, and praise the Lord for his blessings upon mee ; in the schoole I was active & forward to learne which contented my master & father : I thank God for his goodness to mee insomuch as for not saying my lessons I remember not that I ever was whipt ; once I was for an exercise when my master was passionate : it might bee I often might deserve it, yett I made it my aime to learne & lent my minde continually to read historyes : and to shew my spirit let me remember with greife that wch I yett feele : when I was exceeding yong would I project the conquering of kingdoms & write historyes of such exploits. I was much delighted with Cosmography taking it from my ffather. I would project wayes of receiving vaste estates & then lay it out in stately building, castles, libraryes, colledges & such like : & withal wh. was worse, oh ye strange prodigious uncleane lusts when I was yett a child ; how often have I walkt with delight to meditate upon such courses, being too well acquainted with those senes by bookes which I had ; yett I blesse God who kept mee from all outw^d^ uncleannesse ; praise bee to him, & for this I desire to loath & abhorre my selfe.

1631. In processe of time when I was growne up to 14 or 15 yeares of age my father marryed, upon wch he projected to raise an estate for mee, as he had sold his patrimony, for which my grandfather then gave his other lands from him, though the eldest, giving him only 10*l.* : wch according to his will was due to mee, which I had also duly payd to mee after 12 yeares by my two uncles his executors ; but that plott[1] fayled, my father loosing therby above 200*l.* : besides agst all my intreatyes went to farming, wherby he lost most part of his estate.

My fathers love was such towards mee that when I was neare 16 yeares old I went to Cambridge to Jesus Colledge, entred pentioner under Mr Tho : Lant my loving and I hope godly & honest *tutor*;[2] he dealt lovingly with mee, but I was forced to come from Cambridge many times for want of meanes & loose my time in the contry ; yett would I endeavour to gett it up & I thank God notwithstanding all hindrances I was not behind many of my time & standing : & now my fathers love would budd forth in expressions of love & teares towards mee exceedingly, living at Bumpsted in Essex under Mr Symons his landlord & Mr Borradale a godly man his *minister*. 1632 March.

I bless my God to restrayne mee by his grace from lewdness ; and in particular though my father loved me exceedingly & my mother in law, though I hope an honest woman, yett was of a somewhat soure spirit, yett I remember not that I ever caused any debate or division betwixt them for anything, though I was sensible of her disrespect in somethings towards mee : I can call to mind not many things in my life : in reference to my father I blesse God to give mee a spirit carefull to please him so that I had his blessing, being a joy & not a greife of heart unto him. He was greived that he should leave mee no estate, & I told him, if he had enough for himselfe, I hoped God would so blesse mee as that I should, if need were, bee helpefull to him : tis a continuall comfort to mee to thinke of my tender love to him, & my care for him in w^h I was able to do his business, for his creditt, for his estate ; much went through my hand and yett I gave him alwayes a just account, but only for about 5*s.* at one time, which I spent upon my selfe in his imployment & not lavishly.

When I came to Bumpsted I heard Mr Borradale with delight ;

[1] i.e. Plan of raising an estate.

[2] Words in italics have been supplied to fill up mutilations in the text.

whom God used as an instrument to doe mee good; when I heard him, my use was to walke home alone not with other boys or company, & stay not in the churchyard but immediately away, & meditate upon y[e] sermon & example my selfe by the same. I could not afterwards but relate y[e] same to him, who heard it with much joy & comfort; it was my constant course to performe dutyes of prayer betwixt God & my selfe twice & sometimes thrice a day, & to read the Scriptures.

Towards my sisters God gave mee a heart to seeke y[r] good in some measure, my father living and dead, & especially my sister Anna, in hindring her from marrying a widdow, when my father had cast her of, and in reconciling her unto him agayne & this I did before I was 17 yeares old. When my father was dead, in my poverty, I blesse God I did not forgett to doe for them.

Besides w[t] I sayd before of my slips, twice was I mistaken ignorantly & unadvisedly; my God forgive & pardon the same to mee in the bloud of his Christ, which I desire most earnestly; and I had too much familiarity with a neare & deare freind of mine, though I praise my God who kept mee from uncleannesse: the Lord tooke her away young, yett he gave mee all opportunity first to bemoane it with her, and to intreate her to seeke of God pardon & forgivenes for the same: I blesse the L[d] for that Spirit, y[t] having beene a cause with others of erring, the L[d] gave mee grace to lament it with y[e] partyes & aske them forgivenes, & advising them not to bee mislead by my example. I desire to look upon y[e] branch [1] always in respect of my selfe with trembling, and Gods preservacon with thankefulnes: oh y[e] opportunityes y[t] I have had in the affection of *this friend*; I should not have thought y[r] had been y[t] wantonnes in youth if my experience had not manifested the same.

In Cambridge in my studyes I was close & dilligent: my fault was to omitt too many mornings by reason of my tenderness, either in bed or by y[e] fire: y[e] supersticons of y[e] Church were a perplexity then unto mee. God gave mee mercy in blessing me with love and prospering in y[e] Colledge, few fallings out, but one to speake, by o[r]

[1] Tendency.

rashnes, wch wee lamented as being upon a Sabbath day when wee should have been at publique ordinances; their God kept from infection strangely.

For mŷ health, God was good unto mee; preserving mee from the small poxe when I have oftentimes beene neare & in danger.

While I was in this way compassed with mercyes being newly 1636
come up to Cambridge, on Tuesday night Oct: 25 came up my brother Hodson about 10 a Clocke at night and brought mee word my father was sicke, speechlesse, senseles, and like to dye: I rid home that night but had not ye comfort to have one word from him that he knew mee, so as on ffriday Octob: 28 my ffather gave up the ghost, and is now in rest, in joy & glory: he was about 53 yeares old o^r very nigh, and I wanted one quarter to 20. Now was my condicon sad, young, & freindles & pennyles, my father making no will. Octob: 30, wee buryed him in Bumpsted Church-yard: with greife of heart I layd him into the grave, but my God lives for evermore. My mother in law tooke not as I conceived a course to doe us justice; wee could not agree, I departed from her, tooke my degree at Cambridge Batchelor of art, with money I h^d from her, and putt my selfe into apparell, so that of 20*l.* my share in my fathers estate I spent 10*l.* before ffeb: 1, 1636.

But now w^t course should I take? Sometimes I thought upon my fathers farme, then upon the law, but God and the perswasions of Mr Borradale & Mr Thornlecke setled mee againe upon Cambridge; well, I tooke my degree & in ffeb: ult. Mr Thornlecke had word that one Mr Kempe of Sutton in Bedfordshire wanted an usher. I resolved to goe over thither with y^r letter, but I wanted money for my jorney: oh how ashamed was I to aske: one Edward Bell upon my intreaty lent me 5*s.* to pay my charges; oh how hardly with teares in my eyes did I looke upon upon my condicon; much a doe I procured a horse & a sadle: my proud heart thought y^s was very meane: in tedious wheather I went my jorney: providence cast mee upon a carryer y^t went y^t way, otherwise I could not have performed my jorney; I escaped some danger at Potton of miring, sett up my horse their & downe that night to Mr Kempes late ; he entertayned mee, but in conclusion he was provided of an usher and so my jorney was lost ; home I came with a sad heart, a tyred horse, & empty purse ; I rid almost all night because I neither would nor could pay another dayes horse hire ; when I was come home I borrowed 10*s*. of Mr Thornlecke to carry mee into Norfolke to my Unckles : thither I went, having payd my former 5*s*. ; my Uncle Benton entertaynd mee with love & pity & offered mee to stay a while with him ; here was providence, abroad I had none, money none, and frends were not so kinde as I expected ; oh but my God tooke mee up & had a care of mee, forever blessed bee his name. Now I was as it were at an anchor, when loe within 2 dayes, on Satturday at night, comes in a messenger with the offer of a place unto mee ; it came about thus ; Mr Kempe had a letter sent to him from Mr Neale of Deane in Bedfordshire to helpe him to an Usher ; he sent over kindly to Mr Thornlecke, and he to mee in Norfolke ; my Uncle Benton advised mee to accept the place ; I lookt upon it as a gratious providence, returned to Bumpsted, payd thee messenger, and resolved into a country & among persons that I never heard of before : all my things at Cambridge I sold to my sister Anna & in conclusion I gave her them : I made even with all the world, provided mee my horse, and suite of clothes, and coate which I borrowed at 1*l*. 13*s*. 4*d*. upon my Uncle Miles his creditt : when I had fitted all, disposed my bookes & some linnen in my trunke, I left it with a carryer to bring after mee : I tooke horse & rid towards Huntington ; I had in my purse, the charges of my jorney deducted, 1*l*. 5*s*. 9*d*. I was indebted 10*s*. above that formerly expressed for my coate : when I came upon the bridges betwixt Godmanchester & Huntington, I ruminated upon Jacobs speech, with my staffe I passed over this Jordan : my condicon was lowe, I went I knew not whither ; if I had not sett downe in this place, I had been undone : well I considered what a plentifull returne Jacob had : I considered, loe in this condicon thus lowe, a litle money, a few bookes and only 10*l*. my mother still ought mee of my part in my fathers estate ; I stayd and went softly and made this covent with God to serve him & wt ever became of mee, to use no unlawful and dishonest way for my subsistance or prefermt.

In this my sad heart was somew^{t} cheard; at ye foote of the bridge the prisoners were begging; my heart pittyed them in y^{r} distresse and out of my poverty I gave them 3*d.*; riding on my jorney, I found I could not well reach to the end y^{t} night, upon wch I tooke up my inne at Spalditch; their was some charge unexpected: the next morning March 24: 1636: anno aetatis the twentieth & somewhat upwards I came to Deane, alighting from my horse and calling at the doore; the gentlewoman of the House welcomes mee into her parlo^{r} & calls her housband: it rejoyced mee to see their faces, they expressed goodness in their countenances; well in conclusion I agreed to stay; the present schoolem^{r} was not yett gone, but I was to enter upon it as from the next day, he laying it downe March:25: 1637. as that day the end of the quarter: my entrance was harsh, 10*l.* per annum was I to pay for my diett: 3 schollers afforded mee: 7*l.*; the first quarter was worth 4*l.* to mee & I had hopes of increase dayly: now was I in a hopefull way; I applyed my selfe to my schoole & studyes; I was much ingaged to Mr Dillingham for his love & respect: I read through all Chamier[1] there & abridged him. I had acquaintance at my Ld Mandevilles of Kimbolton Castle and the use of his library by meanes of Mr Merrill his chaplaine: I rid sometimes into Essex & Norfolke; once per annum payd my debts, received my money of my mother, had ye countenance of my freinds having now no need of their helpe. Having stayd y^{r} 2 yeares, at Spring 1639 at Easter coming out of Norfolke, 1639. I was taken sicke with an ague & fever, which brought me lowe, as if it would have by a deepe consumption layd mee in the grave; my friends feared mee, yett I did not, but trusted in God for recovery, who sett mee on my leggs againe: in a word at Deane I bought mee bookes, clothes, & saved some money: upon Michaelmas day, anno: 1639, I preached my first sermon[2] at Wormington in Northamptonshire at the intreaty of Mr Elwes upon Acts, 16. 31: some discontents were in my head so that Mr Gifford of Olny coming to mee & proferring mee 12*l.* per annum & my diett, to bee his Curate, I went over to Olny in Buckinghamshire & left Deane Octob: 4

[1] Daniel Chamier, 1570-1621: wrote *de Oecumenico Pontifico.*

[2] He was not ordained deacon till December.

1639, being ffriday; my stocke was *20l. 7s. 9d.* in money & about *1l.* owing mee, so that I putt up in money besides all my expences about *10l.* in money & p[d] my debts.

Olny: The first quarter at Olny I was only assistant to him in his schoole: the first L[ds] day being Octob: 6 was my eye fixed with love upon a mayd, & hers upon mee, who afterwards proved my wife: Decemb: 13 my uncle M[r] Joslin in Norfolke sent mee y[e] offer of a place by him; but my affection to that mayde that God had layd out to be my wife would not suffer mee to stirre, so I gave the messenger *5s.* & sent him away: in that month of December I was ordayned Deacon by the B[p] of Peterburg. The charges amounted to *1l. 14s. 9d.* in my jorney. In my returne I preached at Deane, Decemb. 25[t]. & coming home from thence I read prayers at Olny, and that day found Jane Constable the mayde before mentioned in our house, which was the beginning of our acquaintance. The next L[ds] day I preached at Olny on Acts 16. 31. & so also on Jan: 1 Newyears day: at night invited to supper to Goodman Gaynes. I went in to call Goodwife Shepheard, and their my Jane being, I stayed with her, which was o[r] first proposall of the match one to another, which wrought a mutuall promise one to another Jan: 23: and by all o[r] consents a contract. Sept. 28. 1640: and o[r] marriage Octob: 28 following. Now henceforward I preached once a fortnight & M[r] Gifford gave me *10s.* per quarter more out of his love for my paynes: here I lived with them very comfortably & contentedly; wee used Shovelboard for our recreaton of which I grew weary presently: about latter end of ffeb: I was ordayned minister at Peterburg by y[e] B[p]. & 6 ministers: I would not bowe towards the Altar as others did & some followed my
1640. example; charges amounted to *1l. 6s. 10d.* That spring I went up to Cambridge to visit for my degree of M[r] in arts as o[r] custome was: charges their and for my gowne and cassocke amounted to *19l. 18s.* & somewhat upwards: this was a hard pull; from thence I went to Norfolke, & coming home to preach at Olny fayr, flouds were so great as I narrowly escaped drowning in divers places. I hope I shall never bee unmindfull of Gods goodness to mee in my preservason. Likewise at Olny mighty fall from a chimney into a place,

where I walked presently,[1] as soone as I was passed by. Now being Mr of Arts & minister I began to thinke of marrying, being sure to my wife, but I could not see any convenience how to live. Beginning of July I was at Cranham in Essex & preachd their 2 sermons : about growing in grace ; my uncle & all the towne desird mee to live with them, and I seemed not much agst it : to Olny I return, & having had some offers from my Ld Mandevill which I durst not accept, least I should loose my selfe in a loose family, I repayred to Kimbolton thrice to try providence, but neither time fitting mee, I resolved, twas not Gods pleasure to raise mee that way. I sought him for direction, and about August I was continually perswaded ere 3 months God would lay out a way for my livelyhood ; one day in September getting a part in private to seeke unto God for his direction, as I ended prayer, God perswaded mee I should have a present answer of my desire ; as I stood up at window I heard one inquire for mee. I went downe and it was one sent from Cranham to intreate mee to live with them ; his name was Goodman Tavener ; at length wee came to this conclusion that ye minister allowing 24*l.* per annum & my uncle my diett or 10*l.* & the Towne 10*l.* more I would come over to them ; home he came, made up my proposicons and came over for mee : ffriday Sept : 25 I went my jorney : 26, at London wee mett the joyfull newes of this Parliamt that is now sitting, 1644, and God long continue for his glory, and his Churches good. I was first contracted to my deare wife at Cranham ; I waited 3 weekes for their Minister ; he coming over, wee concluded, so as sent a wagon for my stuffe and came to Olny & marryed Wednesday. Octob. 28, 4 yeares after my ffathers death. On Monday following wee began or jorney & Nov. 4. came safe to Cranham ; returning I thought of my thoughts at Huntington Bridge, & God had brought mee backe, increased with wife, goods, and parts ; loe this was the Lords doing, twas merveylous towards mee.

Being come to Cranham I taught schoole at Upminster, which was great trouble, but no great advantage unto mee ; yr I had a Cranham: 1640.

[1] Just before.

loving people, but I could not injoy my health, being continually subject to Rheumes; I wanted ye conveniency of a house, & offers began to be made to mee so as to my parishes great greife it was probable I would remove from them; the Inhabitants of Hounechurch layd in for mee and made mee good offers of 80*l.* per annum, viis et modis, certayne, without any trouble on my part: only to preach twice on the Lords day, without medling with other dutyes.

Being in y^{s} condicion Mr Wharten of ffelsted was with a freind of his at Upminster and I having some business with him went over to see him, when I found they had told him I was removing from them, upon wch he propounded Earles Colne in Essex a place in a very good ayre; ye meanes he sayd was about 50*l.* per annum: the towne was able to make it more; upon y^{s} I promised him to goe over upon notice from him; being ill I had word from him that they desired mee on the next Lords day. In the meane tyme one of the Towne came over to mee, March. I came over & my loving Uncle Ralph Josselin with mee; wee came that night to Mr Rich: Harlakendens [1] at the priory: I was affected with that family exceedingly & the situation of the Towne: the next day being the Lords day I preachd; upon y^{r} approbacon they desired mee I would come & live with y^{m} as y^{r} Minister; I in a word answered them, if they would make the meanes a competency such as I could live on, wch I conceived was 80*l.* per annum, I would embrace; they gladly entertained it & valewed it thus to mee:

		Per annum.
Earles Colne { Comit. Essex	Tithes they would make good at . . .	40*l.* 0*s.*
	Mr Rich: Harlakenden: wood & money	20*l.* 0*s.*
	His tenants in contribucon:	2*l.* 0*s.*
	Mr Tho: Harlakenden:	3*l.* 0*s.*
	And the towne contribucon	15*l.* 0*s.*

The House, close, churchyard and the dues that accrewed to the Minister, they conceived to bee worth 10*l.* per annum: thus, being Gods providence in it, I accepted y^{r} offer, and their was this proposicon more, y^{t} if I found not the Towne as good as y^{r} words,

[1] Cromwell was related to this family & stayed once or twice at the Priory.

upon 6. months warning wee would part: they desired mee to keep a ffortnight lecture, which though I did not engage my selfe by promise to keepe, yett I did for sometime: things thus acted, wee posted up to London & passed all with the Bp. so that,

March: I tooke peaceable possession, returned to Cranham & 1640.
after a fortnights stay I brought my wife over, my Uncle and Goodman Robson accompanying mee; but not one man of Earles Colne came to meete us on the way, neither did any come to welcome us to Towne, which seemed to mee an unkind part, & made mee suspect that I was deceived in the disposicon of the people.

Well, I stayed with Mr R. Harlakenden untill Apr. 1641, when 1641.
wee went to board with Mr Edw. Cressener; wee pd 5*l.* per quarter; here wee lived, quietly, and very contentdly. I would not desire better usage, tis but ye due commendacon of yr love & respect to us. I fell to my worke in ye Ministery, & now I began to prepare my house; money came not in from the Towne as was expected. In a word I layd out my 20*l.* and Mr Harlakenden, 20*l.* The Towne should have raysed 20*l.* more, but yr was none would take any care for it: to this day they have not brought in 5*l.* that I can give an account of; this was a little trouble wn my quarters came: one or 2 was gatherd not by their care but by my procuring men to doe the same; 2 persons refused at first; my 3*l.* 15*s.* per qter. fell under 3*l.* the first quarter, neither did any take care to make it up: when tithes came I must doe it my selfe: I compounded: with all my toyle, I thinke yt yeare I could make them amount not above 33*l.* and since they are come to lesse, & all the losse to this day hath fallen upon my shoulders: I confesse I was stumbled at yr dealings, & some abuses offered mee about the Protestacon, so that I wonderd at the people, and supposed it would grow bad indeed, that made so bad an entrance; in the country I must confesse I had many private guifts, which helpd to make amends for the towne losses.

June, I rid to my fathers,[1] left my wife yr, came home by Deane, & June 28, I rid to Olny in a day; my father came home

[1] Father-in-law's.

with us, who was much affected with Colne and delighted to bee with us until his death. July, wee rid to my Lady Denies, and then I began to have some hopes of my wives breeding which proved so indeed to o[r] great joy & comfort, blessed bee the name of the L[d]. Returning I applyed my selfe that summer to hasten y[e] compleating the House fitt for our winter dwelling, which being in some measure effected Octob. 20 : with a mayd Sarah Browne to whom wee gave 1*l.* 18*s.* per annum, wee came up to o[r] owne house in y[e] high streete ; no neighbo[r] came to wellcome us to o[r] house but M[rs] Cousins with 2 from Gaynes Colne, & M[rs] King & her sonne & daughter one night : I esteemed it some disrespect and unkindnes, but such expressions I perceive now are not so much used in o[r] towne as in others.

This Michaelmas, upon an order of the House of Commons to that purpose wee tooke downe all images & pictures and such like glasses : thus this winter passed away a time of hopes, & yet sometimes feares, but the King being returned out of Scotland, Jan : 5. 1641 : he attempted the house of Commons in case of the 5 members; but being disappointed he packd away from the house and came to them not to this houre, Aug : 8. 1644, & in ffeb : following the Q. went over beyond seas ; thus spinning out my
1642. time, I began a litle to be troubled with some in matter of separacon. My wife now growing bigge & ill, my mother [1] came from Olny to us upon a Tuesday lecture day, April : 12 : after sermon, having waited upon God in his house, my wife called her women and God was mercifull to mee in my house, giving her a safe deliverance, & a daughter which on Thursday April : 14 was baptized by the name of Mary, M[r] Rich : Harlakenden, M[r] John Litle, M[rs] Mary Mildmay & my wives mother being witnesses. I entertayned my neighbors all about ; it cost me 6*l.* & 13*s.* 4*d.* at least : they shewed much love to mee from all parts : God blessed my wife to bee a nurse, and our child thrived, and was even then a pleasant comfort to us : God wash it from its corruption & sanctify it and make it his owne : but it pleased God my wives

[1] Mother-in-law.

breasts were sore, wch was a greivance & sad cutt to her, but with use of means in some distance of time they healed up : this Spring times grew fearful in the rising of the yeare ; about Midsummer wee began to raise private armes : I found a musquett for my part and the King was beginning to raise an army. The Parliamt did the like. Aug : 1 : wee met at Colchester to underwrite, where for my pt, for my affection to God & his gospell, having endeavoured publike promoting it beyond my estate, I underwritt & payd in to Mr Crane, 10*l.*, but my Rings wanted something, so it fell short nigh 3*s.* Being at London I provided for my selfe Sword, Halbert, Powder and Match ; the drums now also began to beate up ; for my part I endeavoured to encourage others to goe forth ; our poore people in tumults arose & plundered divers houses, papists & others, & threatened to goe farther, which I endeavored to supresse by publique & private meanes ; Edgehill battle being fought, Wednesday following being the fast day, I was told the newes as I was going downe the churchyard to sermon ; the time & place hinted the answer of our prayers on the Lds day, being the day & the time of battle, when I was earnest with God for mercy upon us agst our enemies. Upon this the contry was raised & I for 1643.
my part sent a man out with a months pay, but I returned presently but spent the most of my money. In spring now my wife weaned her daughter and began to breed again : God gave us both our health in a greater measure than I had had before or my wife of late dayes. I should have mentioned or associating[1] in wch service I underwritt a whole armes[2] ; they went out to or great charge, and did litle or no good. I began now to find my meanes grow scant, yt notwthstanding all our industry & good husbandry and many guifts, yt I could have but litle ; upon wch I gave notice to the Towne to prevent it that I might not bee forced to leave them. June : 10 : 1643 my wives father dyed ; the Lord prepare us for our latter ends, & give us mercy with him through Jesus Christ. New Towne came to mee to remain : ffordham, Thaxted, & I went & preached with the last but would not accept the

[1] The Eastern Association.

[2] cf. p. 13. line 8.

Sequestracon. In July upon occasion of a plot [1] to betray the City there was another new Covent [2] propounded & begun to bee pressed. I tooke it but the state lett it fall; things were now sad with us, Waller routed, [3] & ffairfax, [4] & Bristol lost, & Hull like to be betrayed, [5] the City divided: Essex's army also came to nothing, but God remembered us in our low estate.

August: 2: being Wed: I was taken very ill with a quotidian ague; I had 3 fitts; the phisitian told mee I would have one harsh one more, but on ffriday night, seeking God for my health that if it pleased him I might still goe on in my calling, I was strangely perswaded I should have no more fitts; neither had I: Lord lett mee never forgett thy goodnes.

My Towne also rather than I should goe from them, seeing some likely hood of the same, agreed to raise mee, for that yeare, 10*l.* more, which was payd in with about perhaps 10*s.* losse. But now I layd downe my Lecture which I had kept unto ye day.

Septemb. 20: I joyned with Mr Wharton in a day of humiliacon at my Lady Edens & while wee were praying, God was blessing our forces in that great fight neare Newbery, where the E. of Essex had the better agst the Kings forces.

O^{r} ffriends at Olny were miserably plundered at Olny: and I lay in peace without disturbance & my family.

In November, Stanway men made mee a proffer of ye Sequestracon; I yielded not; they gott it for mee, yett I did not accept of

[1] Waller's Plot.

[2] "After this revelation everything was possible for Pym. On the 6th he "made his report on Waller's Plot. Lords and Commons alike were carried "away by their indignation. The imposition of a vow or covenant, which a "few days before had little chance of acceptance, was now voted by the Com- "mons with scarcely a dissentient voice. Those who took it, engaged them- "selves to support the forces raised in defence of Parliament against those raised "by the King 'so long as the Papists now in open war against the Parliament "shall by the force of arms be protected from the justice thereof.'" (Gardiner, *Great Civil War*, i, 149). July in the diary is apparently a mistake for June.

[3] July 10, at Roundway Down.

[4] July 30, at Adwalton Moor.

[5] By the Hothams.

ye same ; oh Ld my desire is to serve thee in Colne if it please thee ; I seeke not great things, only blesse me with thy grace & mine, & make mee an instrumt to doe good to ye soules of others.

Decemb. 29 : or towards morning Decemb : 30 indeed, 2 houres before day, being Satturday morning, my wife was deliverd of her son, which Jan : 14 : was baptized by the name of Thomas ; Mr Tho: Harlakenden & my Aunt Shepheard were his witnesses ; God gave my deare wife strength to nurse, health both to her selfe & babe ; wee were scared with or chamber chimney hearth firing but, espying it in time, it was prevented from any great hurt. This was a great mercy : so hath God kept mee upon my way, by land & water, prevented falls from horse, preserved mee in falling, for which, oh my soule, bee thankefull.

March : 29 : keeping a day of Humiliacon at my Lady Hony- 1644.
woods ; while wee were praying, God was making Waller victorious over Hopton, neare Alsford:[1] and turned backe the forces of Rupert that wee feared would have come on after they had routed or forces at Newark[2] ; oh the sonnes of Jacob never seeke the Ld in vayne. Going in April to Cranham I was taken ill with a cold which sadly afflicted mee for about 3 weekes, but God delivered mee, & gave mee more health, & cheerfulness & content in himselfe, wife, children, his wayes, my people than formerly ; so that my earnest desire is still towards them. July : first weeke I rid forth to Sr Tho : Honywoods Regimt, to Newport Pannell, Northampton, to the Randevow of Sr Will : Waller & Major Browne, neare Geton pastures ; visited my freinds and came home safe; my wife, family, freinds and all in health ; many things I have omitted that may be found in my notes, almanack ; &c. But now henceforwards I shall be more exact & particular ; thus much to this pr sent day.
Aug : 8 : 1644. Aug. 5.

I have bought a part in a shippe : it cost me 14*l.* 10*s.* God send mee good speed with the same ; I have put my part in a bagge of hops to Sunderland ; my sister Mary is come under my roofe as a servant, but my respect is & shall be towards her as a sister ;

[1] Battle of Cheriton, near Alresford, March 29.

[2] Relieved by Prince Rupert, March 21.

God might have made mee a waiter upon others; o[r] former mayde Lydia Weston having dwelt with mee 1 yeare & almost 3 qters marryed into our Towne, the first that marryed out of my family.

The plague, y[t] arrow of death, is sadly at Colchester, brought by a woman that came to visitt her freinds; their have already divers dyed; what a mercy of God is it to respite our Towne; L[d] spare it, and lett not o[r] sins, o[r] covetousness & pride of y[e] poore in the plenty of their Dutch worke[1] cause thee to bee angry with us; I heard from my Mother at Olny of her present health, and also of my sisters; the spotted fever[2] is in towne with them, whereof divers have dyed.

Aug. 12. God good to mee all weeke last past, in my health, in my estate, comforts, freinds, in my family my deare wife and babes; mercifull in carrying mee on in my calling; enabling mee for his Sabbath, whereon I made my last mocon (to respect of my present resolucon) to my parish, to bee careful to gather up my means for mee y[t] I might not want; if they did not, though I shall not cease to love them, yett I must of necessity serve providence in another place; L[d] stirre up y[r] hearts to embrace this offer if y[u] have a will to use mee here, if not, I am thine, thy will be done. And now L[d] I confesse my selfe unworthy of this goodness in many respects, especially my carriage towards y[ee]; make mee more painfull & dilligent in my place, & profitable, more cheerful & contented in my family; helpe mee & heele mee; I blesse thee for delivering mee from grosse wickednes; keepe me in thy pouer to salvacon.

Aug. 26. This weeke my sister Hannah came over to mee, I sent her away in some hopes to helpe her about her house, & with some expressions of love; Lord remember mee & mine & hers in mercy. Aug: 20: being with my men when they layd the hall floure & cutting downe the walls for the doore, an handsaw w[ch] was used agst mee, missed my face very narrowly; L[d] make mee to prise that mercy; the plague continued & increased at Colchester, our towne yett

[1] Dutch refugees had settled at Colchester in the reign of Elizabeth & established there the trade in Bays (Baize) and Says. A specimen of the work of some of the Dutch weavers may be seen in Colchester Castle.

[2] Typhus fever.

in safety; L^d keepe that distroying arrow from among us. Times now very sickly. Ed. Clarke my Christian freind taken sicke & very neare death, divers in our towne & others sickly; L^d sanctify thy hand to them; my wife suddenly ill, yett through mercy well againe; Mr Nettles of London carryed through towne in a coach deprived of his senses, & very mad as they reported; leaping over the pales I scratchd my face, but God bee praised I had no further hurt though I might if providence had not preserved mee, & also in o^r fall w^n my wife and I pulling downe a tree with a rope with o^r pulling all fell together, but no hurt God bee praised: such falls my children have many times & yett safe; Mary fell out of the parlour window with her face agst the bench & had no hurt; a strange providence, all ye witt of the world could not have given such a fall & preserved from hurt, to God bee the praise.

A dronkard came into my house; Lord thy name be blessed in Aug. 27.
keeping mee from y^t sin: I chid him; he seemed apprehensive of what I sayd, the Lord amend him & pardon this sin to him & sanctify him.

Was the publike day of humiliacon. Aug. 28.

This weeke God was good to mee in my health, and in my Sept. 1.
familyes, and in preserving our towne from ye plague, in keeping our sicke neare ye grave from falling into the same, in the hopes of raysing some up againe. Lord sanctify this hand to us all. My ffreinds Mr Benton & his wife with us which shortned my time for studdy, yett God inabld mee in some measure for ye Sabbath: God good to mee in my course towards my family. L^d keepe us in perfect peace all the day long, subdue my corruptions; my sister Mary received her things from Walden which wee feard had miscarryed; Lord blesse mee in all my wayes, direct mee by thy Spirit, helpe mee agaynst vaine thoughts and imaginacons and preserve mee and mine; God gave us very good newes this weeke; wee heard of divers hopkills burnt downe at Captain Chipburnes, and Knights of Hinningham; wee preserved from fire, Lord still keepe us. Wee heard the lost shippe belonging to Colchester was taken by the Irish rebells richly laden; L^d preserve ours in y^e

waves: — oh bee my God and of my Spouse, & our seeds after us, fitt mee for my calling and condicon, and blesse mee in the same. I heard my Cosin Abrahams sonne was dead, my Cousin Benton miscarryed & now through mercy up again; L^{d}, lett thes things cause mee to love ye my God, who sparest mine & dealest more gently with mine, & sanctify thy hand to them.

Sept. 3. Visited a sicke man one Guy Penhacke who was much troubled in mind upon his life: he had strong temptacons from Sathan. I urged him to a Coven^{t} with God to bee a new man if he recovered.

Sept. 4. Mr Will: Harlakenden & my brother Jeremy came from ye army to us; in good health preserved from so many dangers, by enemies & sicknesses.

Sept. 5. Stung I was with a bee on my nose, I presently pluckt out ye sting, & layd on honey, so that my face swelled not; thus divine providence reaches to the lowest things. Lett not sin oh Lord that dreadful sting bee able to poyson mee.

Sept. 6. Liberty of the sermon at Halsted. Sr Tho: Honywood gave mee great respect for my love in going forth with him towards the army; payd my ordinary for mee. I heard y^{t} a child in ye towne was burnt almost to death, & mine safe; oh mercy and goodness to bee adored.

Sept. 8. I heard vile things of one E. C. which I should not have believed; God in mercy keepe mee and mine from the like; L^{d} pardon all my sins, Sabbath & weeke day & fitt mee to doe thee more honour in my place.

Sept. 9. In a breviat of Arch B^{p} Laudes life, I find how the strings of his legge brake without any stepping awry. L^{d} how many sad wrinches have I had in my walking, and yett thou has preserved mee; lett thy gracious protection be still over mee for good.

This day I heard the dolefull newes of the E. of Essex his losse in the West,[1] all his ordnance & ammunicon being a prey to the enemy; it was a sad providence, and speakes o^{r} sins aloude and Gods continuing his displeasure in lengthening the warre; yett oh

[1] At Lostwithiel.

my heart be encouraged in the Ld, he is the same still, and the time of the enemyes ruine is not one houre thee farther of for this yr success, nay it may bee yr blasphemyes shall hasten yr ruine as it did Rabshakehs and his Mrs.

I rid to Colchester; my horse stumbled, God preserved mee from danger, God was pleased to give mee good dispatch in my busynes for ye towne to ye whole Committee;[1] Sr Tho: Honywood payd my ordinary for mee. I had conference with Mr Ellis: he told mee separacon from ye true church was lawfull in some cases, as being not rightly constituted; so did Luther from ye papists & yett yr was a true church among them. Wee from ye Lutherans, whom wee owne as churches, & so the Independents from us. As I came home I heard or shippe was returned safe from Sunderland; the plague is wee hope almost stayd at Colchester. Sept. 14.

This weeke the Ld gratious to mee & mine in or health, (only my wife somewt ill,) and children much comfort. My brother returned to the army againe; this was sad weeke for ye affayres of ye Kingdoms; the Ld can give a turne when it pleases him, and on him wee will wayte for ye same. Sept. 15.

My good ffreind Mr Harlakenden sold one bagge of hops for mee wherin I was advantaged 1*l.* 15*s.* This was Gods good providence. Sept. 17.

We had a collection for one Hastivile, a ffrench Baron yt forsooke ye popish religion & all his honours for ye Protestant religion; I might have beene a beggar whereas I am yett a giver. Sept. 22.

Wee began this day to put the County into a posture of defence; it will cost mee an armes.[2] Sept. 24.

Was a day of publique humiliacon; it would make a man bleed to see how regardless people are of the same, nothing moves them; a load of wool was passing upon the road, our men stopt the same; oh that men would give an outwd reverence to the wp of the Lord. Sept. 25.

I rid to Wethersfeild, injoyed the company of good freinds, saw some manuscripts of things in K. James & Charles his time of consequence; I had yr a good bargaine of bookes. Oct. 1.

[1] The Committee of Defence.

[2] Cf. p. 13.

Oct. 3. I payd 4s. excise for 2 bagges of hoppes; much love in my freinds the Commissioners who payd my ordinary for mee.

Oct. 6. This day I published & exhorted subscriptions for Sr Will Bretheton[1] yt noble Cheshire Gentlemen: I cañot blesse God over all my people; only indeed a few contributed; those that did, did it voluntarily.

I now gave over to gather my quarters my selfe; I left that worke to the Towne; divers brought up their quarters for yr owne particulars, but I would not receive them. I doe not perceive the Towne intends to stirre in it; Gods will be done, I am content.

Oct. 7. In ye morning I went out and God gave mee more than ye day before I layd out in ye publique; I never found I lost any thing by imploying my selfe that way, but God sent mee in more by my freinds, beside ye comfort in my conscience to have done in his cause. I went up to Goodman Bridges & bought his hops at an easy rate. I was used yr kindly. When I came home Stissted men where with mee about yr reference to Mr Boroughs & my selfe, whether Mr Archer or Mr Templer had ye clearer call to yr towne: I found God had gratiously kept my daughter Mary who was strucke with a horse.

Oct. 9. At Halsted, Mr Borough & I mett upon Stissted busynes, about a minister for them; the towne was divided, & would not condiscend one to another; oh wofull, sad divisions.

Oct. 13. Exhorted to contribucons for Sr Will. Brereton, obtayned a litle; wtsoever I have done yt is not right in thy eyes, Lord, pardon ye same.

Oct. 14. A frost & snow, very cold. I rid to Stisted to assist in ye choyse of yr minister; both parts stiffe, divided, a most sad towne, no care almost of any thing; I spoke to them but could not drawe it to a conclusion, though I hope to a good forwardness; Mr Alstone made a serious offer to mee of 10*l.* out of his owne purse, and great likelyhood to carry it, if I would yeald to them, but I would not; I was ingaged in ye busynes & yrfore would not endeavor any such thing to my selfe: ye place hath 140 acres of glebe & ye tith are

[1] Sir William Brereton, a prominent parliamentary commander in Cheshire and its neighbourhood.

worth, about 100*l.* per annum. This day Mr Newbold received or money for Sr Will : Brereton ; ys day invited & promised to assist in a day of humiliacon at Markeshall :

Rcd. in 3 bags of hops from Goodman Bridge at 40*s.* ye hundred ; ye weight was 7 hundred & 3 qters ; goodman Burton run a share with mee. Oct. 17.

Spent part of ye day at Goodman Clarke in settling matters betwixt Mr Harlakenden & him. At night Mr Commissary generall [1] was with us, told us my Ld Manchester was advancing towards ye King. Their is expectacon of a battle. Oct. 18.

This day 3 of my townesmen made an entrance in gathering ye Towne contribucon : it ought to bee at ye least 5*l.* every quarter, and yett I shall not make much above 70*l.* per annum. Wee resolved to try what ye Parliamt would doe for us, for the augmentacon of our small living. Oct. 19.

This day I injoyd at dinnr ye society of Mr ffarringdon ; I saw a young rooke yt fell out of the nest in the priory yard ys day ; I have not knowne ye like in all my dayes yt they should build & breed at this time of the yeare. Oct. 23.

Heard from my deare freind Mr Harlakenden from Cambridge ; this day I begun to practice dayly in Hebrew & Greeke : God blesse me yrin yt yrby I may come to more perfect knowledge of the sense of ye Scriptures. Oct. 24.

A day of or marriage entring or 5t yeare ; God good to mee in yt relacon, blessed bee his name for ever, my sonne well again. Oct. 28.

Bought 2 pigges for 9*s.* the first beasts yt ever I bought in all my dayes hitherto. Oct. 29.

I heard the report of or successe agst the Kings forces [2] ; oh lett God have the glory of or deliverances. Oct. 30.

Concerning the increase of our living by the Parliamt yr was no hope from them for the present ; all yt was to bee done was to be expected from the Impropriator, and yt was Mr Harlakenden : I cannot thinke he will mount higher than he hath already done. Nov. 4.

[1] i.e. of the Commissariat: vide p. 22. "Mr W. Harlakenden, Commissary General to the Earl of Manchester." There was also a Commissary General of Horse.

[2] The second battle of Newbury : October 27.

One old Turner, 84 y. old, dwelling in ye house with one Markham a separatist, y^s^ day drowned himselfe; L^d^ thy judgm^ts^ are secret and righteous.

Nov. 9. This day I injoyed the society of my deare ffreind Mr Harlakenden who came from the Committee to spend a Sabbath with us, and then returne; told us of a man in Some, Camb: y^t^ is about 150 yeares old who had 6 wives 32 children, and very lately carryed 2 comes [1] of pease 2 furlongs, 8 bushels a qter of a mile.

Nov. 10. This weeke ye L^d^ was gratious to mee & mine in o^r^ health, plenty, peace, inward & outward comfort, ffreinds; I & my wife were both ill in o^r^ stomaches; I heard our ship was come home safe; more mercy yett: read an order wherby alehouses are in ye power of the well affected & the minister of ye parish.

Nov. 11. Mary my daughter was preserved from hurt by the fall of a waynscott doore at ye priory; thy name Lord be praised; my deare ffreind M^r^ ffs: children tooke y^r^ leave of us; this day I counted 50*l.* to him to improve for mee; the Lord blesse it for the good of my family, he that endeavo^rs^ not their good is worse than an infidell.

Nov. 15. Three of my parishioners, Rob: Cortle, John Read, Rich: Appleton, gathered up Michaelmas qter; instead of 5*l.* they brought me 3*l.* 0*s.* 1*d*; divers refuse to pay, divers used them crossely, insomuch as they were much discouraged. I am beholding to them yett fo^r^ y^r^ particular love.

Nov. 27. A day of publike humiliacon, the L^d^ was good to mee in the same; our proposicons for peace are gone to the King.

Nov. 28. Mr W. Harlakenden, Commissary generall to the Earl of Manchester was with us in good health. I was at S^r^ J: Jacobs, he went backe in some part from his promise to mee, but I know no remedye.

Dec. 3. Mr Harlakenden went towards London, God prosper him; heard sad newes of ye Earl of Manchester, [2] I hope its false.

[1] Coomb or comb, a measure of corn containing 4 bushels.

[2] " With every sign of bitter irritation, he (i. e. Cromwell) ascribed every " mistake that had been committed to the personal wrong-headedness of Man- " chester. " (Gardiner, *Great Civil War*, i. 83.)

My Lady Honywood sent us tokens [1] shee invited mee to a day of humiliacon, but I could not for many occasions. Dec. 10.

Dind at a strange vaine wedding; a poore man gave curious ribbands to all, gloves to ye women and to the ringers, yett their was very good company. Dec. 11.

Heard of the strange vote [2] of ye house of Commons to call home their members. Dec. 13.

All this weeke God was good to mee & mine in inward & outward mercyes; in my health, in my sight; when I began to pray with confidence my eyes mended. I gatherd liberally for a poore Ministers widow who was plunderd & housband slaine. Dec. 15.

This day my noble freind Mr Harlakenden was made Major of the Horse by the Country & my good freind Captaine Haynes Major of the foote; ye contry did acquitt themselves very well in ye choice and worke of the day in my estimacon. Dec. 18.

I made a serious exhortacon to lay aside ye jollity & vanity of ye time custome hath wedded us unto, & to keepe the Sabbath better which is the only L^ds^ day we are commanded to observe. Dec. 22.

This day Court kept in Towne; ye Jury of Colne Comit. chose for constables 2 men very unfitt to order ye alehouses & loose people of ye Towne. 1644: Jan. 8.

The Arch B^p^, y^t^ grand enemy of the pouer of godlynes, that great stickler for all outward pompe in the service of God, left his head at Touer hill London, by ordinance of parliam^t^. Jan. 10.

This day one of the butchers brought mee in a quarter of mutton, told not who sent it but went his way. I shall inquire whose love it was, & be thankfull for ye same. He that gives to the poore lends to ye L^d^. I have often observed my liberality, or rather my poore mite, imployed for ye publike, or upon others indigent, hath returnd in with gaine and advantage. I must observe ye weeke: on mooneday I sent to my poore Sister 3*s*. & some other small things to others not worth ye mentioning: now y^s^ weeke I received 9*l*. from Sr John Jacob which was in part due long before, and promised but was not payd untill now; divers invitacons of freinds to y^r^ houses: Jan. 17.

[1] Small gifts.

[2] The Self-denying Ordinance.

one sends me a parcel of plums & sugar, another a quarter of good mutton, another a fatt goose, another a capon and cheese, an unexpected income of a summ of mony layd out before; God good to my family & nacon.

Jan. 19. This weeke yr was divers passages of providence for the good of the church in disappointing the attempts and plots of the enemy

Jan. 28. The contry mett to choose yr officers; they waved yr former Collonels & nominated Mr Harlakenden Col; Mr Haynes Major of Horse; Mr Cooke Col., Mr Crane Lieut., Coll. Jermaine Major of foote, men honest and I hope faithfull; how it will be reconciled with the former election I know not, but I feare: det bona Deus.

Jan. 30. Mrs C: gave me in kindnes 3*s*. to buy mee a satten cappe, and my wife. 2*s*.

ffeb. 1. Received advertisemt yt Mr Montjoy had payd my money to Mr Harlakenden: I am glad it falls out so well for mee.

ffeb. 12. Preacht at Chelmsford by desire of ye standing Committee; dind with them and received thanks from them.

ffeb. 17. This day Mr Harlakenden rid with his son to Stortford School; the Lord blesse him yr; heard good newes from Plymouth, but very sad concerning the divisions yt are in our armyes; Lord heale them for thy mercies sake, and give us one heart & spiritt.

ffeb. 18. The regiments of ye County reduced to 2;[1] a base busines in or pts of ye County, but its likely to bee a shame to ye authors.

ffeb. 20. Overheard a separatists sermon agst learning, a most poore peice.

ffeb. 23. When I came out of ye pulpitt I read a letter from Mr Harlakenden wherein he writes excellent newes from Scarborough, taking by storme the sands, Church, 120 ships, 32 peice of ordnance and endangering the Castle; the Lords name bee praised and magnifyed for the same; the Treaty[2] is likely to hold some time longer.

March. 2. This weeke my wife aguish, but pretty chearfull; hott within very much, but now using oringes, sugar & rose water coold.

[1] Troops raised by the Eastern Association had been quartered in Hampshire and Surrey.

[2] The Treaty of Uxbridge, which came to an end at this time.

God was good to mee in my jorney to Braintree and home agayne, keeping me safe and prospering the worke wee had in hand, in ye free choice and election of officers, without any considerable opposicon, although much was perfected and intended; ye division consisted of 10 hundreds; the officers were ye same men, and chosen into ye same places as formerly Jan : 28 : 1644. March. 4.

My Cousin Abraham Josselin came to us from New England, about by ye Canaryes, after a sad long jorney & one tedious fight with a Kings pyratt: heard by him of ye wellfare of ye plantacon for which God bee praised; this summer N. E.[1] had divers losses at sea, and scarce any before: wee rid to my Cousin Bentons; at night heard newes of ye routing of my Lord ffairfax his forces,[2] which was reported as a very great losse, endangering much ye North parts of England. March. 6. 7. 8.

This weeke I saw ye Directory,[3] and an Ordnance of Parliam^t^ to take away ye heavy burthen of ye booke of Common prayer in all ye parts of ye same; this day God was good to mee in ye publike exercise ye sacram^t^ of baptisme, in gatherings for divers poore: I made a serious mocon to all to joyne with the Magistrate in a civil reformacon. March.23.

Our fayre day, through mercy freer from disorder y^n^ at some other times. March.25.

March. A darke day in respect of our intelligence; matters went ill in ye west; o^r^ forces compelled to retreate[4] & somewhat worse was feared by Waller and Holborne; in ye Northwest the enemy preserved and releived y^r^ distressed garrisons[5] and by report fell doune towards us. 1645: March.29.

Returned the account of ye Towne, wch amounted to 1200*l*. and upward, besides ye charge of trayne bands and associacon, which amounted unto 150*l*. at least. March.31.

An anabaptist of our parish being pressd for a souldier, I writ April. 10.

[1] New England.

[2] A false report.

[3] The first ordinance for the Directory was agreed to on March 5. 1645.

[4] Waller had abandoned Somerset and Dorset.

[5] Rupert relieved Beeston Castle, but his farther advance was checked.

and procured his release ; Lord learne mee to doe y^{m} good agst y^{r} reproaches towards mee.

June. 22. My sister Mary went downe to ye priory ; the Lord make her fitt for her place and give her favour in ye sight of y^{m} shee serveth ; Jone my mayd came to us.

May. 19. Payd 2 yeares tenth to ye Parliem^{t} messenger, 1*l.* 14*s.* 2*d.* ; ye messenger received from me for his paynes. 3*s.* ; his power was harsh ; his carriage was yet indifferent curteous ; tis a tryall to bee thus dealt withall ; I blesse God my spirit was under, and I hope ever shall.

June. 1. Y^{e} newes was sad to us wards y^{t} ye king was coming downe to Newarke, had faced Leicest^{r} ; God knowes how soone wee may bee alarmed indeed.

June. 2. At home an alarme, Leicester lost.

June. 7. An alarme to raise o^{r} regiment of Horse ; ye feild officers from home ; I was resolved to have sent orders to have raised y^{m}, but ye Coll. coming home at night I only assisted him in his worke that night.

June. I was out with o^{r} regiment ; wee marchd to Walden, musterd,
10. 11. 12. I sung Psalmes, prayd & spake to o^{r} souldiers on ye Common at Walden & also at Halsted ; God was good to us in accommadating us, and preserving us ; Mr Josselin of Chelmsford brake his legge at Walden, his horse threw him ; o^{r} souldiers resolute, some somewhat dissolute ; the Collonel was pleased to honor mee to bee his Comrade ; I shall never fforgett his great love & respect. I rid to my sister at Walden ; I had not seen her in divers yeares ; the Lord hath made a difference in our outward condicons ; I gave her & her children 6*s.* Lord y^{u} canst doe more y^{n} returne it againe to mee.

June. 14. At my Lady Honywoods wee agreed to meet on Tuesday to seeke God for o^{r} armyes and I went to prayer ; even while wee were in prayer our armyes were conquering. [1]

June. 17. Mr Sedgwicke, Mr Grey, and my selfe, kept a day of humiliacon at Markshall.

[1] At Naseby.

This day was I ordered by ye Committee as Constant Chaplyn to attend upon Coll : Harlakenden's regiment at Masten and to receive 10s. per diem as a salary for the same ; this morning if not last night was Leicester taken ; oh ye speedy returne of or prayers. June. 18.

This was a weeke of much mercy to my family ; to mee my eyes better, my daughter recovered, I was designed to a place of service in ye army. Lord inable mee for it and make me faithfull and usefull in the same to ye nation in ye great victory and the consequences of it, as also in smaller fights in divers parts of ye kingdome ; God was good to me in ye Sabbath his name be praised, in ye ordinance of baptisme, I baptized after the order of ye Directory ; I gave notice of a fast, and a day of thanksgiving. June. 22

A day of publike humiliacon. June. 25

A day of thanksgiving for ye great victory in Naseby feilds over ye Kings army, by Sr Tho : ffairfax. June. 27

Coll : Harlakenden payd me 50s. for waiting as preacher upon his regimt. to Walden ; this is the first mony that I received of ye States ; God can this way pay in my payings out in his cause and service. Aug. 10.

This day I baptized 3 children. John Read held his own child ; the first that I ever baptized so. Aug. 17.

In ye night I heard the drummes beat at Nether Yeldham ; it proved an alarme upon ye Kings coming downe to Huntington. Aug. 24.

ffast day. I preachd once, after yt I rid to my Coll : quarters to great Chesterford, when wee had an alarme of ye enemyes advance to Cambridge, and presently of his intentions to fall upon or owne quarters. Aug. 27.

I preached at Royston one sermon where or quarters were for present ; God good to us in or march, in or accomodacons. Aug. 31.

Returned home safe with or troops : no damage to any man, one horse shott in ye legge through a mistake : my horse eye hurt : God good to mee in enabling mee for my jorney. Sept. 4.

This weeke God good to us in or returnes of peace ; the enemy fled before us and gone downe to other parts of ye kingdome. Sept. 7.

Some fayling that had promised to goe along with mee, I went Sept. 9.

alone toward Major Haynes, came safe to Cambridge, heard he was at Grantham or Lincolne, upon wch I resolved home, & so went to bed in Sydney Colledge.

Sept. 10. Having ye opportunity of a convoy I resolved to find him out; wee came safe to Huntington; y^{r} I refreshd my selfe with Mrs Taylor; hearing that divers of ye Cabs rold (*sic*) upon ye road wee made ready for o^{r} defence & marchd on; before wee came at Stangate hole, Captaine Warner & divers in his company overtooke us; at Stilton I mett ye welcome newes that Major Haynes at 9 of clocke was at Stamford; much a doe I perswaded y^{m} to march that night to Wainsford bridge, 7 miles in ye night; o^{r} supper was a hard egge, and tough cheese, and pretty course lodging; blessed be God wee had any thing.

Sept. 11. I and 3 more in ye morning rid to Stamford 5 miles; found ye Major who was riding into Grantham, very glad of my company; wee quarterd at Mr Wolphs, a grand malignant here; wee had good lodging and diett.

Sept. 12. A day of publike humiliacon for Scotland, preachd once at St Maryes Stamford.

Sept. 13. Continued at Stamford. Heard the good newes of Bristol. Saw ye sad face of Burleigh house; a litle surfetted with eating grapes.

Sept. 14. Lords day: continued at Stamford; preachd 2 sermons; very ill with my cold; one hurt with his own pistoll upon ye guard.

Sept. 15. An alarme y^{t} ye enemy with Horse was entring o^{r} quarters, ye guard sayd they discryed a great body of y^{m}. Y^{e} Major had a fall; God preserved him; it proved false & was soone quieted.

Sept. 16. Wee marched through Rutlandshire a pleas^{t} litle County to Bilsden in Leicestershire. Coll. Rossiter with 4 troopes of horse came up to us; wee quarterd y^{t} night at Houghton at a poore house; pittiful blacke bread; I gott a white loafe crust; o^{r} lodging was upon straw & a quilt, in o^{r} clothes; I slept well I blesse my God; heard y^{t} Montrose was entred England.

Sept. 17. Marchd out with a short breakfast; randevoud at Leicester, where Coll. Rossiters troopes marchd from us; beheld ye ruines of a brave house,[1] sometimes ye Earle of Devonshire's; nothing standing but ye stone works; from hence wee marchd towards Ashby; refreshd o^r^ selves upon ye way, but o^r^ meat smelt; I pocketted 2 white loafes agst ye worst.

Quarterd at Ibstocke, Lauds living, now Dr Lovedyns, a great Cavalier; o^r^ diett very good, and lodging indifferent. Sept. 18.

Marchd in ye head of two troopes to Rounston in Derbyshire, thence to Ashby, much infected with ye plague; wee faced ye house; I prayd with ye Councell of Warre; wee summond ye house; we drew off about night: lost 2 men: one shott in ye breeches & yett had no hurt; killed one of ye Cavaliers: heard ye newes of routing Montrose, Sept. 13.: ye next day to ye ffast: here I eate some of my bread; wee had no beere all day long: marchd backe to Ibstocke: rid in a pretty while before o^r^ troops; 6 men in toune they said of Leichfeld; it scard our men and made them ready to run. I was in ye house & heard nothing. I have cause for ever to praise God for the mercyes of this day; one of ye men was slaine on the ground where I had stood closely a litle before, not knowing of the perdue in the ditch, who shott ye man presently after. Sept. 19.

Marchd through Leicester; saw ye ruines of some part of ye towne; so to Roulston, quarterd y^r^; o^r^ usage good. Sept. 19.

Randevoud at Shemington. 3 troopes marchd off with Rossiter to Grantham, and the other 5 came safe through providence to Stamford. Sept. 20.

Preached 2 sermons at Stamford; God good to mee in ye same. I hope not without good to ye people: wee spoyle one of ye Church ffeasts ye day; people are still for y^r^ old wayes. Sept. 21.

Left ye Major and came safe to Cambridge; suppd with ye Comittee; angerd y^m^ at Huntington. Sept. 22.

Returned safe to Colne to my deare wife & freinds, my place supplyed in my absence I praise God: Sept. 23.

Publique ffast; preachd once. Sept. 24.

[1] Leicester Abbey. It had been the headquarters of the King from May 30 to June 2, but was demolished by his troops, probably to prevent its being useful to the enemy.

Oct. 10. Ye County newes about presbytery,[1] and ye alarme of the Kings coming with 2000 horse to Newarke.

Oct. 12. Wee gathered for poore Taunton, wherin God was good to mee in opening my mouth and opening my peoples hearts; wee gathered 8*l.* 4*s.* 4*d.*, beyond any presidents[2] about us.

Oct. 14. Reported the plague is at Kelvedon. Mr Sawyer chose burgesse of Colchester, an unworthy act but suitable to the men.

Oct. 16. Came the wellcome newes of ye taking of Basing; its to be razed; of a truth many habitacons are layd waste.

Oct. 18. Heard the newes of Major Haynes his routing 300 of ye enemies horse and taking an 150 of them; Lord prosper that man; my mayde went away; send mee one Ld that feareth thy name.

Oct. 21. Rid to Chelmsford, motiond my busynes with Mr Archer to Col. Cooke.

Oct. 23. Finished or busynes: Earl of Warwicke payd my ordinary 2*s.* 6*d*: in so great a meeting not an oath sworne.

Oct. 24. L: Coll: Grimes with us; God preserved him hitherto from many dangers, not to loose one drop of blood, no wound, but dry ones, great blows & bruises.

Oct. 27. This day in ye feilds I found a bucke; Mr R. H. was with mee, with his greyhounds; after much sport wee kild her in ye river; this was an unexpected providence.

Oct. 31. Two of Thaxted were with mee early about accepting their place; I gave them an answer of my unfitnes, advised them to consider how to make the place comfortable for a minister.

Nov. 2. In the Sabbath made a mocon to the Towne, now to settle my meanes, or else to leave mee to my due liberty; my sonne troubled with bleach, but very jocund.

Nov. 5. My townesmen made some beginnings to better my meanes.

Nov. 6. 7. Thaxted men came not; a good providence, for my townesmen had not yet settled their busynes.

Nov. 10. My good ffreind Mr Harlakenden perplexed about his shrivaltey, an offer of an under sheriffe unto him; Mr Crane with him about it.

[1] vide Gardiner's *Great Civil War*, iii. 6, 7.

[2] Precedents.

Heard of ye returne of Mr Harl : sworne high sheriffe for Nov. 29.
Essex.

Major Haynes wee heard was coming home with his men : 1645 :
Heard of Major Haynes his returne into ye County. Jan. 6.

Received 6 weekes pay of the Major as his chaplayne ; it was Jan. 10.
a good providence of God towards mee to supply all other wants.

Decemb. 8. at night, on Monday, new moone, it began to frize, Long & Hard Frost.
and so continued exceeding violent ; ye ice of wonderfull thicknes, after a months time it thawed, a little, and raynd, but continued to frize untill Jan : 28 : it begun to thawe, & raynd ; ye frost wonderfully in the ground, and the ice of wonderfull thicknes ; nigh half a yard in some places ; a quarter of an ell at least in my pond : by reason of thawes it was wonderfull glancy : the thawe was as earnest as ye frost : admirable in its kind ; ye frost & ice was sooner out of ye ground then expected.

Wheras a supply of bookes is necessary for me, & my meanes Jan. 30.
but small to purchase them, I haue layd downe a resolucon, to buy but few, and those of choise & special concernm^{t}, and to allott towards the same a moity of all those moneyes, that providence doth by guift or otherwise unexpectly & freely supply mee withall ; and to purchase them at the second hand, out of libraries that are to be sold.

This day I resolved upon & entred agayne upon the practice ffeb. 4.
of Hebrew ; I find it so usefull that I resolve to spend a good part of my time therin, and the Lord blesse and prosper my endeavo^{rs} y^{r}in.

Rid to Wormingford; kindly entertayned by my Lady Waldgrave. ffeb. 16.
17. bought Mr Pilgrims library for 16*l.* 18 : brought it to Colne a very rayny afternoone ; the bookes had no hurt, unloaded y^{m}. dle. 19.

Lent M^{r} W : Harlakenden. 30*l.* ; God hath shined upon mee & ffeb. 24.
increased us somewhat in the midst of all thes difficult times.

Since the last fast God hath beene gratious to our forces at ffeb. 25.
Chester, in ye West at Torrington ; and though many in South Wales, especially in Glamorganshire, have revolted, the Lord is able to turne it to ye best.

March. 5. A day of P. thanksgiving for Chester, and ye victory at Torrington, God good to mee in ye same.

March. 6. 1645 : carryed 4. qters of barly wch I bought of Mr Litle at 18*s.* per qter to Goodman Potter to malt for mee.

1646 : March. 25. Heard of ye route of ye Ld Ashley, thus Gods enemies fall everywhere.

April. 16. Kept a P. day of thanks, for o^r western successes & over Sr Jacob Ashly[1] : wherin the lord was good to mee, as also in breaking up a match of wrestling in the Towne, wherat were gathered nigh 500 people ; Exeter was now in the catalogue of o^r mercies.

April. 19. I mett $Lieu^t$ Coll. Grimes, who received an 100*l.* guift from y^e $Parliam^t$ for the newes of Exeter which he brought to the houses.

Rosebuds. Wee had damaske rose buds in o^r garden before the middle of April this yeare 1646.

May. 8. Good society at the Priory ; Mr Harlakenden returned safe from London & his company ; newes that the king in a disguise was gone from Oxford: *sic transit gloria mundi* : a report that their was a chardge drawne up against him about the death of King James : its reported when he was dressing of him the Duke of Richmond asked him what he meant, what he intended to do, & whither to goe ; he told him he must goe, but whither he must not tell him. But I goe, sayd he, to my freinds and thine ; whereupon some supposed he intended the Scots army & Contry, but I imagine he intends either to lye hid somewhere or els for Ireland, which is most probable.

May. 8. At my Lady Honywoods : heard of ye sad end of one Rust, who drowned him selfe ; my preservacon is of God ; of a monster borne about Colchester, first a child, y^n a serpent, y^n a toad which lapped. The King found in the Scots army ; Lord preserve the kingdomes in union.

May. 19. P. Day of thankes.

May. 20. This day I had in my garden a full ripe & blowne damaske rose : May : 17 : the L^{ds} day before, my wife had a fayre bud : I conceived it argued a very early spring.

[1] Defeated at Stow-in-the-Wold.

Day of Humiliacon. May. 29.

My last quarter was now brought in & that fully by Mr Elliston & M^r high sheriffe. May. 31.

Gatherd nigh 40*s*. for poore Leicester. June. 21.

This day I held against Oates the Anabaptist, morning & afternoon, argum^t that they had no ministry, and y^t particular Christians out of office had no power to send ministers out to preach; he confessd it, and held only to doe what he did as a disciple; I shewed him it was contrary to Scripture; our discourse was without passion; the man boldly continued in Towne till Wednesday, exercising all three dayes. June. 29.

A motion made to buy the widow Bentals land July. 18.

Mr Harlakenden & I went up to the widdow Bentals, to view the land, which was hers by inheritance; John Kent her father had an estate in it for life, if redeemed, but at present, it was in mortgage for 150*l*. to two of Coggeshall; her father promised to joyne in the sale; shee asked me, *220l*. as shee had been bidden, and I bid her her price within 3*l*. and parted till next day. July. 20.

Wee mett againe, I gave the widdow her price; her father and shee surrendered it to mee, whereupon wee tore a bond of 300*l*. that Kent had given not to trouble the widdow nor her heyres in the estate; so I came home very well satisfyed: but going up to John Read, he holds the surrend^r was good for nothing, because the morgagors stand for present possest of the land; this perplexed, especially because of Kents bond that was rent, wherupon I went up againe to them and giving them bond for their money they entred both into 300*l*. bond to strengthen y^r act, with any further surrender at the next Court; this wee feard Kent would not have done, but by providence he was willing. July. 21.

I rid to Colchester to advise with my Cosin Josselin the steward, who advised mee to press the morgagors to surrender to mee, or Kent & Bentalls act was good for nothing; wherupon I rid to Cogshall, and spoke with them & found them very willing to doe any reasonable demand, wherupon I sent to the steward who came over unto us, July. 22.

This day, & kept Court: Coxe Gray surrendered the land to mee, July. 23.

paying them in their money, which I had all of M[r] Harlakenden, to whom againe I surrendered the land for his security.

July. 24. I lett my farme for 3 yeares to Brewer old Spooners sonne in lawe, without wood to dischardge Lords rent, tith, and pay mee 12*l.* 5*s.* per annum : I am to get it in repayre and he is to keepe the same.

July. 25. I put of [1] the fallow to my tenant for 13*s.* 4*d.* rent, and 10*s.* plowing ; the rent I promise him, when he leaves it againe.

Aug. 4. Rid towards Chelmsford with M[r] high sheriffe a great trayne of gentlemen, & about 30 liveries ; he dined us all at his owne cost ; I procured a chamber & entertainm[t] for the Ministers ; I lay well accomodated at my Cosin Rogers to God be praise.

Aug. 5. Preached the assize sermon before Judge Bacon, & Seargeant Turner Judges of Assize on Rom : 12 : 3. 4 : wherin God was good to mee, for voyce, and memory, and spirit. I dined with the judges who used mee with respect.

Aug. 8. I stayed all the assize time as chaplayne to M[r] high sheriffe waiting on him at his board to say grace ; he used me very lovingly & kindly.

Aug. 13. My Cosen Josselins opinion was I had a right to Josephs land.

Aug. 16. Heard of the peace betwixt the Rebells, and the Kings party in Ireland. Lord helpe, for designes are layd to enthrall us againe, & againe.

Aug. 28. A comission sat in y[e] contry for charitable uses to inquire into lands disposed or moneyes for such end, and had not beene performed.

Aug. 31. This Monday my wife & I rod to Havingfeild : I from thence, Sep : 1 : to Cranham ; found my uncles well, & fayre respect in the busines of my uncle Josephs land.

Sept. 6. The plague increaseth & devoureth at London, y[e] Lord in mercy aswage the same.

Sept. 7. Rid to Colchester, God good to mee, going & returning; my Cosin Josselin told mee my cause in the busines of Josephs land was good, & he wished mee to proceed therin.

Sept. 8. Sent by M[r] Toby Cressener letters to both my Uncles, the exe-

[1] Let.

cutors of my grandfathers will to acquaint them with my clayme & intent to stand by my title unto the land : bought some of Mr Turners litle pasture with money Mrs M. Church gave mee, whom God stirred up to bee a faithfull, loving & constant freind to us : the plague very much in London, and sicknesses in ye contry.

A merveylous wett season, winter coming on very early ; a great hop yeare : wheat this yeare was exceedingly smitten & dwindled & lanke, especially on strong grounds ; all manner of meates excessive deare, beefe at cheapest 2½*d.* per *lb.* butter & cheese very deere & yett it was a very rich grasse yeare. Sept. 15.

On Monday Septemb. 14 : 1646 the noble Earle of Essex died : his death is a great weakening to the Peerage of England. Essexs death.

A Publike thankesgiving. Sept. 22.

This day was a day of much mercy ; some freinds fayling mee, I was supplyed with an horse for my jorney, & Mr Jeffery Little rod with me : this day was exceeding pleasant, the like not in divers weekes before ; I had like with a packe horse to have been beaten into a deepe loome pitt but God preserved mee ; I rod safe & returned safe, praise to the Lord that kept mee. I found my uncle Simon at home, I made a demand of the land before three witnesses, wch is in ye box with my writings of Mallories ; my uncle seemed perswaded & convinced of my right, & to delivr up ye land to mee wthout any suite or trouble ; when I came home I was very ill, I had a great inclinacon to vomitt, which through mercy I did & brought some water off my stomacke ; upon wch I was well, went to bed & rested comfortably to ye Ld bee praise. Sept. 23.

Mr Lorkyn with mee for his certificate of his qualificacon for a minister : to whom I gave my hand : I nevr gave my hand to any other but only Mr Cane as yett to my best remembrance : & herin desire of God caution & warynes. Sept. 26.

I received a letter from my uncles ; the Lord direct my spirit what to doe ; I made a motion to my people, that ye yeare being out, if they continued yr contribucon & made it good 80*l.* a yeare I would continue with them God willing ; if not I must cheerfully serve the providence of God : & so I doe resolve by Gods grace. Heard of ye tumults at Halsted, great disorders. Sept. 27.

Sept. 28. Writt to my Uncles to meete at Chelmsford Octob : 8. with either of us a freind to make a finall end & conclusion in our busines if possible.

Oct. 1. Dind at Mr Braclyes : my wife went with mee ; Mr Ludgater brought mee this day my money ; I payd the widdow, now Penhackes wife, all y^t^ I ought her, so that now all my debts are come into Mr Harlakendens hands.

Oct. 8. Rid to Chelmsford ; y^r^ by 9 of ye clocke and very dry, and so also homewards, though very much raine fell y^t^ day, and before us on the road ; my uncles mett, not only Simon ; wee resolved to goe over to Josephs execut^rs^. Mr Grimston kind in giving mee advice in my case ; some hopes to get an augmentacon for our living out of ffeering Berry being an impropriacon of ye B^ps^ of Londons, whose estate is now sequestrated.

Oct. 11. This weeke the weather continued very wett and sad in respect of ye season, litle rye & mislen [1] or wheat sowne.

This weeke I drew up a peticon for augmentacon of o^r^ meanes ; it was presented to Mr Grimston, who promiseth all fayre respect ; y^s^ was Octob. 9 & 10.

Oct. 14. 15. Rod to my Uncle Hudsons ; God gratious in his providence towards mee, in providing me with horse, fayre season, out & home, in finding my way, preserving mee safe in my jorney. My Uncle Simon mett not, my other Uncles are very confident they shall injoy the estate, which if they justly doe I am content ; wee agreed that our Counsell should discourse in the businesse.

Oct. 20. 21. Mr Harlakenden kept his Courts : they were payring Courts, men coming in with their wives to take up houses ; most poore people ; one man purchased a house to him & his wife, and y^r^ heyres, & for want of such heyres to the heyres of the survivor. Wee chose two honest men for our constables Edw. Clarke & Christopher Mathew.

Oct. 23. Payd Mr Harlakenden 50*l*. I borrowed of him.

Oct. 24. Received a letter from Mr Harrington that my money was ready and that I should have it when I sent for it, for wch I blesse God ;

[1] Mixed corn, e. g. wheat and rye.

at night I heard by Major Haynes that our shippe wherin my part was about 18*l*. was cast away, three men drowned, but the merchants saved their goods; this was the first froune upon my estate from my first being of age; the M^r of the shippe oweth mee about 6*l*. for hoppes, which I duobt will come in heavily.

A wonderfull sad wett season, much corne in many places abroad, rotted & spoyled in ye fields, grass exceedingly trodden under foote & spoyled by cattle through the wett which hath continued almost since the Assizes; worke very dead, woolle risen to 16*d*. in the pound & upwards, butter and cheese, and meate very deare, and corne rising: litle corne sowne, and a very sad season still continued; great divisions & feares of our utter ruine in ye kingdome.

Mr Sayer writte us word that an augmentacon was conferred upon mee out of the impropriacon of ffeering; if it prove effectuall, it will ease mee of much care & enable mee more closely for my studdyes. Oct. 31.

This weeke the wettnes of the season continued with litle or no intermission & so it hath continued for above two months. Nov. 1.

Heard my 50*l*. per annum was likely to come to nothing; Gods will be done. Nov. 8.

A frost, and pleasant day, at night I was subpenad into the Chancery by my Uncle Hudson, & Ri: Josselin: it was in the businesse of Josephs land. Nov. 12.

This day I went to Stansted hall and received 8*l*. Sr John Jacob ought mee; I feare I had 6*d*. to much which I intend to restore to him; injoy much love and good society at Mr Litles. Nov. 18.

This day was ye P. ffast; it was wett in ye morning so wee went not to Church untill eleven and I continued preaching untill sun was sett, wherin I found God exceeding good to mee; the sad wett season still continued: Some sewd mislain Novemb 23. et 24: I shall observe how so late sowne rye prospers; it was on lusty lands. Nov. 25.

Mr Harlakenden came from London; he received 56*l*. for me of Mr Harrington; I made it up, threescore and twelve pounds towards the paym^t of the hundred pounds I borrowed of him. Nov. 27.

He and Sr Tho: Honywood joyntly obtained an order to receive the bishops rents out of the impropriacon of ffeering 10*l*. or 12: out of Wittam 12*l*. out of Wethersfeild 15*l*. out of great Dunmowe 36*l*, and to divide it betwixt the two townes of Earles Colne, and Markshall.

Nov. 29. God good to mee in society of divers honest neighbours at Gdman Mathewes, where speaking concerning our intermission of the Lords Supper, I told them, that perhaps some feared offending people in point of my maintenance; they would deny mee my stipend, I told them for my part, loving his ordinance, and to pursue the injoying of it by scripture rules, I would willingly trust God with my meanes and would not have them intermitt for that: and this I may doe & trust God who in his way will provide.

Nov. 30. ffinding ye exceeding misse of Hebrew, (whereof, although, I have a little smattering) yett I begun this day to assume my dayly studdy yrof, which I intend God willing to prosecute, and not give over if the Lord give mee life, untill I have obtained some indifferent skill yrof; oh my folly to forgett my schoole entrance, and to neglect this studdy at Cambridge & with no more dilligence to pursue it since;

Dec. 6. I went on in my endeavors in the Hebrew, & made good progress therin, blessed bee my God; things are duobtfull for the Scots and us, but Ormond in Ireland playd deceitfully.

Dec. 9. Mr high sheriffe with me; I drew a peticon for him to ye Lds to take of his burthen; he was much afrayd it would continue another yeare. I ventured with him it would be passed in both Houses, a sheriffe for Essex, before Christmas, or I was to give him 5*s*. for two bokes, which if,[1] I was to have them for nothing. Mr Wm Harlakenden went towards London; I gave him 5*s*. to buy me two Hebrew Grammers; his cheife occasion was about the sheriffes businesse.

Dec. 11. Mr Wm Harlakenden made a speedy, and safe returne from London; our high sheriffe likely to bee of, yr being another passed by both Houses; I received my two bookes from him; I am glad

[1] i.e. If a new sheriff were chosen.

he is so neare an end of his troubles, & care in that office ; the goldsmith of Chelmsford kild and robd upon y[e] road, as he returnd from Braintree markett by three troopers ; its Gods mercy and goodnes that preserves mee, my house, and that I injoy in safety.

M[r] Harlakenden received his dischardge from his shrivaltry, one M[r] Pyott being sworne in his roome for next yeare ; I hope ere long he will act as Justice for the good of towne & contry. Dec. 21.

On Tuesday. 22 : I saw an order wherin the rents of 12*l.* per annum out of ffeering: 12*l.* out of Witham: 15*l.* out of Wethersfeild & 36*l.* out of Dunmow, in all 75*l.* was allowed toward the augmentacon of my meanes, and y[e] Ministers of Markshall equally which is 37*l.* 10*s.* yearly, and this the sequestrators are to pay at the due time. Dec. 23.

Monthly fast. I preachd but once ; heard the King was slipt into Holland, but I hope its not true. Dec. 30.

This day I went downe to the Pryory to M[r] Harlakenden & fully dischardged my morgage, & made even with him ; I gave him a bill of my hand for tenne pounds, & then when his fine is payd, I am in a good forwardnes out of debt. Dec. 31.

This day wee begun to digge a well, which I let to ffossett at 9*d.* per foote : Jan. 7. WELL.

About M[r] ffaulconers businesse :

I distinctly remember that M[r] ffaulconer sold to Goodman Taller of Aldham a portion of tithes, which he had in lease from S[r] Robert Quarles, which anciently did belong to the priory ; he was to receive 10*l.* presently, and 10*l.* att the making of the deed, or setting over his right, as Councell should advise, & that within a short time.

Now wheras M[r] ffaulconer saith that M[r] Harlakenden was to assist him so that he might receive something from S[r] Robert Quarles heire, I remember no such agreem[t] in my presence, but this I remember, that M[r] ffaulconer, giving in bond to redeliver the deeds to Goodman Taller, was to have the use of them if he could therby make any advantage agst the heyre of Quarles :

And wheras M[r] ffaulconer saith he was to make neither bond or promise, I remember no such condicon agreed unto : only thus much that he was only to set over his owne right, and to bee at no further charge.

Jan. 18. Went down to Gaines Colne, present at giving possession of land; the manner thereof: Any one cutts up a clod & sticke, & stickes it in ye clod; the man that is in possession remains alone in the ground; he to whom he delivers possession enters to him to whom he delivers the clod & so possession of the whole according to agreement; then he comes forth & leaveth the other in possession who then presently comes out.

Jan. 29. I am now preparing for London to answer the suites of my Uncles about Josephs land; my resolucon is this (by Gods grace) to repaire to learned Councell, & if they say the right is mine, to endeavo^r^ an arbitracon, and make an end of the controversie peaceably if possible, and to stand to the end of the arbitrato^rs^ w^t^soever; if I have no right I will no way molest or trouble, but endeavo^r^ that those that have right may injoy it.

ffeb. 2. Rid safe to London, well entertained at Mr Cresseners, but very weary of my jorney; I spake with both the seargeants in our suites; gave seargeant Turner a peice for his advice in both my causes; he declared to mee the way of my Cousin Josselin's opinion, the issue I leave to providence.

ffeb. 3. Went downe to Westminster, spake with both ye seargeants, concluded a meeting to end our businesse, March. 3. at London; bought a few toyes, payd my tenths to Abbott, returnd safe, to Cranham, praised bee God, but very weary & sore; the wind blew hard in my face.

ffeb. 4. Came home safe, to God bee praise, and received a penny at my owne doore as a poore man, being unknowne to all mine.

ffeb. 6. Newcastle ours, the King with our Commissioners, & the Scots going out of the Kingdome; hope of good agreem^t^.

ffeb. 21. This weeke heard ye King came die 16. to Homeby with our Commissioners.

ffeb. 27. Received notice by letter to bee at London March 11. to end our suite, all parties willing; I intend God willing to bee their, although it is ye day after the fast.

ffeb. 28. Cromwell called home from ye army to attend ye affayres of y^e^

house according to the ordinance upon which ye new Modell was raised: reported so but not true.

This day heard that Sr Tho: ffairfax his army was come to March. 6.
quarter in our parts of the kingdome; the Lord in mercy turne it unto good; some of the generalls owne regiment att Halsted.

Rid to London safe, mett my uncle Simon, went downe to March.11.
Sargeant Turners; he could not attend to end our businesse; went downe to Westminster; wee delivered two peticons to ye Lds & Commons to remove the souldiers out of the County; the Lords gave us thanks for our good affection, and promised to take it into consideracon; went to Mr Kequiches: found his sister Mrs Elizabeth King sicke of the small poxe, but in good hopes of her life: as returned into London, I mett my uncle Ri: and Hudson; wee weht togither, lay togither, and that night & next morning, wee concluded our business, I to injoy the land, and to pay to them an 100*l.*; came safe to Cranham.

Came safe praised bee God to Colne; no souldiers with us yett, March.13.
blessed bee the name of God; found all mine well, and Mary rid of her ague, to God alone bee glory and praise; my charges besides jorneyes came to 1*l.* 10*s.* & no more; the Lord bee praised for this comfortable, contentfull end, the Lord blesse them & theirs with ye mony, & mee & mine with the lands.

This yeare I begun in a visitt of the Generall his Excellency 1647:
Sr Tho: ffairfax, at my lady Veeres in Hinningham, where I had March.26.
the honor and favor to discourse with him, and dine with him; he is a man thankefull for respects, and yett casts away honor from himself; wee rid outwards on his way with him, tooke or leaves, and returnd in safety praise bee unto God:

Or constant loving freind Mrs Mary gave my wife a gold ring, and my selfe a silver tooth and eare picke, as a remembrance of her love; my dearest wife would needs also bee so bounteous as to give mee a silver seale, to use and not loose for her sake.

Above 60 of Major Desboroughs troope quartered with us one April. 5.
night; I was free through providence; by them heard the gentlemen sent up about the peticon,[1] yt caused the declaracon of both

[1] Vide Gardiner, *Great Civil War*, iii, 254, etc.

Houses, were returnd; the matter quiett; that all officers in commission were shortly to meete att Walden; the Lord in mercy direct affaires for the best, and prevent our jealousies: the souldiers are civill; divers of them cast out evill words, agst presbyterians, and ministers, particularly. L. E.; (*sic*) the presbyterians are so bitter, he did not desire but to quarter with some honest Independent.

April. 6. Captain Laurence, a very faire civil gentleman, with some part of his troope, came and quartered among us.

April. 28. P. Day of humiliacon.

April. 30. This day rid to Bollinghatch; all my uncles met, and gave mee free & peaceable possession of those parcels of land given to Joseph; I payd the executors of Joseph 20*l*, gave them bond for 80*l*, received 7*l*. 16*s* of the mony of my uncle Simon for rent due: God good in his providence towards us, outwards, and homewards; this land part of our antient inheritance; now I have about 20*l*. per annum in land, besides my wives land, and my stocke, but I owe in all about one hundred pounds.

May. 4. Souldiers removed y^r^ quarters from us.

May. 9. This weeke gave us some hopes of blowing over the discontents of the army, and hopes of accord through the meanes of Skippon entertaining the command of Ireland, & the houses yeelding to the souldiers in divers particulars.

May. 12. This day I received in 50*s*. quarteridge [1] from the towne, a greater summ then I had received in divers weekes before.

May. 17. Heard high language of ye souldiers intencons & resolucons, though I scarce may creditt they should be so bold. Reports of souldiers foote, abusing of women; they are now coming towards us; ye Lord be ou^r^ guard & protection from y^r^ violence & insolency. I had some rugged wordes from one of them, a Lieuten^t^, about quartering, wherby I perceive hnw unable poore men are to containe y^r^ spirits, if ever they are in imployment.

May. 23. This spring was forward; yett all things continued excessive deare; if grass had not come on, our wants would have beene very great; wee had plenty of roses; stilled some May. 22.

[1] He should have received £3. 15, 0, one fourth of the £15, the sum due to him yearly.

May. 30. My towne full of foote souldiers but very quiett & orderly, without any disturbance from them hitherto.

May. 31. Payd Mr H : his fine, 8*l*. for my land ; he used mee reasonably, and lovingly.

June. 1. 160 souldiers came to quarter in or towne ; they should have marched & disbanded this day, but they refused, fell into distempers, & marcht towards yr generall ; the Lord in mercy give a good issue unto things : the souldiers marchd from us, June. 2, quietly, but afterwards they were a greater burthen where they became ; it was a providence of God towards us, the lord doe us good by ye same ; ye reports of the souldiers distempers continued, and yr words very high ; wee are still in the hands of God, and his purposes shall and must stand.

June. 6. This weeke yr is a sad turne and change on the face of the kingdome ; what God will doe wee knowe not, the counsell of Jehovah shall stand ; the poore ministers are in straites on all hands, but the name of the Lord, is a tower unto his.

June. 13. Spent much time & tooke especiall care to drawe up a faire peticon to ye house that they would have a speciall respect to our safety & ye content of ye army, & this wee did as farre as possible wthout passionate overswaying affection to either part ; & this we rather did to prevent the subscribing divers heady peticons that went up & downe ye contry tending to disturbance.

June. 20. Wee endeavourd a faire peticon to the house ; it was generally resented in the house ; I hope it will prevent higher ones in the County from taking place.

July. 1. Or gentlemen went towards London with our peticon ; the Lord prosper and succeed them in the worke and undertaking, and give them favor in the eye of our Magistrate. Mett at Mr Owens for conference ; ye peticon was well accepted, and thankes returned.

July. 6. The charge agst the 11 members was this day delivered into ye House of Commons.[1]

July. 8. Thomas Prentice married ; I preachd and married them in a method that gave great content to honest people ; Tho : ffrends offerd freely ; he tooke about 56 pounds.

[1] vide Gardiner, *Great Civil War*, iii, 298.

July. 26. This day the parliam[t] was forced by the Londoners in the matter of their militia; the busines was plotted, and brake out on this occasion; as some report, its like to be the rise of troubles to us; the King endeavourd to make escape from the army and joyne with the Londoners.

July. 27. House of Commons adjourned untill 29.

July. 29. This day the most of the Lords & members being withdrawn, the members that continued mett, chose a new Speaker one Pelham, voted themselves a parliam[t]; Massey was chosen to command the city forces, Skippen resigning.

Y[e] army marching up towards London to redresse tumults, the City makes great preparacons to defend themselves, and impute y[e] combustions to y[e] army, medling with y[e] militia, w[ch] they told them would raze y[e] foundacons and cause tumults.

July. 31. 2 Troopes of Dragoones were sent by the Generall to surprise the blocke house at Tilbury in Essex to command the Thames, which was effected.

Aug. 5. Sett apart to seeke God in regard of the straites and difficulties by reason of y[e] London tumults; wee mett at Coggeshall, and y[r] y[e] newes mett us of a preparative accord betwixt y[e] City & army & much good newes concerning y[e] same, y[e] L[d] answering our prayers while the thought was in our heart; y[e] day was very comfortable. 8 ministers prayed & in y[e] midle one preacht; God was very good to us his name have y[e] praise of all.

Aug. 8. This weeke y[e] Lord began to blowe over our feares of a new warre; the citye was in division & not as one man for a new warre, blessed bee God; and that made way, especially by the meanes of South-warke complying with the army, for an accord, which, in my apprehension, was one of the greatest acts of the army, performed

July. 27. on so great a city; a pretended parliament sitting to encourage them what was in their power, and that from Tuesday when they had the first notice y[r]of, by Wednesday sennight following, in nine dayes the army entring Southwarke Aug. 4, and y[e] accorde made that night with London, the army being scattered, the head quarters at Bedford, some souldiers in Suffolke, others 100[d] miles and more from London; they say in their declaracon some were gone from them 200 miles; this was wonderfull in o^r^ eyes.

Times of great sicknes and illnes, agues abounding more then in all my remembrance, last yeare and this also; feavers spotted rise in the contry; whether it arise from a distempered and infected aire I know not, but fruite rottes on ye trees as last yeare, though more, and many cattle die of ye murraine, this portends something. Aug. 15.

A fayre day; land is through mercy in a good case, and the seed time good; the Lord send us plenty: all provisions are excessive deare & scarce to be gotten for our money. Aug. 16.

The Lord good in the season which was very faire, and as fitt a good time as ever came; things are at that rate as never was in our dayes, wheat 8*s.* malt 4*s.* beefe. 3*d.*[1] butter 6*d.* ob.[2] cheese 4*d.* candle 7*d.* currants 9*d.* sugar 18*d.* and every other thing whatsoever deare; the souldiers also returning to quarter againe with us, and that in a great proportion viz: 25: Sept. 26.

Y^s^ day wee had 25 Troops came to quarter with us, somewhat bold and vapouring; through mercy I yett escaped free from them. Sept. 27.

P. ff. Some few of the Troopers were with us hearing. Sept. 29.

Troopers removed y^r^ quarters having staid with us 10 dayes. We had 25 of Capt. Tailours troops in ffleetwoods regiment. Oct. 7.

Y^e^ season was very faire and wholesome; the plague abated in London and Chester blessed bee God; the kingdome in a strange unsetled frame. Oct. 17.

P. ffast. Oct. 27.

The King Nov: 11: about or before supper time escaped from Hampton Court and went downe to the Ile of Wight to Coll: Hammond, who is one of the Coll: of the army (and is to marry Cromwells daughter) and its conceived this businesse was not done without the privitie of many great ones in the army; this is certaine, letters dated that even, conjecturing whither the King Nov. 14.

[1] Beef was usually 2*d.* a pound. "The year 1646 was the first of a series of six years in which the harvest was deplorably bad." Gardiner, *Great Civil War*, iii, 195.

[2] Obolus=halfpenny.

was gone, mention it as most possible to the Ile of Wight. Great endeavo[rs] to divide the army, but not effected hitherto.

Nov. 18. Payd the last 40*l.* of the hundred for my land at Roxwell.

Dec. 5. Troopes among us, very erroneous fellowes, but otherwise indifferent civill.

Dec. 25. People hanker after the sports and pastimes that they were wonted to enjoy, but they are in many families weaned from them.

1647: Jan. 9. Heard of the votes of the Commons, which seeme to tend to the laying aside of the King; the Lord direct them.

Jan. 13. Our souldiers removed from us; I have through providence to this day never beene troubled to quarter either horse or foote, nor received any affronts from them.

Jan. 14. P[d] in the most part of our 6 months assessm[t] into the hands of y[e] high collector & received dischardges.

Jan. 15. At night, 60 of Major Swallows Troope in Whaley's regiment, that were on y[e] guard that night the King removed from Hampton, came to quarter with us; though ill I was forced to make the ticketts.[1]

Warme January. This month of January passed without any frost to mention, or much wett, but was dry, and open, and warme, and free from winde even to the admiracon of persons; roses leaved out: fruite trees beginning to shoote out and so appricockes more, hedges budding out, gooseberries had litle leaves on them.

ffeb. 6. This time was a sad deare time for poore people, onely their worke beyond expectacon continued plentiful and cheape; money almost out of the contry.

ffeb. 11. On ffriday morning my wife was delivered of her second son.

ffeb. 20. Y[s] night againe my sonne very ill; he did not cry so much as y[e] night before; whether the cause was want of strength I knowe not; he had a litle froth in his mouth continually; in the morning y[r] came some redd mattery stuffe out of his mouth, w[ch] made us apprehend his throate might be soare: Lord thy will bee done; he cheerd up very sweetly at night, and in the night was very

[1] i.e. To arrange for quartering the troops in the town.

still; what God will doe I know not, but it becometh mee to submitt to his will.

This day my deare babe Ralph quietly fell a sleepe, and is at rest with the Lord; the Lord in mercy sanctifie his hand unto mee, and doe mee good by it and teach mee how to walke more closely with him. This correction though sad was seasond with present goodnes, for first the Lord had given it us untill both my selfe & wife had gotten strength, and so more fitt to beare it, then if in the depth of our sicknes; the Lord gave us time to bury it in our thoughts; wee lookt on it as a dying child 3 or 4 dayes: 3 it dyed quietly without schreekes, or sobs or sad groanes; it breathd out ye soule with 9 gaspes and dyed; it was ye youngest, & our affections not so wonted unto it. ffeb. 21.

As often times before, so on this day did I especially desire of God to discover and hint to my soule, what is the aime of ye God of heaven more especially in this correction of his upon mee; and when I had seriously considered my heart, and wayes, and compared them with ye affliction and sought unto God, my thoughts often fixed on thes particulars: ffeb. 23.

Wheras I have given my minde to unseasonable playing at chesse, now it run in my thoughts in my illnes as if I had beene at chesse; I shall be very sparing in ye use of that recreacon and that at more convenient seasons.

Wheras I have walked with much vanitie in my thoughts and resolved agst it and have served divers lusts too much in thought, and in actions, wheras both body and soule should bee the Lords who hath called mee to holynes, God hath taken away a sonne; I hope the Lord will keepe my feete in uprightness that I may walke alwayes with him, and I trust it shall bee my endeavo^r^ more than ever:

And also y^t^ I should bee more carefull of my family to instruct them in the feare of God, that they may live in his sight and bee serviceable to his glory.

This weeke after a long restraint, God was pleased to sett mee at liberty againe; I went abroad now commonly againe to any of my freinds & neighbou^rs^ houses; in my restraint I read over March.19.

Meads[1] "Clavis Apocalyptica," and Vaser[2] his "Successio"[3] also; my wife went to church with mee, the Lord bee praised for this mercy in raising her up againe.

Library: Made a full end about the library, I receiving from Mr Layfeild the mony and the residue of the bookes.

1648: March.31. Rid to Colchester; mett Mr Newcomen, & divers other Ministers; wee had much discourse concerning falling into practice[4] and in the first place, seing that elders are to bee chosen, by whom shall it be done; the parliam^t^ proposeth by the people y^t^ have taken ye coven^t^: others, as Mr Owen, conceived this too broad, & would have first a separacon to bee made in our parishes, and that by the minister, and those godly that joyne unto him, and then proceed to choosing.

April. 6. A hearer at Coggeshall; heard that the Ministers with earnestnes endeavord to promote church government.

April. 8. Subscribed a peticon for government to ye parliament, as also an encouragem^t^ to those London Ministers that appeare agst errors; the Lord heale a sad divided kingdome; Mr Newcomen sent to us to meete on Wednesday at Mr Thompsons about proceeding in the matter of church government, but by reason of occasions it was intended the Wednesday following.

April. 10. Meeting at my house; our discourse was concerning baptisme; Mr Harlakenden was afraid of a writt from my Lord of Oxford by a stranger from London, but he came about another businesse, by whom I heard of the sad tumult and rising of divers prentises & other rude people at London, wherin 5 or 6 persons were slaine.

April. 23. Our times grow sad, and threaten stormes every day more than other; places growe very much disaffected unto the parliam^t^; our County now sett on a very dangerous peticon, but I hope in my Towne it is prevented, and not likely to proceed.

May. 1. Heard a report of a tumult at London, Norwich, and this day at

[1] Joseph Mead, B.D., b. 1586, d. 1638. Fellow of Christ's College, Cambridge.

[2] James Ussher, b. 1580, d. 1655.

[3] *De Ecclum Xtianum successione et statu.*

[4] Adopting the new practices.

Colchester, and through mercy all this time wee are in peace : that at Colchester more in feare and rumo[r] then in anything else, upon which the Trayne band was raised.

This day I paid unto Thomas Cowell 10*l.* that formerly I borrowed of him ; now my debts amount to about 50*l.* I hope through Gods goodnes towards mee in some short time to pay them all, if no troubles arise to hinder mee. May. 2.

This day rid to Castle Hinningham, preached the lecture, on Cant. 1. 3. Dined at the ordinary with the gentlemen, who paid my ordinary. May. 9.

Among all y[e] severall judgments on this nacon, God this spring, in y[e] lattter end of April, when rye was earing & eared, sent such terrible frosts, that the eare was frozen & so dyed, and cometh unto nothing : young ashes also y[t] leaved were nipt, and blackt, and those shootes died, as if the Lord would continue our want, and penury, wee continuing o[r] sins. Rye blasted.

The Lord good and mercifull unto us in good and comfortable tidings out of Wales, in quelling the power their in armes [1] in such a sad time, when all the Contrie cried out against the parliament and army and mutinies were in most places, plundering honest men, and continuall threatnings against such. Mens minds exceedingly inraged ; all the base false reports raised that could be to dishearten good men, and to encourage others ; multitudes of base bookes written to stirre up to sedicon, and render the parliament odious unto the kingdome: truly words cannot convey to the understanding of men, the ability to judge what y[e] times were. May. 14

Vile men have lifted up themselves exceedingly, and presumed by the people to bring about their old wayes, and that this cause, thus farre advanced, should fall to y[e] ground & come to nothing. May. 21

The schoole M[r] y[t] is nominated for our towne came over unto mee. May. 29

P. ffast, preacht once, I spent three houres. May. 31

Our Committee men putt out a declaracon of the sense of the Counties peticon ; I was earnestly pressed to appeare in it from them, but I refused. June. 1.

[1] Poyer had seized Tenby Castle and declared for the King.

June. 2. Our committee men met at Chelmsford and were secured by the peticoners[1]; the morning was very wett, wherby Sr Tho. Honywood and Coll. Cooke who intended to bee their, were reserved at home to doe y^r^ country service as they did.

June. 3. Captaine Maidstone brought ye newes[2] to Sr Tho. Honywood. 2 Deputy Lieutenants, Mr Tindall, Mr Sawyer, burgesse for Colchester, refused to joyne with S^r^ Th. H., in raising forces to oppose in our owne defence, wch yett wee agreed to doe, wherin some few did y^r^ best for y^r^ poore contry: for my part I went daily to Coggeshall to observe the worke, wherin I was no hindrance; I went and returned commonly by my Lady Honywoods whom God used as a pretious instrument in this worke.

All this weeke full of rumo^rs^ and feares, the enemies increased apace; our Towne went in on Tuesday: 6: day to Coggeshall, and were the first of the contry that appeared. June. 8. Mr H. came in unto us; wee begun to send out parties of horse this way and that; brought of the Magazine from Braintree; the way was stopt that wee could have no intelligence. Goring and the Kentish men were come into Essex; wee were all young and raw men, yett God in mercy disposed our spirits to resolvednes and a willing laying out ou^r^ selves; we had many alarmes but all false, the enemy never attempted on us at Coggeshall.

June. 11. The enemy marcht on to Braintree die: 10: and this day, being up and downe, plundering and taking away Mr Nicholson 2 miles beyond us upwards to Colchester; our people assembled in armes; wee were not able to drawe into Church for the keeping the Sabbath, but were deprived of that opportunity: wee sett good guards in the towne; at 8 of the clocke y^t^ night the enemy advanced from Braintree to Halsted; wee heard they intended Colchester, but wee knew not for certaine this.

June. 12. On Monday morning the enemy came to Colne, were resisted by our towne men. No part of Essex gave them so much opposicon as wee did; they plundered us, and mee in particular, of all

[1] Gardiner *Great Civil War*, iv, 146 puts the date of this as June 4.

[2] i.e. Of the siege of Colchester: vide Gardiner, *Great Civil War*, iv, 146, &c., for the full account of this siege.

that was portable, except brasse, pewter, and bedding; I made away to Coggeshall, and avoyded their scouts through providence; I praise God for this experiment; it is not so much to part with any thing as wee suppose, God can give us a contented heart in any condicon, and when o^r^ losses may serve to advance Gods glory, wee ought to rejoyce in the spoiling of our goods; this day I borrowed mony for to buy hose, and borrowed a band to wear, having none in my power. I was welcome unto, and pittied by my Lady Honywood.

I returned home, mett with danger by our owne men, who by June. 13. some suddaine accident mistaking mee, fought for mee, but I escaped their hands through Gods mercy, who in their fury might have done mee wrong; I was called for by my freinds and acqainted that y^r^ was no danger, and espying the men still in the streete, my poore babe Mary cryed and pittied mee; but one desired mee to goe out of her house for feare shee should be plundered: it cutt my heart to see my life no more regarded by her, and it was the greatest damper and trouble to my spirit for present that ever I mett with; a true freind shewes, if in adversity, and such I found Mrs Church and her daughter; I am perswaded it cutt the heart of the gentlewoman for what shee said, and y^r^fore I willingly in my spirit passed the unkindnes by. My deare wife was with mee, much amazed: I went to my Lady Honywoods that night, and my wife and all the children, where wee have been kindely entertained; the Lord requite her love; I my wife, and children, could not shift us, untill my Lady furnished us with ye same; that night the Gen. marcht to Colchester, were was a sad skirmish; wee retreated to Lexden, and resolved to drawe a line about the towne.

I went divers times to the leagure, but through Gods providence, I mett with no danger, yett the musketts divers times, and the Drake[1] bullet flew with divers noises neare mee.

[1] "The drake was a brass field gun used in the Civil War, 9 ft. long, weight 143 cwts., carrying a 5 lb. shot and a charge of 4 or 5 lbs. of powder. Many old pieces of artillery were named from animals, a dragon was a carbine; culverin came from the French couleuvre, an adder; a drake and a saker from birds." (Note in *Verney Memoirs*).

June. 10. I preacht at Markshall and Mr Clopton for mee; I preacht in my litle coate as I goe every day; I could not with that confidence venture to Colne at first as afterwards, but being wonted to the troubles, and rationally considering the same, and submitting unto, and resting in Gods providence, I was daily more and more emboldened.

June. 25. This Lords day I preacht at Earles Colne to my owne people, who were glad to see mee preach to them.

June. 28. This was the P: ff: I was perswaded not to preach, but I did, and had the greatest audience, I had many dayes before; but truly our hearts are not cleansed nor our wayes reformed; the Lord goeth out against us in the season, which was wonderfull wett; flouds every weeke, hay rotted abroad, much was carried away with the flouds, much inned but very dirty, and dangerous for catle; corne layd, pulled downe with weeds; wee never had the like in my memory, and that for the greatest part of the summer; it continued to August: 14: when it rained that it made a litle floud, and commonly wee had 1 or 2 flouds weekely, or indeed in the meadowes their was as it were a continuall floud.

Wett summer.

July. 2. I preacht at home, and so I did every Lords day that month, and on the fast day; wee were not troubled with one alarme, but the carts went continually to the leagure, and so did persons, that yr was no distinction made of Sabbath, so that warre truly is ready to make people more vile, a rare thing to see men made better.

Aug. 13. The 2 Lords dayes in this month I preacht to my people. My lady Honywood continueth to afford entertainment still to mee and to my wife and children.

Aug. 16. A very great floud with the great raines last day & night: the season sad, and threatning.

The nacons sins are many & sad, Lord lett publike ones be pardoned; the nacons judgments are, 1: continual raine to the spoyling of much grasse, and threatning of the harvest; 2: the sad charge by warre to the undoing of ye contry; the sad decay of trade in reference to our poore, to our undoing except God finde out some other way of subsistence.

The Warre in the nacon, the divisions among our selves, our cryings out after peace on any termes to save o^r^ skins and estate, w^t^soever become of others, Lord remove thes judgments from us for thy name sake.

My Lady sent home my 3 children, gave us 2 paire of sheets: our children and wee were y^r^ 9 weekes and 4 dayes and had continued their still if Mr Honywood had not fell sicke. Aug.16.17.

Mett in a day of humiliacon at my lady Honywoods; at night wee heard the newes of the Scots rout, a confirmation whereof wee expect. Aug. 22.

Dayly raines, but especially this morning, wee found it exceeding wett; it caused a very great floud, aboundance of hay rotten, much corne cutt and not cutt groweth, and yett men repent not, to give glory unto God: this day a thanksgiving at ye Hith church [1] for ye victory in the North; [2] the enemy in Colchester demanding very high termes on which to surrender the towne. Aug. 24.

Great hopes that Colchester would have surrendered presently, but so great a worke must aske a longer time to effect ye same. Aug. 25.

Wee kept a day of humiliacon: y^t^ night wee heard of ye Scots route, on Friday the season sett in comfortably, and on ye Lords day, Colchester agreed to surrender; speedie and sweet answers of prayers. Aug. 22.

Colchester yeilded; infinite numbers of people went thither; ye Councell of warre adjudged 3 to be shott to death. Sr Charles Lucas, Sr George Lile who accordingly suffered, & Sr Barnaby [3] Gascoine an Italian who was spared. [4] Aug. 28.

Aug: 30: a wett night, and wettish day, as if God would have called men to his w^p^, but their was no regard of the same; my thoughts growe strong within mee to give over preaching at Colne at Michaelmas, and to declare the same beforehand, to the cheife P. ff.

[1] The Hythe was the landing place for boats arriving from the mouth of the Colne.

[2] At Preston.

[3] This should be Sir Bernard.

[4] "Gascoine, who had already taken off his doublet to die with his comrades, was told that he was reprieved. His foreign extraction, combined, it is said, with the devoutness of his preparation for death, had saved him." Gardiner, *Great Civil War* iv, 204.

inhabitants; Lord direct mee what to doe, I have given out speeches of my enforcement unto it; I preacht once this day on Amos 8 : 11. 12, concerning the famine of the word wherin having occasion to speake of the conditon of this land I delivered my thoughts to this purpose.

People, when our armies had conquered all our enemies, my thoughts were sad concerning the displeasure of God remaining towards England; and I told you Essex must not escape, which is come to passe by the marchings of Goring & his army and plundering many places, persons, the sad ruine of Colchester by fire, the decay of trade by their losses, the charge of the countie in mainteyning their forces at the seidge, and sending in provisions for above 11 weekes for many thousands of horse and foote; my thoughts were and are sad concerning England still, not from the rising of many counties agst the parliam[t], the strong invasion of the Scots upon us, for my thoughts verily were God would breake them; but when I consider the decay of the power of godlynesse among christians, y[r] flightinesse of Spirit towards Gods ordinance, the wofull uncontroulable encrease of all manner of wickednes among us, y[e] awe that was on mens hearts towards God and his wayes being removed, the slighting all the warnings of God in judgments and by his ministers, maketh mee thinke God is yett angry, and he will leave our great Counsell to their wonted partiality in their wayes, and bring more ruine one way or other on the nacon, or give us up to the cursed wayes of our owne hearts, taking away his ministers and s[ts] apace from England, and few arising in their stead.

August. 30. 1648. after y[e] route of Hamilton, taking of Colchester, discovery of the City plott, [1] when all our feares seemed gone, and our enemies hopes quite dasht.

The raine that fell caused a floud: the Suffolke forces went home yesterday, all the residue of the army was drawne up in a body, and almost all the Essex forces were disbanded: the prisoners were many of them sent unto Kelvedon this night.

[1] Vide Gardiner, *Great Civil War*, iv, 196, 197.

A fayre day. Septemb. 1, it was very wett and hindred men in yr harvesting; wee feared it would cause a floud. Major Haines returned from ye North where they have taken about 13000 prisoners. Aug. 31.

The prisoners taken at Colchester are dispersing apace; divers gett away. Sr Wm Compton, yr Sergeant Major Gen, 2 Coll. by meanes of our waggon-Mr-Generall made an escape. Coll: Culpepper, Coll: Chester. Sr Abraham Shipman, escaped out of Mr Warrens house. Sept. 5.

A publike day of thanks for the great and notable mercy in the route and dissipating of the Scotch army[1] by the forces under Cromwell and Lambert. Sept. 7.

I drunke my beere for 3 or 4 dayes with as much content out of a dish as at sometimes out of a silver bowle. My thoughts much working within mee about leaving Colne, seing they have not regarded to bring in promised maintenance unto mee. Sept. 10.

Being as it were forsaken and neglected by the inhabitants of Earles Colne, and destitute of competent maintenance to live upon, I sett this morning apart to seeke unto God for direction in this matter, whether providence called mee away, or whether I should continue with them still; now the good Lord who is the God of prayer answer my desires and request, and make mee to understand that which is most pleasing in thy sight. Sept. 12.

First my case in reference to maintenance is this: first for tithes, the general maintenance, the last yeare I received in from the Towne, at severall times, with much calling upon, 25*l.* 6*s.* 9*d.* and perhaps this yeare may afford thus much; then Mr Jacob is to pay 4*l.* wch perhaps he will continue to pay: Mr R. Harlakenden he its likely will performe his 20*l.* per annum: so their is about 49*l.*, if the tithes bee gotten in: for the other 31 pound I have not received 4*l.*; but suppose their should 8 or 9*l.* pound of it bee paid, ys amounts not unto 60*l.* by the yeare, out of which I am to pay taxes, which will amount to 3*l.* per annum: tenths to the Parliamt, and reparacons, which will bring it downe to a matter of 50*l.* a yeare, and for this I have my selfe, wife, 3 children, mayde,

[1] At Preston.

my wife a childing woman, so that this summe cannot at the great price all things now beare mainteine us in a very lowe manner.

But yr are 2 things more incumbent on mee, and that is to bee hospitable and mindfull of the poore ; Titus : 1: 8 : and our Towne is full of poore, and a roade way, and their are great occasions for a liberall releiving hand, which those yt have not cannot performe; this then brings a scandall on the ministry, as if he had much but would not releive them.

Farther, a man is bound to provide for his family, and lay up for them ; this Scripture alloweth, commendeth, requireth : Gen : 30 : 30 : and now when shall I provide for my owne house also : 2 Cor : 2 : 14 : 1 Timoth : 5 : 8 : and in a probable way when a mans children are young, and he is young, is the fittest time to doe this duty ; but when the yearely income cannot mainteine, what is their to lay up ?

Againe, what a distraction it is for men to be intangled with thoughts of providing for their tables, when wee should be attending our studdyes : under the law, tithes were brought in to the preists ; now wee must run out after them ; its a great discomfort when a man is not mainteined freely, and cheerefully, though it be sparingly.

Ob :[1] But God hath increased your estate here at Colne.

Ans : It is true, ye secrett treasures being his, he hath done it ; but those dayes are past ; how to subsist with any freedome I knowe not nowe, and if I could I professe I would not remove ; I have bought something while I lived at Colne, but halfe I have gained hath not beene from Colne but on other occasions.

Ob : But it may be Colne doth for your maintenance what they are able.

Ans :1. Not ; ye towne is able to mainteine a minister, and his family with an 100*l.* per annum, if they were willing : but people are regardles and careles of the wp of God, as if they could well spare it.

2. Ye litle promised by contribucon and tithes, is payd very unwillingly : the contribucon not regarded to be gathered of them; a man or 2 is willing, but not any other are willing so much as to gather it up from others.

[1] Objection.

3. The parliament hath added augmentacons to other livings; our townesmen neglect ours; true an addicon was granted, but it is ineffectuall, neither doe wee take any course to make it effectuall:

Upon this and many other consideracons, seing my ministry thus barren, and slighted in Colne, I have cause to be humbled, and search my heart, and see whether it bee rather a punishment on mee for my sin, or a providence of God withall to remove mee from them.

I cannot but acknowledge many iniquities in mee, and neglect Ans: 1.
in my calling, and indeed great unfitnes and inability for this weighty worke, and this, Lord, I lament from the bottome of my heart; & questionles when the Lord makes people neglect their ministers, yr is a respect to them in it, [1] though perhaps not principally.

But in regard the state of things I stand thus: I have continued Ans: 2.
to beare many wants, contented my selfe with small meanes, stirred them up to regard ye condicon of the Towne & so others have also, and yett nothing done but my condicon is worse and meanes than before; I continued about 11 weekes at my Lady Honywoods, and it was knowne it was for want of meanes to keepe house, yett in all that time, though I was plundered, did my people consider my condicon, gather up any of the moneyes due unto mee? So that it seemeth cleare to mee providence invites mee away, my heart being also more inclined to lay downe, having no offers of a place, but leaving it to Gods providence to provide, then I ever was when I had offerres of good places made unto mee.

And in this condicon it seemes to mee cleare that I may depart. I doe not leave them untill they have forsaken mee; I desire no great meanes to live richly in the world, but convenient food and rayment, & the Lord ordaines that they which preach the gospell should live upon the gospell, and that in many places of Scripture, 1 Corinth: 9: 14; and surely then, when any place doth not afford him a subsistence, he may observe his providence in going

[1] The fault rests partly with them.

unto another; and when the preists had not their tithes brought in whereby they might waite in the Temple but were scattered into y[r] severall cities and feilds for bread, here is the worship of God neglected, the preists leave the Temple: whose sin and fault was it, being they wanted their meanes of livelyhood? It was the peoples, and the princes; they are blamed for the same, Nehem. 13. 10. 11. and he gathers them togither and setts them in their places, and provideth for them. v. 13. 14.

So then I lay it downe as a conclusion that my Towne affords me not a competent maintenance; if they make it appeare they have, then lett the blame of it rest on mee, and this is the reason I will insist on; and I will not be my owne judge; lett any understanding men judge whether 80*l.* bee not as litle as a man can live on in thes times, and this place, & seing they doe not, it is a just & a warrantable reason by Scripture, and nature, to provide otherwise, according as providence shall direct.

So then, after looking into the Word to be my counsello[r] and seeking unto God to direct mee, my resolucon is to acquaint M[r] Harlakenden with my condicon and what I must of necessity bee inforced to doe; and if by him and the townesmen I bee provided for, in paying in my dues last yeare, and in securing the next yeares, if I live with them; if not, that then I must, though with lothnes lay downe at Michaelmas & leave the townesmen to take care of the same, to provide another minister, & for my perticular to cast my selfe on Gods providence to provide for mee, as hee seeth best.

This resolucon I intend to prosecute, and to observe God in the same, and, whatsoever his providences are, to take them with as much patience and quietnes of Spirit as may bee, and with a thankefulnes unto God, for w[t]soever he appoints mee unto.

I shall also alwayes acknowledge that their are some in this Towne, that to their power, and beyond their ability, have beene loving to mee, and done their part to continue the Ministry of the word among them, whom it greiveth my soule to part with; but for what they have done they will have God and y[r] owne conscience bearing them witnesse, and affording them peace and comfort in whatsoever condicon cometh upon them.

I went downe to Mr R. Harlakenden, acquainted him with my purpose to leave Colne; he is sorry, wisheth it were otherwise; but y^r is no proposall of remedy & indeed ye fault is not particularly in him.

This weeke die 20. 22, was very wett, the season very sad both in reference to corne and unto fallowes, very few lands being fitt to bee sowne upon; some say that divers catle that feed in the meadowes dye, y^r bowells being eaten out with gravel & durt.

On the 17th of August I intimated that it was probable I should not very long stay with them, but truly very few in the towne regard it, or seeme to take any notice of it.

Some of the womenkinde of the parrish desire mee not to goe away, and Mr Elliston, who promiseth his endeavor to ye uttermost to better the meanes, but other men stirre not, say nothing. Aug. 24.

Some time in this weeke I spent in reading Hebrew and I resolve, now I am neare 32 yeares old, to sett my selfe more closely to the studdy of it. Things are yett very deare; I gave 8*s.* 2*d.* for a bushel of new wheate, the greatest price I ever gave in my time of housekeeping. Oct. 8.

This weeke I bestowed some time in the studdy of Hebrew; vita brevis ars longa, and much time I have & doe misspend, and find it hard to redeeme the time. Oct. 29.

In the latter end of October I begun to reade Bell:[1] de 15 staires or ladder steps to God, a prettie discourse; it containes 418 pages in 16°. I also read in mornings fferi[2] Specimen, a learned discourse, it containeth p. 559: I observed the most materiall things in him. Oct.

A very rainy day; heard that Coll: Rainsbrough was stabbed in in the North[3] by 2 that pretended to be sent from the Lieu^t Gen. with a letter unto him. Nov. 4.

Wee begun this morning to rise early, and to spend some time by fire and candle; I intend in morning to read over the liberall Nov. 6.

[1] Robert Bellarmin, Cardinal, b. 1542, d. 1621.

[2] Paul Ferri, of Metz, Protestant Divine and Preacher, b. 1591, d. 1669.

[3] at Doncaster: for his career see *Dict: of Nat: Biography.*

Vossius institute orat. arts, and began with Vossius[1] Rhet. Tom. 1. in 4°. It containes 433 p.; ceptis aspira nostris, domine, that hereby, being more skild in the tongue and arts, I may be more usefull in my generacon.

fferrig. This night I perfected the reading of fferius Specimen.

Nov. 13. Hookers and Cottons treatises: Begun the reading, and noting the principal things, out of 2 treatises concerning church goverm^t by Mr Hooker, called a survey of the sum of church discipline; the second treatise by Mr Cotton, called The way of congregational churches, cleared in in 2 treatises, one historicall, against Baylie disswasive, the other polemical. The time I allotted for this was in the forenoone togither with my Hebrew studdies; viz what time I could picke before dinner, having read Vossius ante solem, and being to learne a part every morning in the Heb. Gram.

Nov. 15. Bellarmin's scale &c. This night I made an end of reading Bellarmines scale ad Deum, a booke that containeth divers sweet meditacons in it, and now I intend on nights to reade ov^r the ecclesiastical history.

Nov. 16. Cent. 1^ce lib. 1. This night I began by candle light to reade the ecclesiastical history, called the Centuries of Magdeb: This I intend, if God give mee strength, to read on nights, that therby I may understand the state and affayre of that body wherof Christ is the head, and observe from history the witnesse of the several gratious preservacons of Gods truths, and servants in all ages.

Nov. 18. I finisht the reading of Vossius his first tome.

Nov. 30. Mr Harlakenden with me from London: he did nothing about the augmentacon, neither doe any regard to bring mee in any moneyes to live upon.

Dec. 11. I was hard putt to it for money receiving none from my people.

Bakers Chronicle. Finisht the reading of Vossius Rhetoricke. I read Bakers Chronicles of England[2] now and then for my recreation, and the Archb^ps triall.

Dec. 21. This day Mr Harlakenden and Mr Elliston went about to gather

[1] Gerard John, 1577-1649: Dutch classical scholar and Protestant theologian.

[2] Sir Richard Baker, b. 1568, d. 1645. "The Chronicle of the Kings of England, inexact and uncritical, but written in a pleasant and readable style, quickly acquired a high reputation. It was continued to 1668 by Edward Phillips, Milton's nephew." *(Encycl: Brittan:).*

my money y[t] was much in arreare; they brought me in 3*l*. 6*s*. and a good report generally of a willingness in the people to doe something towards my maintenance.

This day M[r] H. and M[r] Ell: went to gather up some contribucon for me, and found some persons willing to contribute, which were not yett in the bill; they brought me in in money 3*l*. which was a good refreshing to mee. Dec. 25.

This weeke I had some moneys from my people. Dec. 31.

I finisht the reading of S[r] Ri: Bakers Chronicle; also this day I entred upon a great worke, wherin I intend some care & paines to collect the places of Scripture, that seeme different one from another, and the reconciling of them: Lord assist mee with health, strength & wisedome for this great worke. Jan. 4. Bakers Chronicle read; Reconciler.

This day 7 yeares King Charles came to demand the 5 members, and it was thought with an intention to have offered violence to the house; this day the Commons of themselves ordered the tryall of the King; many men cry out of this worke y[t] it will ruine y[e] kingdome, the army, religion &c. For my part I conceive it strange, extraordinary, and that it will occasion very much trouble betwixt the prince, and his freinds, and the joyners in the new representative,[1] but if the worke bee of God it will prosper, if not it will come to nothing.

Y[s] day, I went abroad to S[r] Tho: Honywoods, I found him home, and heard by him good hope that the augmentacon granted by Parliam[t] may prove at last effectuall; if so, I shall blesse God; if not I shall bee content. Jan. 4.

This weeke the Lord good and mercifull to me and mine in our health, peace, in providing for us, notwithstanding the great dearnes of every thing, beefe at 3*d*. ob per pd, wheate 7*s*. 6*d*. rye 6*s*. 4*d*. cheese 4*d*. butter 6*d*. ob per pound, and men expect it will bee dearer and dearer. Jan. 7.

[1] "The rejection of this ordinance by the few Peers who remained brought about a fresh resolution from the Lower House, 'that the People are, under God, the original of all just power; that the Commons of England in Parliament assembled—being chosen by, and representing the People— have the supreme power in this nation'" etc. (Green, *History of the English People*, 554).

Divers people in imitacon, or in abuse, sitt with y[r] hats on when wee are singing psalmes.

Jan. 13. My hall chamber was finisht by M[r] Harrington; the masons worke & stuffe one way or other amounted to about 50*s.*; the timber I found, onely he payd the carpenters.

Hooker and Cotton. This weeke I finisht the reading of Hookers discourse about church goverm[t]; I find it a peice worthy the perusing, I observed the most materiall heads out of it.

Jan. 15. Smalcius p. 29. I began to read Smalcius [1] the Socinian, agst the incarnacon of Christ, in latine; it containeth 29 pages in a large quarto.

Jan. 16. Amama p. 240. Began to read dilligently over Amama's [2] Heb: Grammer.

Jan. 17. Finisht the reading of Smalcius discourse, a man of subtle witt. This day and y[e] 18th M[r] Harlakenden kept his courts.

Lessius. I read over Lessius, [3] and the treatise with it, and though I am not satisfied concerning a constant measure of provision, yett I concurre with him, that a full diet is not best; *plus necat gula quam gladius;* a slender and a hard diett and exercise is very much conducing to o[r] health, and to mine in particular, and therefore my thoughts are to bee more moderate in my diett then formerly.

---

33 : y[r] : 1648 :

Jan. 25. This day I have completed my 32 yeare, & enter now upon my 33 y[r].

Jan. 28. I followed my Hebrew studdies this weeke, but not so seriously as I intended. I did somewhat also in my reconciler, to the 15th of Genesis.

Jan. 31. Heard K. C. was executed, but that was uncertaine: he was

[1] Smalcius, German Unitarian writer, circ. 1620.

[2] Amama, Dutch Orientalist, 1593-1629.

[3] Lessius, Dutch, wrote on the Immortality of the Soul. 1554-1623.

adjudged to dye Jan. 27. 1648. Bradshaw, the lord president, pronounced sentence; this day was a fast, a very cold day.

I was much troubled with the blacke providence of putting the King to death; my teares were not restrained at the passages about his death; the Lord in mercy lay it not as sinne to the charge of the kingdome, but in mercy doe us good by the same; the small poxe on some familyes of the towne but spreadeth not, to God be the glory therof: this weeke I could doe nothing neither in my Hebrew, nor in my reconciler. ffeb. 4.

The death of the king talked much of; very many men of the weaker sort of Christians in divers places passionate concerning it, but so ungroundedly, that it would make any to bleed to observe it; ye Lord hath some great thing to doe; feare & tremble att it, oh England.

Monday it was debated about Kings and Peeres; on Tuesday the house of Commons ordered to null the house of Lords as uselesse, & on the next day to lay aside the Goverm^t^ by Kings, & to sett up a councell of state.

Great dearth and want of all things, I gave 4*d*. per pound for porke. ffeb. 18.

I was dealt with to subscribe a manifest of the Minist. agst. the present proceedings, and the Agreem^t^ of the people,[1] and a dissent in the matter of the King; y^r^ are some things are well done, but for Ministers to intermedle thus in all difficulties of state I, question the warrantablenes therof, and therfore I could not concurre; but my advice is that the civill part might be undertaken by some able statesman and the religious part by some able Ministers, and then proceed to a subscription. ffeb. 19.

That part of the army before Pomfrett hangd a Minister, a Cavalier; they condemned him for holding intelligence with the enemy in the Castle, and that he had a hand in betraying the same; this weeke their seemed to appear some differences in the Councell of state, and in the army especially, a dangerous peticon as they say being sett a foote;[2] and truly the enemies onely course is to divide them on the peoples interest and their owne; for ffeb. 25.

[1] vide Gardiner, *Great Civil War*, iv, 281.

[2] vide Gardiner's *Commonwealth and Protectorate*, i, 34.

probably, if they[1] continue united it will cost a sea of bloud, and a world of trouble to alter what is now in setling.

March. 18. Cheese now at 4d. q. & ob per pound, butter sold by some at 8d: porke 4d. q. or ob, beefe 3d. ob. q. great feare of the decay of trade.

March. 22. Mr W. H. came home from the assizes; he was sworne y^r justice of peace; we have 3 justices now within 2 mile of our Towne on either hand with him; the Lord make him serviceable for our good; y^r are but few in ye countie, its a good providence that wee are so well supplyed: y^r fell out worke for him as soone as he came home, pretences[2] of slaughter; heard by him that L. Col. Lilburne and his partie did gather about St Albans to goe on with their pretended principle of libertie, and to ease the subject of taxes; tis true y^r are burthens on us, and divers pretend to amend them, but they are but easy easyers; they rather increase then ease our burthens; Martin,[3] and some others its s^d joyne with him, and encourage him.

March. 25. I was very neglectfull in my Hebrew studdies this weeke; but I
Meditacons & Vowes. 1649. begun a peice of work which I hope will not be unprofitable to mee in my spirituall estate, viz. as I read over the Scriptures, some places yeild me much spirituall solace, matter of rejoycing and some of ingagements,[4] which I take notice of in a booke for that purpose; I went on more speedily then formerly in my reconciler; I finisht Numb: Cap: 12. this weeke.

March. 27. Yesterday I bought mee a new felt, it cost mee, 7s.; this morning Mr Nicholsons stable being robbed, Justice Harlakenden came over to mee; I made out two hue and cry's after the horse on the road; the first that I ever writt in my life.

April. 15. This weeke the Lord was good and mercifull to mee and mine in all outward mercies, when as their is a great scarcitie of all things,[5] beefe ordinarily 4d. per lib: butter 7 o^r 8d. cheese 5d.,

[1] The Council and the Army.

[2] Charges.

[3] Henry Martin, who afterwards abandoned the Levellers.

[4] i. e. to God:

[5] vide Gardiner, *Commonwealth and Protectorate*, i, 44.

wheate 7s. 6d. rye 6s. 8d. yett we wanted nothing needfull or fitting for us.

This day by act was sett apart for a day of humiliacon but was not kept in most places by reason the act was not divulged abroad, wherby ministers and people might have timely notice to prepare for the same. April. 19

My deare wife had beene very ill for 3 weekes, now towards night paynes came fast on her and shee was delivered before nine of the clocke of her 5t child, and third sonne, God giving us another sonne in stead of my deare Ralph whom he tooke away; my wife was alone a great while with our good freinds Mrs Mary, and her mother; some few women were with her, but the midwife not, but when God commands deliverance yr is nothing hinders it. May. 5.

Great difficulties by reason of the proceedings of divers souldiers designed for Ireland. May. 15.

This day was a day of publike humiliacon; many men in great straites and difficulties in regard of the Levellers attempts to raise troubles, and many of the souldiers discontents; God was mercifull to mee in giving me strength for the duty of the day wherin I spent publickely above 4 houres. May. 17.

This day I payed Mr Harlakenden of the priory 12*l.*: I now owe unto him 23*l.* for which I gave him a bill to pay it upon demand, and I intend God willing to pay him well and truly with all speed: my lady sent her daughter Mrs Elizabeth and kinswoman with her cost (*sic*) to give my wife a visitt; wee testified the utmost of our respect unto her. I gave her the choice of any booke in my library, which shee accepted very kindely and lovingly from mee. May. 18.

Heard the newes of quashing the Levellers, a glorious rich providence of God to England.

This weeke the Lord was good to us, in our peace, in health, and providing for us notwithstanding the great scarcity of all things, rye at 6*s.* 8*d* bushel, butter at 7*d* pound, cheese 6*d*, beefe 5*d*, lambe 7*d*. May. 20.

I received this day my money from Mr Tho: Harlakenden and pd Mr Harlakenden 4*l.*; I now owe him but 19*l.* wherof the greatest part I hope to pay very shortly. May. 22.

May. 25. This day I pd for beefe about 4*d*. ob. q. a pound, and 5*d*. the pound for mutton, but beefe was commonly 5*d*. y[e] pound : 9*s*. and 10*s*. the score, the best in the markets.

May. 26. Sleidans Commentarie Begun to read this history [1], horis successivis, its in a large octavo, but a smal character and close ; it containes the merveylous dawning and spreading of the reformacon of religion in the latter dayes under Luther, and y[e] progresse y[r] of for divers yeares.

Medes discourses. Begun to read M[r] Medes discourses on several texts, and to observe some of y[e] most materiall things y[r] in.

June. 3. This day was very warme & comfortable, I gave 8s. 2d. for a score of indifferent beefe. I spent a litle time in my Hebrew, did a litle in my meditacons and reconciler to Deut : 12 : and spent some time in Sleidan, where I observe the strange progresse of the gospell in Germany and other places, many princes and families renouncing the pope, and of late yeares none have ; neither hath the gospell any entertainm[t] in Spaine, Italy, Sicily, and in the territories of the Venetians ; I did somewhat in Medes discourses.

June. 18. Rid with M[r] Harlakenden to Stortford ; 19, wee and M[r] H. son rid to Cambridge where I viewed with delight my old colledge ; the M[r] and fellowes, very good men, hope of y[r] good : 20, M[r] R. Harlakenden admitted fellow commoner of Jesus.

June. 27. Spent most of this day in a day of prayer, entreating God for John Burton who was to be cutt of the stone, for my owne distemper, that God who healeth his would bee an healing God to mee and to others.

July. 1. The newes from Ireland this weeke was sad, that the enemy was come before Dublin ; [2] the Lord in mercy provide for them if it bee his pleasure, and give us successe against them.

July. 7. Received newes and true that Major Heynes, my good freind, had procured me 15*l*. for my pay as chaplaine to the regiment for Colchester service ; it was a singular kindnes in him towards mee : my good freind M[rs] Mary Church brought mee in 20s, from her selfe, and 20s. from M[rs] Mabel to buy mee a booke.

[1] Sleidan, 1506-1556. Historian of the Reformation.

[2] Ormond occupied the grounds of Phoenix Lodge on June 21.

This weeke reports were heard from Ireland; wee looked when Cromwell should goe, but yett he did not. John Burton for whom wee sought God June 27, was cutt for the stone July 6, and good hopes he will recover, and doe well; God of his mercy say Amen thereunto. Made a collection for Lancashire which is much afflicted with famine and pestilence. July. 8.

Ye newes from Ireland this weeke is sad, Culmore Castle lost, and so no releiving of Derry by water: Tredagh likely to be lost, yr magazine being blowne up with powder by ye treachery of some aldermen; tis many times Gods season to helpe when wee are low; Cromwell marcht out of London in great state;[1] they goe with wonderfull confidence; the issue is in Gods glorious armes disposing. July. 14.

I began formely and now to bee sensible of a distemper and weaknes in my backe about the reines; I have had ye same divers yeares, what it tends to I knowe not. July. 15.

Kept a day of humiliacon at ye priory, for the good successe of Ireland. I brought home a bible for my sonne Thomas, which cost me 3s. 2d.: this booke is now very cheap. July. 18.

Finisht the reading his 26 bookes of Commentaries July 20: I begun to reade his discourse on ye 4 empires & finisht it July 29. Sleidan.

Mr Harlakenden would not goe to ye assizes; the other justices went. July. 24.

This day I bought of John Beereman a parcell of land, now Sarah Haukesbees; it containd 3 acres and more; rent 2*l.* 10*s.* besides the lords rent; it cost mee 36*l.* 15*s.* I am to pay all his mony even downe and to take the rent due at Michaelmaes. I payd him 15*l.* home with him; this is Gods providence to blesse mee, and to adde to that litle which I have. July. 26.

This weeke or newes was sad for Ireland; no forces gone & Tredah, and Trim, and Carickfergus, and Carlingford lost; Dun- July. 29.

[1] "On July 12 he set out for Bristol with unwonted state in a coach drawn by six grey Flanders mares and protected by a lifeguard every member of which was 'either an officer or an esquire'. Above him floated a milk-white standard, symbolising as it would seem, his hope to bring back whiterobed peace from amidst the horrors of war." (Gardiner, *Commonwealth & Protectorate*, i, 108.)

dalke beseidged,[1] and also Dublin close beseidged by the enemy; Cromwell not yett ready to goe over; publisht this day an order for a day of humiliacon to seeke unto God, for a blessing on the forces designed for Ireland; Gods providence hath beene very good towards mee; I have payd since last yeare I was plundered already full 40*l.* which I ought and I have payd 15*l.* on a purchase, and hope through Gods goodnes to pay of shortly twenty pounds more; John Burton came home from London cutt of the stone, his life spared, his wound healed, I hope cured, answered very sweetly in o^r prayers.

Aug. 1. A day of P. Humiliacon for Ireland and a blessing from God upon ye forces that are designed thither; the Lord in mercy goe along with them, and blesse and prosper them; I expect that Dublin should become a prey to the enemie; the Lord alone is able to prevent it; we spent from three of ye clocke untill sun downe at the priorie, in continuing the exercise; the Lord remember us for good for his owne names sake.

Aug. 6. This weeke I went about to gather up some tithes; I find mony scarce.

Aug. 14. Sometime reported that Dublin was lost, sometime that a part of Ormonds army was routed, 100^{ds}, and sometimes thousands slaine.

Sarah Hausb. land. This day wee perfected the agreem^t between John Bearman and my selfe; I payd him all his money, viz. 21*l.* 10*s.*; he bated me 5*s.* in regard the lords rent was more y^n wee supposed.

Aug. 19. A weeke of harvest, corne abated in price a litle. The glorious successe in Ireland[2] ye next day after the publicke fast; the first rumo^r I heard of it was August 14, in the morning.

Aug. 29. This day a P. Th: for the great victory over Ormond.

Sept. 7. Mrs Crane gave mee a payre of gloves which she ought me about a wager when her housband was prisoner with the Cavaliers.

Sept. 10. I was with Mr Harlakenden; his crop of hops wonderfull small;

[1] Gardiner, *Commonwealth and Protectorate*, i, 110, 111.

[2] Jones had defeated Ormond at Rathmines on August 2nd. "In the city wagers were freely offered that Dublin had already surrendered at the enormous odds of £100 to 5/-." Cromwell only heard the news on August 12th.

much about 800 weight upon twentie acres ; my freinds have given mee enough for my use.

This day I went to visitt Mr Jacob ; heard of some stirre at Oxford by the regiment their upon the levelling score.[1] Sept. 11.

The disturbances at Oxford over in a good season and by a very finger of God ; the rate of things continueth dearer and is likely to encrease. Sept. 16.

At night begun to study a litle before supper, I begun with the first part of the Ecclesiastical history of the Magdeburgensis.[2] Oct. 3. Magd.Cent. 1. lib. 1. Colum.372.

I begun about the begining of ys month to reade Senertus[3] institucons in a large 8°. smal print ; this I did in the day time. Senerti. Inst. Vol. 1. p. 917.

This day I finisht Josephus, of the antiquities of the Jewes, whereof I read a great part, especially where the history of ye scripture is silent & I intend to read the residue of his booke.

This weeke all things very deare, wheate. 8*s.* 6*d.* rye 6*s.* barley 5*s.* a bushel, cheese 4*d.* ob, butter 7*d.* ob the pound. Oct. 7.

The contry full of reports of Cromwells route in Ireland, but its hoped yr is no truth therein. Oct. 28.

My boy is now lively, somewhat fuller of spirit, of a good memory, a good speller, apt to learne, and attaine the hardest words in his bible or accidence in which he reads. This day we kept a publicke thanksgiving for the successe against Tredah, and before we heard the great newes of the taking Wexford, and putting the garrison, and some say the inhabitants, to the sword. Nov. 1. Thomas.

Ye times were wonderfull hard, wheate at above 9*s.* and rye Nov. 25.

[1] "On Sept. 8 the garrison called on its officers to join in demanding a free parliament according to the Agreement of the People.... Failing to elicit a satisfactory response, they seized New College where the Magazine was stored and placed their officers under arrest." (Gardiner, *Commonwealth and Protectorate*, i, 182.)

[2] An ecclesiastical history of the first 1300 years of the Christian Era, in which the records of each century occupy a volume.

[3] Daniel Senertus, 1572-1637. He introduced the study of Chemistry at Wittenberg. He was accused of blasphemy and impiety on the ground that he taught that the souls of beasts were not material.

about 7*s*. a bushell: God was good to mee in my sonne Thomas who learned well, and I wish if ever he bee a man he would remember I undertooke the teaching the schoole at this time cheifely for his sake, among the boyes, though my highest aime was to doe good while I live; God was mercifull to mee in giving mee and my deare wife bowells towards the poore; we begun this weeke to fast our selves a meale or 2 in a weeke, and give away a meales provision in meate, broth, or money to the poore. The times were very sad in England so that men durst not travell, and indeed rich men were afrayd to lye in their houses, robbers were so many and bold; men knew not how to carry moneyes, and many gentlemens houses were sett upon and pilfered: the affayres of Ireland went well; the hand of God was notable, that when our interest was lowe their, then y[e] natural Irish, and the meere popish party joyned not with Ormond but rather assisted us;[1] but seing no hope from us, when Ormond was lowe, and our forces begun to prosper, then Oneale and his party fell in with Ormond.

Dec.1.to16. This time all things were wonderfull deare, wheate 9*s*. malt 4*s*. 8*d*, rye 7*s*. 6*d*, oatemeale 8*s*, per bushel, and cheese 4*d*. ob; all things deare, yett the season was indifferent warme and drye; beggars many, givers few, Lord of thy bounty provide for the poore; I constrayned my selfe to doe more then ordinary for our poore; it is better to give then to receive; and yett poore people were nev[r] more regardles of God then now adayes.

Dec. 18. This day I rid to Witham, and 19, to Chelmsford, where I subscribed the Engagement, the first in y[e] County of Ministers and y[e] 13th man of y[e] County. I subscribed the Engagement[2] as I considered it stood with y[e] Coven[t] while y[e] gov[r]ment actually stood establisht; and my faithfulnes is not to create any troubles, but seeke y[e] good of y[e] Commonwealth.

[1] For the convention arranged between Monk and O'Neill, see Gardiner, *Commonwealth and Protectorate* i, 87, 88, etc.

[2] "I do declare and promise that I will be true and faithful to the Commonwealth of England as the same is now established, without a King or House of Lords." (Gardiner, *Commonwealth & Protectorate*, i, 196). All Members of Parliament and officials generally were ordered on Oct. 11 to sign this.

Mr Harlakenden troubled at the greatnes of his sons expenses at Cambridge, I writt to Mr Richard, to be frugall of his fathers purse, & to improve his time for learning & pietie, God blesse my advice to him. Jan. 9.

This day I began to teach the schollers for Mr Harrington. Jan. 10.

Jan : 4 : 1649 : yr was much mischeife done at London by blowing up divers barrels of powder, which blew up divers houses, and persons; it was thought neare all 100d; the fluxe is much in London, and in some parts of this kingdom; it hath cutt downe many of the army in Ireland. Jan. 13.

This day Mr Wade of Halsted sent mee a dozen of candle, and Mr Hickford a sugar loafe, a liberall & bounteous guift. Mrs Church gave mee 5s. Jan. 15.

Ffeares and jealousies of troubles from among or selves by reason of ye ingagement, and other sad affaires among or selves ended the yeare. Jan. 24.

Jan : 25 : 1649 : an : aetatis 34.

I was sensible it entred mee into a new yeare, and I eyed God in perticular for his presence with mee. Jan. 25.

Mrs Church invited us to supper, where wee were kindely entertaind: Gdee[1] Mathew sent us a lovely breast of veale; this love and kindnes is from God; at night my right side aked very much. ffeb. 6.

Made an end with my Tenant; he is to plowe no more than what is plowed; he is not to medle with my wood, and to lay 8 load dung on the mowing peice, and to quit the farme at Michaelmas, 1651. ffeb. 25.

Gods hand was towards us for good in our children. Maries eyes mended somewhat, & so did little Ralphs; his glisters[2] did him good, and the best outward meanes were rose oyntment & plantayne water steeped with white sugar candie; this day my sonne Thomas began to learne his accidence by heart as wee say, memoriter; he is now 6 yeares old and about two months. March.

[1] *i. e.* 'Goody'.

[2] Poultices

March. 2. debts. Reviewed what I owe, and I perceive all my debts, one and other, amount to somewhat above 40*l.* and I have so much and more owing mee this present day.

March. 15. This day, I was warned to appear at Westminster die 20th.

March. 17. I received 6*l.* of my Committee money [1] from Chelmsford, and a botle of sacke from London, from Mr Linch.

March. 18. The subcomittee voted mee 43*l.* per annum augmentacon.

March. 23. Gave over teaching the schoole for present.

1650. March. 26. Rid to Braintree; Coll. Cooke promised to doe for mee what he could in the matter of the schoole; returnd safe praise to God; heard when I came home that ye schoole was disposed. I goe about this whole businesse with submission to Gods providence, which I conceive hath layd it out for mee. I payd a considerable debt this day.

March. 27. debts. Cast up my debts this day and they are 45*l.* 0 : 1*d.* including 23*l.* 12*s.* which I shall owe to Mr Haukesbee, and now my estate is as followeth.

Value of my estate, which God hath given mee.

Land : Mallories part Bollinhatch 2 closes in Colne	27*l.* per annum
Moneyes in Major Haines hand to bee payd to Mr John Littell.	50*l.*

My debts are much about 10*l.* more than my moneyes that are owing unto mee; this increase is from Gods goodnes, and providence towards mee.

March. 27. Perfected an agreement with Goodman Paine; he is to have ye close at ye old rent 3*l.* per annum until Michaelmas in 1651; he is to lay on 80 load of dung, and sowe it with barley this yeare, and with oates the next, and when either of his crops of corne are taken of, then am I to have the pasture, and the layer of my catle in it for the winters.

April. 11. This day I tooke ye surrender of Sawyers from Mr Wm Haukesbee to ye use of my daughter Mary Josselin, and her heyres for

[1] The Committee for plundered ministers. vide Jan. 17-1650.

ever; the purchase cost mee 50*l*., which I fully paid to him & received an acquittance from him for it, and bond to make it good.

Sent a letter to Major Haines to send into New England, containing three sheets in my small hand, being a relation of affaires foreigne, and domestique from y[e] rendicon of Colchester untill Aprill. 16. 1650, this present day. April. 16.

Bee cautious of speaking to M[r] Harlakenden in the point of his royaltie, for being intent on the proffits of them, he takes it ill, as I found this day, which I hope shall learne mee some prudence in the world. I would willingly bee a gainer by other mens tempers. April. 20.

Wee made our rate this day; I tooke it kindly from the townesmen, who did not raise my rate upon the close I hold in my owne hands. April. 22.

It rained a most sweete showre; God is opening his hand to fill us with his bounty. M[r] Harlakenden and I had great discourse about our Lords rent; I find & he acknowledges by comparing the copies, and the rentalls, that 10*s* for the Aldarcar[1] part of Oxenfen is sett on my head, and Kents, and 7*s*. for Mills[1] fen &c. is sett now on Osbornes, and Tills head; he was somewhat moved; I blesse God who gave me a patient command of my selfe. April. 23. Lords rent.

This day M[r] Harrington pd mee in 7*l*, for keeping the schoole, from Jan. to March 25. 1650; he promiseth to dischardge all to mee, and the moneyes I am out, when he sendeth for his sonnes things; the matter of the schoole in a great uncertainty.

Hay was very scarce and deare, at 3*s*. and 3*s*. 4*d*. per hundred weight. April. 25.

My tenant this day at Mallories paid mee 6*l*. 10*s* for Lady rent, I sett of 10*s*. for taxes, forgave him 18*d*. w[ch] was his part of them. April. 27.

This day M[rs] Mary Church made a disposall of her estate, which amounts to 21*l*. per annum in land, the trust whereof, shee layed on mee, a burthen heavy but I durst not refuse it, in regard providence lead mee to it. May. 17.

My litle Mary very weake, wee feared shee was drawing on; May. 22.

[1] Many of these old names still persist down to the present day, e. g., Aldercar, Mills Farm, Dagnall, Mallories, Hobstevens.

feare came on my heart very much, but shee is not mine, but the Lords, and shee is not too good for her father; shee was tender of her mother, thankefull, mindefull of God, in her extremity, shee would cry out, "poore I, poore I."

May. 25. Hopes of Maries life especially towards night, but it was onely hopes; God is her life, shee shall enjoy it in heaven, not here; Ralph ill.

May. 26. This morning all o[r] hopes of Maries life were gone; to the Lord I have resigned her and with him I leave her, to receive her into his everlasting armes, when he seeth best; shee rests free from much paine, wee hope, in regard shee maketh no dolour; the Lord makes us willing shee should bee out of her paine; my litle sonne in all peoples eyes is a dying child, Lord thy will bee done; thou art better to mee then sonnes and daughters, though I value them above gold & jewells.

May. 27. This day a quarter past two in y[e] afternoone my Mary fell asleepe in the Lord; her soule past into that rest where the body of Jesus, and y[e] soules of the s[ts] are; shee was 8 yeares and 45 dayes old when shee dyed; my soule had aboundant cause to blesse God for her, who was our first fruites, and those God would have offered to him, and this I freely resigned up to him; it was a pretious child, a bundle of myrrhe, a bundle of sweetnes; shee was a child of ten thousand, full of wisedome, womanlike gravity, knowledge, sweet expressions of God, apt in her learning, tender hearted & loving, an obedient child to us; it was free from the rudenesse of litle children, it was to us as a boxe of sweet ointment, which now its broken smells more deliciously then it did before; Lord I rejoyce I had such a present for thee; it was patient in the sicknesse, thankefull to admiracon, it lived desired and dyed lamented, thy memory is and will bee sweete unto mee.

May. 28. This day my deare Mary was buried in Earles Colne church by the 2 uppermost seats; shee was accompanyed thither with most of the Towne; M[rs] Margaret Harlakenden, & M[rs] Mabel Elliston layd her in grave, those two and M[rs] Jane Church, & my sister carryed her in y[r] hands to y[e] grave; I kist her lips last, & carefully laid up that body, y[e] soule being with Jesus, it rests y[r] till y[e] Resurrection.

Called up this morning to see my deare freind Mrs Mary Church, who departed to an eternall rest and Sabbath about 9 of the clocke; my deare Ralph very ill, we cannot long enjoy him; the Lord wash his nature from his filth, and defilement, & doe him good. My deare Ralph before midnight fell asleepe whose body Jesus shall awaken; his life was continuall sorrow and trouble; happy he who is at rest in the Lord; my deare wife ill as if she would have dyed. June. 2.

This day my deare freind Mrs Mary Church, and my sweete Ralph were buried togither in the church; I preached her funerall on Mathew 25, 34 verse; God hath taken from mee a choyce speciall freind. In some respect I see great mercy therein, for Satan lieth in waite to corrupt our affections & that mine were not was Gods aboundant grace, who keepes mee, that, though I fall, yett I am not utterly cast downe. June. 4.

When Mrs Mary dyed, my heart trembled, and was perplexed in the dealings of the Lord so sadly with us, and desiring God not tó proceed on against us with his darts and arrows; looking backe into my wayes, and observing why God hath thus dealt with mee, the Lord followed mee with that sin no more, "lest a worse thing happen unto thee;" and the intimacon of God was he would proceed no farther against mee or mine, and he would assist mee with his grace if I clave to him with a full purpose of heart, which I resolve; oh my God helpe mee! oh my God faile mee not! for in thee doe I put my trust.

Mrs Church this day delivered unto mee the will of Mrs Mary deceasd; many suppose shee hath given mee all her land, others shee hath given mee nothing, but what is done is Gods providence: lett Harris ye house at Coggeshall till Michaelmas, the first tenant that I agreed withall. June. 6.

In the affaire of Mrs Mary their are divers discourses, but the uprightnes of my heart therein affords through God peace to mee, and I trust will more & more; others esteeme I shall loose very much by it. June. 9.

Began to teach the schoole; 8 children came, but none of their parents. June. 10. Schoole.

June. 19. Had some discourse with Mr Harlakenden about Mrs Maries businesse; wee agreed very lovingly in the value of the land, Mrs Marys part, *6l.* per annum, the other at *10l.* per annum : the free at *5l.* per annum : he sett both the fines at *20l.*, he acknowledged they were too hard.

June. 23. I find I goe through ye matter of ye schoole without any extraordinary burthen ; ye times of schoole I make my times of studdy. Ye Lord was good to mee in the Sabbath, in ye word preacht and opened ; ye unreverent carriage of divers in sitting with yr hatts on when the psalme is singing is strange to mee.

June. 24. This morning I bought Smiths cow ; her price was *6l.* 10*s.* 0*d.* I also bought of him the pasture of Dagnall till Michaelmas for *3l.* 10*s.*; he is to pay me the tith which I told him of; and to pay all towne taxes untill Michaelmas ; I am to enter on them on Wednesday. I borrowed the mony of Goodwife Math : 40*s.* I now paid him in hand : if I buy cowes I am to putt them now on the ground : the Lord my God give a blessing unto mee herein.

June. 25. Went to Messing, received 10*s.* of Allhayes, *7s. 6d.* of Medcalfe, 11*s.* 8*d.* of Bridge Shaw, promiseth his August : 1. Yr is some improvemt to bee made towards our repayres, which will cost nigh *10l.*; this night wee begun to milke our cow bought of Smith. God good in my iorney, I went 18 miles, spent *6d.*

June. 27. This day I fetcht a cow from Westney's of Halstead, it cost *6l. 5s* ; I had great trouble in ye cowes unquietnes ; God enters mee into many of my affayres with trouble. I pd Smith *8l.* ye residue of his bargaine ; I lent Polly *20s.*; I receivd in *30s.* from my schoole rents.

June. 28. Heard Huggins was undone; care taken about my rent in seizing the crop ; Hedge bad mee *18l.* per annum. & Dawkin *19l.*; receivd from Overell *4l.* 17*s.* *6d.* rent ; and the gurney (sic) booke from Mr Harrington.

June. 30. Heard this weeke of ye consuming plague in Ireland. Cromwell is made Gen : ffairfax hath layd downe the commission.

July. 7. God afflicts Ireland with the plague most sadly, and now Scotland and wee are likely to engage into bloud ; arise and save us, for in thee we trust, and doe us good for thy most holy name sake wee entreate thee !

Proved Mrs Maries will at Kelvedon, and returned safe; 10, In'd July. 9.
3 jaggs of hay from my vicaridge close ; I had about 45*cl.* of very good hay. Die 11, I lett my farme at Ardleigh to Hedge for 19*l.* per annum for 3 yeare ; one Heckford undertakes ye rent for ye 3 yeares.

Rid to Colchester, dined with ye Commissioners that were y^{r} July. 13.
about the livings of the ministers.

The Publike Courts for o^{r} Manors were kept, in which I was July.23.24.
admitted in reversion to all the land of Mrs Mary Church, and my sonn Tho : to the land of M^{r} W : Haukesbee.

Mr Bearman came, and I was admitted to both the parcells of July. 25.
his wives land, being now tenant of both manors ; this is not of my selfe, but it is ye Lords blessing upon mee ; as a pricke in ye flesh I am troubled with rheumes, my goomes swelling.

Pub : day of Thanksgiving for the route and slaughter of the July. 26.
popish Irish army under Cloghers[1] command, which I kept with rejoycing in God, who hath given them bloud to drinke, who had shed y^{r} selves so much.

This day I payd Mrs Church her 20*l.*, so I have now p^{d} her 50*l.* July. 27.
and 5*l.* to ye poore, and other charges layd out in money, 1*l.* 19*s.* 6*d.*; so in all I have layd out 56*l.* 19*s.* 6*d.* this day on Mrs Maries estate.

Y^{e} day reports common all lost in Ireland, Cromwell beaten, July. 31.
tumults at London ; but their was no truth y^{r} in.

Heard that ye Scots were routed and thousands slaine.[2] Aug. 2.

Heard reports of great successe in Scotland. Aug. 21.

Resolved henceforwards w^{t} soever money comes in on guifts, or curtesies, all incomes, and receipts on the schoole besides the rents, and whatsoever is saved by preaching at any places, shall bee layd out in bookes.

P^{d} : 11*s.* 3*d.* for driving my fetherbeds & bolsters ; wee made us Aug. 29.
a very excellent downe bed. I payd Mr Harrington. 1*l.* 5*s.*; I owe him now 2*l.* 10*s.*

[1] Macmahon, Bishop of Clogher.

[2] Scotch repulsed at Musselburgh : the number of the slain is exaggerated.

Sept. 2. Rid to Colchester; at y^r^ feast and banquetts; when I returned home, I found the small pox at Gdman Abbotts & Burtons.

Sept. 3. This day heard of ye taking Redhouse in Scotland: the Lord give a good issue to that dangerous affaire. Receivd a bushel of good new wheate at 5*s.* 4*d.* tollfree, a comfortable abatem^t^ from 10*s.* & 11*s.*; the Lord make us thankefull.

Sept. 6. This day my cowes were driven away from Smiths from off his ground with his, for rent by his landlady. I apprehended it might have beene some trouble to mee; I followed after them, overtooke them, and had my cowes delivered quietly to mee.

Sept. 8. The Scottish affaire very difficult; give a good issue unto it for thy glory & peoples good, wee entreate thee; its not so much layd to heart as formerly; heard of the route of the Scotch army, that 4000 were slaine[1] 10000 prisoners, 22 peices of ordnance taken, and this done Septemb. 3; newes London die. 7°.; this was reported to mee just when I came downe out of pulpitt.

Sept. 15. The small pox proceeded no farther this weeke. This weeke wee returned thankes to God for our Irish victories; the Scots victory true; wee heard of the wellfare of Major Haynes after o^r^ victory, for which the Lord bee praised; this weeke the Lady Elizabeth second daughter of ye King dyed in the Ile of Wight whither shee and her brother were sent; this is the first of them that fell by the hand of God in all thes troubles; y^r^ are 5 more of them still living, 3 sons & 2 daughters.

Sept. 22. The season is very sad in wet, hinders seed time, raiseth corne already, rotteth o^r^ muttons.

Sept. 26. My schoole lands ordered to pay taxes which will bee 7*l.* a yeare to my hindrance.

Oct. 2. The engagem^t^ is prest in Cambridge to out many honest men, and to admitt divers young & rude blades because engagers.

Oct. 8. A day of thanks for the great victory in Scotland.

Oct. 23. The engagement outs many deserving men from ye fellowships; its thought y^r^ will fall a sad blowe upon the ministry, the universities and y^r^ meanes; the report is that one moved whether y^r^

[1] Gardiner says 3,000.

should bee any standing ministry in England, but that is somewhat too much yett for this early day.

Received my tith from Goodman Abbott, very lovingly & quietly for which I blesse my God. Oct. 28.

Pose, die. 8, 9, 10. I had a pose, some litle stuffings in my head and chest, and on the 13th my gummes swelled as usually. I am advised to take 5 pils *sine quibus esse nolo.* Nov.

Writt and sent by Mr Harlakenden a lattin letter to Dr Wright, in humble thanks for conferring the schoole upon mee. Nov. 11.

God taketh away our enemies abroad viz the Prince of Orange[1] which is a great worke as things stood there and here. Nov. 17.

Warrants out to raise the horse & foote in or County, because of ye troubles in Norfolke[2]; this matter is in the darke to us as yett, though talkt of divers dayes; God I trust will give a good issue hereunto; gave in a perticular of my schoole rents as they were Septemb. 29. 1650. viz. 62*l*. 3*s*. 4*d*. yearly; its pretended to ease us of or assessments, which if so, I shall bee glad, but I duobt not. Dec. 3.

In the morning called up, and acquainted by Mr Harlakenden who was sent for to Chelmsford, that the Norfolke businesse was somewhat allayed, it being only an attempt of a few mad blades to proclaim the King; and this proved true, God shewing us the rod, and telling us what might have been done, but not letting mans rage prevaile to doe us ye least hurt. Dec. 4.

Begun to peruse the Revelacon, and Brightman upon it. Dec. 9. Revelacon Brightman

Heard this morning as if Carr and his Scotch forces were routed by or horse.[3] Dec. 12.

Heard farther good newes out of Scotland or army getting health, ye enemies now sickening, yr divisions still confirming me God is casting downe princes and that family in perticular, that he shall not be crowned, nor reigne long their, but die an untimely death to himselfe, but in good time for his kingdomes. Dec. 17.

[1] Died October 27 of small-pox.

[2] A Royalist outbreak; the leaders lost their lives on the gallows.

[3] Gardiner, *Commonwealth and Protectorate*, 381, 382.

Dec. 23. This day sealed a lease of Pickstones to ye widdow Overral for *22l.* per annum; ye first lease I sealed of the schoole lands. 24. pd Mr Harlakenden my fine for Mrs Maries land viz. *12l.*; ye times are hard; tis a great mercy that in these declining dayes I am able to pay any of my debts.

Dec. 29. Still ye Lord keepes us from ye small pox, wch continueth still in some families.

Dec. 31. This day heard yt Edinburgh Castle was surrendered Decemb. 24 past to General Cromwell; nothing can withstand Gods purpose, nor hinder that which he intendeth to accomplish; this castle was counted invincible; it endured about 15 weekes seidge.

Jan. 1. This day sett of to Mr Richard Harlakenden, his qter. *3l.* 15*s.* and pd in money *4l.* 15*s.* in all *8l.* 10*s.* towards the bond of *25l.* due to him Jan: 27 or 28 next; now my roll of debts is *77l.* 18*s.* 0*d.*

Jan. 4. Heard for certaine of ye spoiling P. Ruperts fleete upon ye Coast of Spaine Nov: last[1]; ye Spanish shew great affection to or Commonwealth[2]; ye ffrench since gave ye Spaniard a great overthrow at Rhetel[3] neare Mouron. Philip one of ye Q of Bohemia's sons slaine yr.

Jan. 9. Mett at Goodman Matthewes to endeavour to unite so as to receive ye sacrament of the Lords supper; divers willing.

Jan. 13. The reports from Ireland as if they intended a generall rising of all ye Irish to destroy the English, and also from Scotland; yr King crowned,[4] they would all rise, and many in England, to destroy this interest.

Jan. 17. My deare freind Mr W. Harlakenden had an invitacon from Cromwell to take an imployment with him in ye army.

Jan. 19. This weeke ye Ld Good to mee and mine in or health, my sonne recoverd from his ague, my wife this day better yn former, blessed bee my good God the Lord good especially in giving me a spirit more free from annoyances of Sathan, I having been a through-

[1] "The destruction of Rupert's fleet by Blake was almost complete." (Gardiner, *Commonwealth & Protectorate*, i, 338.)

[2] Spain recognised the Commonwealth December 26.

[3] Turenne and the Spaniards defeated by Mazarin.

[4] Charles II. had been crowned at Scone.

fare for many vile uncleane, worldly thoughts, oh deliver mee for thy goodnes sake.

Now I come to review this last yeare of my dayes past viz 34, and I find the Lord hath made good the intimation that he sett upon my heart to provide for mee for my livelyhood: he hath in mercy given mee an indifferent proportion of meanes from my people: a large supply from the Come for plundered Ministers, and also somewhat from the Come of the County towards my losses by Goring, and the death of my deare ffreind Mrs Mary Church occasioned her to entrust mee with her estate, wch I question will be no hindrance to mee, who also gave my daughter Jane one hundred pounds, and this yeare also God gave mee Earles Colne schoole. The Lord hath beene good to mee in my health, not so much subject to rheumes and colds, my navel though sometimes moist, yett not sore; it drieth of it selfe so as I have not dressed it for about 4 months, neither have I beene much troubled with my issue in the summer as formerly, nor seene it as yet this winter; but in these mercies I have found chastisement, the death of my deare Mary & Ralph, but they were not mine but the Lords, and Mrs Mary Church all togither in the space of 7 dayes; and yett this mingled with mercy, in the preserving my two that yett live, and giving mee hopes of another seed by my deare wife.

Or publicke affaires ended with peace at home, the nations Jan. 24.
abroad fearing us; only the Scots having crowned their King, prepare great armies to invade us.

The summer past yr was a great earthquake in Archipelago, Candia, and reported by Mrs King an earthquake for a short time at Geddington in Northamptonshire where shee was: great inundacons in fflanders, and of ye Seyne by Paris doing great hurt; these signes portend something.

35 Yeare of my age. 1650.

Sensible it entred mee into my 35 yeare, Lord bee with mee in Jan. 25.
ye same.

This day preacht in order to the sacrament; this day I sayd Jan. 26.

freely clearly as seing it, that one of the bitterest pangs of Englands travaile was yett to come, in this latter push of the Scots troubles, and stirrings within our selves.

Jan. 29. Heard from M[r] Clopton as if my 40*l*. per annum were ordered by y[e] Com[e]. and that he had an order to receive 30*l*. upon which mony is expected very shortly.

Jan. 30. A day of publike thanks for divers successes in Scotland and at sea. I apprehend a great noise of trouble over England, and a great sound of praises of y[e] saints who shall be delivered from it.

Feb. 9. Y[r] are expectacons of some bustles in Ireland & Scotland; ffrance is tampering about Mazarine.[1]

The Lord was good to mee in y[e] word & worke of the day; the next weeke I appointed two meetings to receive y[e] names of persons y[t] intend to receive y[e] sacrament togither, and to receive informacon concerning y[r] fitnesse to joyne in y[t] ordinance; the lords presence bee with us y[r] in for good.

Feb. 11. Mett at my house as appointed; Gods providence good to us in it, which I desire never to forgett.

Feb. 23. This week paste y[e] Lord was good to us in o[r] peace, plenty, health, and in the meeting of both sacraments this day, which had not for neare 9 yeares.

Lords Supper. This day after the humiliacon at my house wherein Gods presence was much, M[r] Harlakenden propounded if christians would, wee might proceed to administer the Lords supper, which I entertained with joye, and so did divers; twas propounded to divers christians about us, but wee had no helpe nor joyning from them but from W[m] Cowell; but meeting privately about it, wee were still letted, but God gave us a resolucon to goe on; wherfore wee desired Mole y[t] hindred, if he would not helpe to stand of and not hinder, who dissented, and reckoned no pastors now in the earth, as wee could gather, disowned baptisme; I declared if men did not in some measure owne all ordinances, I could not owne y[m] in this: so now wee resolved on the worke how few so ever would joyne, and to trust God with ye same, & to give

[1] Mazarin had returned to France from Brühl in Cologne, whither he had retired in the previous year. His return had roused much popular feeling.

publike notice to prevent offence, and yett to admitt none but such as in charity wee reckon to be disciples. Jan : 30, wee mett at priory ; divers presd y^{t} persons must make out a worke of true grace on y^{r} hearts in order to fellowship & this ordinance ; I was ill with ye toothake, yett I could not but speake, and turned them to all places in ye Acts, and shewed that beleeving admitted into Communion, and none rejected that professed faith, and then if y^{r} lives were not scandalous y^{t} wee could not turne away from them in this ordinance ; this gave good satisfaction to our company, wee went on, appointed two meetings at my house to take names and admitt by joynt consent. ffeb. 11, was ye first ; when divers came y^{t} wee could not comfortably joyne with, my heart quakt and our company feared ; before I did any thing, I sought God in private, and he sweetly answerd mee "who art thou that art afraid of a man, and fearest not mee," which came with life, & brought of my heart upon it ; I spake as God enabled mee, y^{t} wee should search peoples knowledge and admonish them in point of scandall, and Mr Harlakenden agreed with mee; then praying I dismissed ye company, and gave a liberty to go forth, and bade our company give in y^{r} names ; most went, few gave in y^{r} names : Thursday came Feb. 13. when stranger faces appeard. I sought God, he answerd not ; I was resolved to rest on his former answer ; I sought again, and he answerd, "I will never faile ye nor forsake y^{e}," which word came with power, and commanded my heart. I admonisht divers, admitted others with consent ; divers christians hung backe. Wee mett Feb. 20, in a day of humiliacon at priory, and y^{r} God was on o^{r} hearts and o^{r} company gave up themselves to this worke, about 34. After ye ordinance was done, and ye collection for ye poore, ye rest withdrew, wee stayed, & proposed whether any had any thing agst another y^{t} wee might joyne as one bread ; wee gatherd for bread & wine, and proceeded Feb. 23 to celebrate ye ordinance.

Wee all sat round and neare ye table ; ye bread was broken not cutt in blessing it ; ye Lord pourd out a spirit of mourning over Christ crucified on me and most of ye company, and my soule eyed him more y^{n} ever, and God was sweete to mee in ye worke.

No vaine thoughts but wholly intent on ye worke; no difficulty among o^r^ selves, a savor on my spirit, but not y^t^ healing to my soule at present I desired.

Received an account from many of o^r^ society of the sweete and comfortable presence of God with them, the livelynesse of the actions in breaking the bread, and in powring out the wine; the Lords name have the glory of all.

March. 1. Y^e^ season cold and very sad, worke scarce, the poore in a sad condicon, and its feared it will bee farre worse with the spinner.[1]

March. 2. The season cold, and things hard, price of corne and commodities rise, and litle or no worke; the worke at present staid in Scotland; all things for present quiet in England blessed bee his name.

March. 5. I bought two cowes of Day at Halsted, & brought them home this day; they with y^r^ calves cost mee 10*l.* 15*s.* the Lord prosper them with mee.

March. 9. The small pox is in 6 families, Lord still preserve mine.

March. 16. Three married women died out of one house of ye small poxe; blessed bee God that hath kept mee and mine. The state seeme to act towards banking meanes for ministers and schooles, which what it may prove towards mee I knowe not, but to my God I committ my selfe & wayes, who hath and will provide for mee.

March. 17. Ardleigh taxes at 32*s.* 7*d.* ob.; repayres cost mee, 1*l.* 10*s.* 0*d.* wch I allowed. this day I payd Mr Har: 16*s.* for use of his bond on which I owe 10*l.* I payd R. Johnson 3*l.*; I owe him 8*l.*

March. 18. Brownebacke calved, ye first of creatures y^t^ brought us young; God blesse o^r^ stocke.

March. 22. Reported y^t^ Cromwell was dead, the Lord liveth, and reigneth, and dependeth not on any instruments for his worke; at night our newes came, and Major Haynes letter of 8 of March which s^d^ the Gen. was sicke and could not bee spoken with.

March. 23. Mr Owen[2] hath a place of great proffit given him, vz Deane

[1] The weavers, etc., in Colchester & the neighbourhood.

[2] "As minister of Coggeshall, he attracted the notice of Fairfax on his way to the siege of Colchester, and by Fairfax he was carried to London, when he was selected for the arduous duty of preaching before Parliament on the day after

of Christ-church; 18 com^rs^ are gone downe to order ye affaires of ye army in the unfitnes of ye generall to doe it.

Bought two peices timber of Mr Jacobs bayly at 6*s.* 6*d.* March. 24.

Sett Day of Halsted a price of my farm called Mallories, viz 245*l.* I am very indifferent to sell or not; Lord direct me in all my outward affaires for ye best; the small pox appeared anew in 4 families more, two neare us. Wee lost in attempts on a castle in Scotland 180 men as its said. 1651. March. 25.

Y^e^ value of my outward estate which God hath given mee. March. 29.

Imprimis land as formerly Malleries Bollinhatch. 2 closes Colne	27*l.* per annum.
In Mr John Litles hand money as was formerly mentiond.	50*l.* 0.
This yeare I have p^d^ ye fines for my closes at 4*l.*; built and layd out for ye schoole about. 26*l.*	
I have in money on Mrs Maries land and ye improvem^t^ of it March. 25. 1651. past.	81*l.* 0. 0.
stocke, 5 cowes at 5*l.* round, my nagge, 3*l*,. my hogges and hay, 4*l.*	32.

I was then in debt 45*l.*; now I am about 70*l.*, wch is 25*l.* more than last yeare, which taken out of my stocke y^r^ remayneth 7*l.* wch added to 81, is 88. & so much estate is betterd blessed bee my God; but I hope my soule hath gained infinitely from God whom I praise for all.

the execution of the King...... 'Sir,' said Cromwell, tapping the preacher on the shoulder, when he next met him at Fairfax's house, 'you are the person I must be acquainted with.' Taking him aside, Cromwell insisted on carrying him as his chaplain to Ireland. In 1651 Parliament, doubtless at Cromwell's instigation, named Owen Dean of Christ Church in succession to Reynolds, who had refused to take the engagement...... Some little time afterwards he appointed him to the Vice-Chancellorship, thus committing the Puritan reorganisation of the University into his hands." *(Commonwealth and Protectorate,* ii, 25. etc.)

April. 1. Mett to choose officers; wee agreed not; most scurrilously abused by old Wm Adam for dawbing with untempered mortar, for Kendalls bond, for going to Halsted for 20*s*. per day.

April. 2. Heard of the relapse of Cromwell, the Lord raise him up. Y^{r} are 2 dead now in the towne of the small pox.

April. 3. Mett, cast up the ov^{r}seers accounts; it amounts unto 14 quarters within a litle; wee chose our officers without any trouble, and did our business with as much peace and ease as might bee.

April. 6. Cromwell well recoverd; the boates come to ye ffirth upon wch wee expect action.

April. 9. This day was goodwife Day with mee; I perceive shee is resolved to give mee my price for my farme of Mallories, and I intend to lett it goe.

April. 13. The Lords hand is abated in the distempers of ye small pox; in the Towne they are up and well in all families except two. Wee gave over our jangling chiming as they call it.

April. 14. The small pox in a family upland; feared ye Wid. Rugles will have it.

April. 20. Many suppose our Commonwealth lost. Spaine & ffrance & Holland against us. Ireland & Scotland heavy worke, & not to bee effected; ye English divided, and worne out with taxes and burthens, the merchants trade even ruined, and so all tending to poverty; but if ye worke be Gods, y^{r} is enough in his arme to effect the same, and up to him his people looke to bee y^{r} salvation.

April. 27. Great buzzines as if the D. of Lorraine[1] would undertake ye protection of the Irish; great feares and jealousies are abroad and among men.

April. 30. This day I surrendered Mallories and the appurtenances to Day of Halsted and his daughter. I received 193*l*. downe and bond for 50*l*. more; they are to pay mee 3*l*. more very shortly; ye surrender in Mr Littells hand; they are to abate ye 14*s*. for ye wood to my Tenant.

May. 3. Seaver tooke of mee all the bushes in Dagnal to stubbe up by

[1] Charles had applied to him for help, as his father had done before him.

ye rootes & to pull all ye broome; he is to cleare ye grounds; for y^s I am to give him 10s. & the broome, which I doe account to bee 13s. O.

Jone Rayner buried of ye small pox taken with conceit [1] in y^t place where often I have smelt a smell. May. 10.

The smallpox continued in some families in this towne; its reported that the Irish and the Duke of Lorraine are agreed; [2] he is expected in June next to bee with them. May. 11.

Mrs Wm Harlakenden sicke of y^e smallpox; tooke y^m with a conceit of a keepers touching her hand. May. 12.

Heard as if the Scots were near Carlisle; the Lord o^r God stand up for o^r helpe in whom I putt my trust: the great $rumo^{rs}$ of this weeke came to nothing; Cromwell recovers apace for wch Gods name bee praised. June. 6.

The state of England although worne with civill warres, and scarcity and ill trading for many yeares, being but in bad termes with Holland, [3] and not altogither sure of Spain, proclaimed open warre with Portugall, [4] and is in open warre with ffrance, o^r fleets being in ye midland Sea [5]; wee at ye same time are endeavouring to conquer Scotland, and Ireland; attempt Silly with a fleet, & yett send a fleete also to reduce the ilands of Barbados in America; [6] & yett the nacon is much discontent & divided, yett feareth not ye attempts of any forreigner against them. June. 9.

[1] As she conceived.

[2] vide *Commonwealth and Protectorate*, ii, c. xix.

[3] Vide *Commonwealth and Protectorate*, i, 361.

[4] The Portuguese ambassador was on May 16th ordered to leave London within fourteen days.

[5] In the Mediterranean, Penn's fleet had captured some French prizes.

[6] "As for the masters themselves, they long lived in harmony in spite of the distracting influence of the English Civil War. For some time anyone calling another either Cavalier or Roundhead was bound to give a dinner of pork and turkey to all within hearing when the offence was committed. Of late, however, this happy agreement had been brought to an end. Young English Royalists, smarting from defeat and sequestration, had flocked to the Island, where, headed by two Devonshire brothers named Walrond, they made themselves masters of the colony by a combination of force and intrigue...... Parliament gave orders to prepare a fleet of seven ships to sail under Aysene for the reduction of Barbados." (*Commonwealth and Protectorate*, i, 354.)

June. 19. Heard of a great route given ye Irish, a very seasonable mercy. Two families in towne more visited with small poxe.

June. 24. This day I paid Mr Harlakenden 4*l.* 7*s.* for his rent for Dagnal; the roll of my debts now is about 57*l.* 13*s.*

July. 6. Y^e successe of o^r forces in Connaught in Ireland is very great,[1] none being able to stand before them; from Scotland wee expect action in as much as ye armies are on ye march; the Lord bee with o^r forces to prosper y^m. Our ambassadors are returned from Holland, it is apprehended without doing the businesse for which they were sent.

July. 13. One or two more in former families sicke of ye small pox. Heard y^t Mr Love[2] was condemned to be beheaded July 15; he and divers peticon for life, others call for impartiall justice; one Joyce, y^t commanded the guard that surprized the King at Holmeby, reports y^t the Scots commissioners and divers English engaged to rule ye King by force & to put divers factious persons of ye Commons house and in the Country to death.

July. 15. This day I payde to Wm Brand 5*l.*; I now am out of his debt, but I owe him love for his great kindnesse to mee; my roll of debts is
52*l.* 13*s.* now 52*l.* 13*s.*; it was apprehended Mr Love, a godly Presbyterian Minister, would loose his head at London this day; but upon his peticon, his wives, & the Ministers of London, he was repreived unto Aug: 15 next; blessed bee ye name of God for this act of compassion extended towards them.

July. 22. This day Mr Harlakenden went about casting his ponds;[3] my 8*l.* I lent him, he repaid mee, whereof 4*l.* I paid to Johnson; I am now cleare with him but 13*s.* for a loade of wood; my roll of debts
48*l.* 13*s.* now 48*l.* 13*s.* 0*d.*

July. 25. I lent to M^r Jo: Littell this day 50*l*; I shall make this up an

[1] Coote captured Athlone, Loughrea and Ballinasloe.

[2] For participation in a plot to put an end to the Council and Parliament and to restore Charles. Mr Love, a Presbyterian minister, was involved with others; a strong appeal for mercy was addressed to Cromwell, but Mr Love was executed on Tower Hill, Aug. 22. Milton appears to have written articles in "Mercurius Politicus" in support of the sentence.

[3] Cleaning the ponds.

100*l*; he had 20*l*. before, in all, 70*l*; he offers mee his meadowe at 5*l*. per annum, which I conceive is very deare.

Heard of action in Scotland; the Scots tooke from us Newarke house in y[e] West, wherin wee lost 140 men; wee tooke from them Callendar house [1] in the view of y[r] Campe; Major Gen Lambert, Harrison with his Brigade, in Fife routed a brigade of the Scots, slew a 2000 on the place, tooke many prisoners; [2] the armies on both sides are marcht, action is expected, the Lord in mercy remember us. July. 26. 2500 slaine 1533 prisonners most deadly wounded.

Sawe Cromwells letter to M[r] Speaker of this Scotch action; he writes not so like a servant in my minde as when he was in Ireland. July. 28.

Heard Aug: 1 that Sligo was taken by storme and 3000 put to the sword on the affaire of Scotland. I heare that divers suppose a weeke or two will putt an end to that businesse. I say, stay till December next and then judge. Aug. 1.

Matters went very well in Scotland; great expectacons of crushing, and ruining that Scotch army; some suppose they will for England; wee lost about 90 men at Limbericke in Ireland; that army very sensible of Gods stroke, and humbled for y[e] same; Lord arise & helpe us! The Lord was gratious to mee in keeping my heart in some measure close to him, in helping mee against old corrupcons; sometimes they show y[r] hornes, but Gods carpenters are ready to cutt them of; wee heard as if y[e] Polanders had routed the Cossacks, [3] and their complices; slaine and wounded on the place 48000; of them, 14000 slaine; about 80000 slaine & wounded on both sides; if so it is the most memorable battaile hath beene in Europe for an 100 yeares. Aug. 10.

Reported for certaine at Colne, that the Scots were at Dumfreeze entring England, and that Cromwell and his army was then before S[t] Johnstons; the Co[mes] in the several counties ordered to take Aug. 11.

[1] Near Falkirk.

[2] About 1500; total Scotch force, 4,000: at Inverkeithing.

[3] June 1651. Battle of Beresteczko in Galicia. The Cossacks, led by Bogdan Khmelnitski, in their revolt against the Poles were defeated here; they eventually (1654) transferred their allegiance to the Czar of Russia.

care of the kingdomes peace; the forces in the North ordered to March up towards Alnwicke to resist them.

Aug. 13. Heard ye Scots were in Lancashire, and that they had not mett with any opposicon; there emissaries are gone into all the kingdome.

Aug. 16. Heard ye Scots entred England with y^r^ King & 11 or 12000 men, August 5, about Carlile on August 6, and were August 10 at Lancaster, ye 9 at Kendall; that day, viz ye 10th, Harrison was at Rippon.

Aug. 21. The enemy wee heard was in Cheshire; all our foote ordered to march to Dunstable.

Aug. 22. Rid to Colchester; heard the enemy intended that night for Lichfeild, but that day he entered Worcester; o^r^ horse ordered all to march, the County left emptie of all force whatsoever.

Aug. 23. The Scots coming in at first was a great dampe to Gods people and all men, but they presently recovered and beare up very comfortably.

Aug. 24. The enemy for London as reported, I feare not but God hastens him to his fall.

Aug. 27. Heard the enemy had been at Woster; still s^d^ they intended London.

Aug. 29. Orders to disarme and secure malignants in the County, and to raise Voluntiers for the security and defence of ye same; heard the action likely to bee at Worcester.

Aug. 30. Heard Derby routed in Lancashire; divers of quality slaine, many prisoners; the levies intended in the West of Scotland broken. Sterling Castle taken; and our army gone towards Dundee. Cromwell at Warwicke; all marching towards Worcest. where they are before this time.

Sept. 2. At night heard by many hands o^r^ freinds abroad were well, and y^t^ Cromwell was before Worcester & the Scots in it, and their horse in the Contry round about.

Sept. 5. About noone heard at Colne, y^t^ ye Scots were routed, y^r^ horse gone; towards night confirmed y^t^ they fell out of towne, y^t^ they were beate in againe; 4000 slaine, 300 prisoners; our forces did gallantly; done while wee were praying at Markeshall.

Sept. 7. Heard after sermon of the taking of Worcester; 6000 prisoners,

2000 more slaine; even in y[e] place of prayer I heard it; God good to mee this day, though I sinfull & unworthy.

Received a letter from London signifying the Lords Mayors pleasure unto mee to come up and preach before him, and his brethren the aldermen at Pauls, which I intended to doe, & serve providence in it. Sept. 13.

The weeke past die. 10, wee kept a day of praise unto our good & gratious God at Cornelius Brownsons in Earles Colne. Sept. 14.

This day our souldiers returned.

This Friday morning my wife was very well delivered of her fourth sonne, and sixt child, much about seven of the clocke; I intend to name him John. Sept. 19.

R[d] this day a letter from London y[t] my L[d] Mayor expects mee at my day; I shall not faill with Gods leave.

When the Hollander rejoyced in the false newes of o[r] fall, y[e] enemy fell at Worcester; God hath beene very terrible to Scotland; many of y[r] nobility, slaine, imprisond and fled into strange lands and that in a very short season; y[r] breake began Aug. 28, at Ellett; y[n] somewhat more, a litle after at Dumfreeze, then Sep: 1, at Dundee and then Sep. 3, at Worcester, and in y[r] pursuit they are even almost all taken; oh feare, England, and hono[r] God, least he turne the wheele upon thee also. Sept. 21.

30. P[d] M[r] Harlakenden all lords rent due until Michaelmas past, viz. 3*l.* 8*s.* 8*d.* ob; I r[d] also his q[ter]. I now owe unto him still 10*l*; my rol of debts I now esteeme to bee about 45*l.* 12*s.* 6*d.*; this day M[r] John Littell of Halsted received of mee so much mony as made up that in his hands an 100*l.*; now he oweth mee an 150*l.* and his brother Jeffery, an 100*l.* Lords rn[t]. 45*l.* 12*s.* 6*d*

I preached this day at Pauls in London by order from y[e] L[d] Mayor; the audience was great; my text was Luke 24. v. 28. I dined with y[e] L[d] Mayor, and by his intreaty preached before him, at his owne church; the Lord was good to mee in the worke & service of the day; this was the first time that I preached in the city of London. Oct. 5.

Reported that Cardinal Mazarine of France, abiding at Colen in Germany, had tampered with the electors and wrought with y[e] Major part of them, and wonne them to transferre the Empire from Oct. 12.

ye house of Austria, and to elect the eldest sonne of the Duke of Bavaria King of Romans.

The Prince of Conde and ffrench King in armes one against another.[1] Divers forces in England ordered to bee disbanded; Major Generall Deane one of the Admirals chosen to command in cheife in Scotland.

Oct. 16. Heard Dr Drake had discovered the whole plott, and actors to bring in ye Scots King; and this weeke came the good newes of their pardon of the Ministers and the other companions in that businesse.[2]

Oct. 19. Paid unto Wm Hickford what I owe him viz 12*l.* 8*s.*; so y^t^ my

39l. 2s. 6d. roll of debts is now but *39l. 2s. 6d.*

Oct. 22. This day I received 8*l.* 19*s.* of Nathan Perry, and made even with him until the last michaelmas, and now all the lords rent for that part is payd unto mee, and I am cleare also with my uncle, and all about the same; this day also I received 47*l.* 10*s.* from Goodman Day of mony for his purchase of Mallories; heard also as if ye prince were escaped into Holland, which if, then its likely to continue o^r^ troubles and bring on forreigne ingagements; God will have it so, and I am perswaded God will make them fall under us; its said he was in London in the habit of a footeman & escaped over in that of a seaman.

It was said by many he was slaine, but what is man unto God? his life shall contribute to Gods works more than his death could.

Oct. 24. A day of publicke rejoycing for the eminent victory at Worcester.

Oct. 29. This day lent to Mr Pelham and his sonne on their bond, 50*l.*

Oct. 30. Now I heare ye King[3] is in France; I said by October wee should heare where he was if alive, on this ground that a King is too great a person to conceale long; some s^d^ he was kild, some said he was here & there & they say Lorraine intends to waft over forces into Ireland, but I feare them not, if this notion hold. Heard Jersey iland was taken.[4]

[1] Louis XIV had been declared of age, and Parliament declared Condé and his followers guilty of treason.

[2] The other ministers arrested with Mr Love.

[3] He landed at Fécamp on October 16.

[4] Not taken till December 12.

Paid Nicholas his 3*l.* 10*s.* I borrowed of him; my roll of debts is now, 35*l.* 12*s.* 6*d.* Nov. 1. 35*l.* 12*s.* 6*d.*

The King escaping and appearing in ffrance, matters growing very high in y^t nation; the state of England in this latter end of October, wonne Jersey iland in the lap of france and the castle, as also Man island[1] and Limbricke in Ireland,[2] which giveth us hope of good successe in o^r affaires at home, y^t wee may more vigorously attend forreigne designes; the Scots also are much divided, and divers tender compliance with England. Nov. 2.

Received from Mr Harlakenden my sermon at his wives funerall which he printed; I had a litle peice of my drawing printed in Mr Harlakendens booke, but this was my first at the presse.[3] Nov. 16.

Writt up to London for our augmentacon businesse. I am now in arreare 1 yeare 3 qters; at 40*l.* per annum it is 70*l.*; if I receive in all 60*l.* I will make ye Lord a sharer with it for his worke in new England to ye sum of 5*l.* when they gather for the advancement of the Gospell in new England. Nov. 18.

Lent Young of Halsted 3*l.* who was in great straites to make his rent up to his landlord; I bought of him 4 bushels wheate at 4*s.* 6*d.* the bushel; Nov. 19.

The state of England hath in a manner reduced Scotland and Ireland; w^t probability is their of continuing their command over them, for surely the seed of liberty will remaine in those nations, if not of revenge also; and if ever our troubles and discords, or y^r happines & valor of some perticular person appeare, they may give a turne; to destroy the nations were barbarous, to plant them with English colonies is very hard and unlikely, and Scotland will not invite our men, and yett this must be done besides good garrisons. God who hath done what is done, will effect his owne purpose, and therefore I beleive it.

The small pox continueth still in Towne in many places. This weeke wee heard the house voted Novemb. 18, they would sitt Nov. 23.

[1] Surrendered October 31.

[2] October 27.

[3] The sermon was entitled "The State of the Saints departed, God's cordial to comfort the Saints remaining alive." Published in London in 1652.

but 3 yeares more; the Cavas [1] give out y[e] King of Denmarke is dead, and Charles Stuart called to that kingdome, that he should marry y[e] daughter of Spaine—strange things: Its said the P. of Conde hath sent over unto us for souldiers, but our state demurre. [2]

Nov. 26. W[m] Webb and his brother tooke my ditching, to throw the marle into the feild, to cutt the hedge, sett on one againe, and to goe three spitt where need is; to throw of a spitt where I intend to quicke and to raise it up with new earth; I am to give them *3d.* ob. per rod, and where worth it *4d.*

Dec. 1. This day we kild a good hogge; through mercy the price of things, and catle abateth very much; this afternoone, my litle Scotch hobby that I bought my sonne Tho. died, the first of such creatures that ever dyed from mee; Lord its mercy that it was not a greater and a nearer losse.

Dec. 7. Heard as if some of Lorraines men were come over into Ireland. [3]

Dec. 9. I received *25l.* of my augmentacon arreares, which my good freind Major Haines procured from M[r] Stanbridge.

Dec. 12. 13. R[d] the *3l.* I lent Young; I paid him *17s. 4d.* for four bushels of wheate; I paid Nich Hurrel *4l.* I borrowed of his mony from my sister; I am cleare with him; Caplin paid me the last of my *5l.* and this day I lent Jo. Smith oatemeale man, *4l.* until Dec. 26. Coxal destitute sent for me to preach, profferd me *20s.* but I refused; this day wee heard that Ireton Deputy generall of Ireland dyed at Limbricke in Ireland No: 26. Ludlow who was L. gen. commands the forces in cheife for the present.

[1] ? Cavaliers.

[2] He sent over an agent, La Rivière to England to ask for help.

[3] "On October 7 Synott returned to Galway with an agreement between the Duke of Lorraine and the two Commissioners, Plunket and Browne, in accordance with which the Duke was to be styled the Royal Protector of Ireland holding powers little short of those of Royalty itself. On the 20th this offer was summarily rejected by Clanricarde as entrenching on his authority derived from the King...... The Mayor and Corporation of Galway even chose an agent of their own to re-open the negotiation, which the Lord Deputy fiercely denounced. The Duke was not likely to lead an army into Ireland on the simple invitation of the Corporation of Galway." (*Commonwealth and Protectorate*, ii.)

Releasd from going to Halsted, saw Manasseh Ben Israel, [1] or Dec. 20.
the hope of Israel. Lord, my heart questions not the calling home the nation of the Jewes; thou wilt hasten in its season, oh my God; oh, thou God of the ends of the whole earth, hasten it Amen ! Saw the good newes of taking of the private excise on beere; the several oppressions of men will spew them out in due time so that their places shall know them no more.

The Holland Ambassadors had y^{r} audience : Dec. 19 [2] : no Dec. 28.
actions this weeke ; our worke will bee to setle our conquests, and to order things at home with justice to content ; heard that 12 men, 4 lawyers & 8 gentlemen are chosen to frame a moddell of regulating the Law : its said the Gen. in the House offered them his commission now Ireton is dead ; its questioned whether the power of Lieuten^{t}ship shall bee continued to Cromwell, or which way his place and that government shal bee managed.

Heard y^{s} day of ye reducement of ye two Ilands of Jersey and Jan. 3.
Guernsey to the obedience of parliament. Elizabeth Castle yeilded Decem : 12 ; ye 15, our men tooke possession according to agreement : Cornet Castle [3] was ye last of ye kingdome of England y^{t} held out agst ye parliament for ye King y^{t} was yeilded up.

My eye is on ye troubles of France ; God is disquieting them. Jan. 6.
In 48 ye Germane peace [4] was concluded ; who would have thought

[1] "On November 5 (1655) Manasseh published his Humble Address to the Protector, defending Jews from calumnies raised against them, and arguing with some defect of worldly wisdom, that as England was the only country rejecting them, their re-establishment would, according to the prophecies, be the signal for the coming of the Messiah. A few days later he prepared a request for the admission of his race on an equality with the natives of England...... Though the Protector solaced him with a pension, he was forced to cross the seas discomfited, together with a number of Jews who had accompanied him and shared his hopes." (*Commonwealth and Protectorate*, iii, 218-221.)

[2] "Before the end of the preceding year the States General, alarmed at the Navigation Act, resolved to despatch an embassy to procure if possible its repeal...... At their first audience they were informed that the Navigation Act was irrevocable." (*Commonwealth and Protectorate*, ii, 107.)

[3] In Guernsey, surrendered December 17.

[4] Peace of Westphalia.

that had not beene a step to reconcile France & Spaine, or afforded liberty to forreine princes to ingage agst England ? but ye troubles of the world shall come on them suddenly as paines of a travailing woman.

Jan. 18. God good to mee and mine in our outward mercies ; y^{s} is a still time for present in England ; the French troubles come on, [1] no body knoweth why, and so in England no body can state the cause of the quarrel.

Jan. 24. This day was the last of my 35 yeare.

All ye threats of o^{r} enemies ended in ye ruine of ye Scotch designe at Worcester, and the flight of y^{r} King into France ; all Scotland even reduced by force, and disbanded on treaty ; our forces also prospered in Ireland, where ye sword, famine and pestilence hath made a great waste. Wee are not in good terms with Holland ; the new hopes of the enemies are that these 2 states will fall out to eithers ruine and make way for the Spaniard and Stuard to recover y^{r} owne againe in both.

France is likely to fall into flames by her owne divisions ; this summer shee hath done nothing abroad. The Spaniard hath almost reduced Barcelona, ye cheife city of Catalonia, and so y^{t} kingdome ; ye issue of that affaire wee waite. Poland is free from warre with the Cossacks but feareth them. Dane and Suede are both in quiet, and so is Germany, yett the peace at Munster is not fully executed : the Turke hath done no great matter on ye Venetian, nor beene so fortunate and martial as formerly, as if that people were at y^{r} height and declining rather.

The Iles of Silly, Jersey, and Guernsey, Man, and all ye proper possessions of England now reduced, and no great feare of any power within ; God prevent breaches among our selves, o^{r} fleetes are strong at sea.

Y^{r} have been great inundacions in Spaine at Bilboa, and in Italy ; letters from Silly mention an earthquake their on Decemb. 25, past.

[1] Condé had been declared guilty of treason and France was involved in civil war.

Jan: 25, 1651. y. 36 of my age.

This was the Lords day, and I was sensible, that it ended my 35, and begun my 36 yeare. Jan. 25.

Mett at my house; wee gave a sharpe reproofe to some of o^r company in their weake carriage. I was with Thomasin, poore troubled heart; helpe her oh Lord! heard that Jo: Lilburne, [1] when he received his sentence Jan. 20, 1651, refused to kneele, wherupon they ordered him to be banisht within 20 dayes wch end I apprehend ffeb: 8:, he said, "I shall outlive this sentence of yours, as I have all the rest of them." Jan. 27.

Bought 12 bushels white oates at *22s. 6d.* only ½ bushell branke [2] given in.

A report out of Scotland, as is whisperd from the West y^r of, y^t the Rebels had burnt Dublin; this lookt on as a tale, and perhaps is so, but when such a thing doth come, its a signe to the English nation of dismal dayes coming on them. Jan. 31.

Lett Bowles my ditch at Bridgmans for *6d.* per rod. Feb. 10.

Was Iretons funerall. Feb. 6.

Heard y^t 20^m. Danes were landed in Scotland, perhaps some, not so many; perhaps none, but surely y^r is much trouble yett coming on England, and wee shall not enjoy y^t constant victorious successe that wee did formerly; yett God will crowne the issue with much good to his remnant. Heard ye Q. & K. were banisht out of France, they sending ambassadors to us. Both these proved reports as farre as we could discerne; ye French troubles advance. Feb. 30.

Went to Halstead; in my way mett with Captaine Maidstone, who prevailed with mee to preach the assize sermon at Colchester on March 2 next. Feb. 26.

Rid to Colchester, where I preacht the assize sermon; the Lord was good to mee in my comfortable jorny outwards & homewards; I bought Mr Dells booke; cost mee *3s.*; I hope I might doe good, and receive good from the occasions of that day. March. 2

[1] *Commonwealth and Protectorate*, ii, 7.

[2] Buckwheat.

March. 8. This day a sweet warme raine. I sold to Mr Wm Harlakenden 20 Q. hay at 2*s*. per Q.

March. 24. 1651 : A review of my outward estate which God hath given mee.

Bollinhatch pt. and 2 closes in Colne, as formerly.	
Mallories sold in lieu of yt I have in Mr J. L. & Mr J. L. hands.	250*l*.
In Mr P. hands yt wch was in Mr J. L. formerly.	50.
25. March 1652. now at hand in mony & improvemt of Mrs Marie's land.	85
My stock in all much as last yeare.	32

I was then in debt, 70*l*. I am now in debt about 12*l*. so I have paid 58*l*. and have added 4 to Mrs Marie's land ; this yeare through mercy gives mee an improvemt of my estate to about 70*l*. for which I desire to give praise & thanks to my good God. I have moreover in G. Y. hands....... 10*l*.

1652. This day I renewed ye resolucon of Aug. 23. 1647 about bookes to put it in execution, and to sett out the 10th of all receipts in mony that are paid unto as rents, or profits, towards charitable uses, thus. viz in 10*s*. because of giving many things in kinde at the doore, every 4*s*. towards bookes and necessary things for my study, and the other 6*s*. to dispose towards such charitable uses, as God shall give mee a fit opportunity for ; and this I desire to doe out of obedience unto God, and love to the service and commands of God and Christ.

This day a great eclipse ; see memorials of this day.

June. 9. A fast day in London.

June. 10. Presented Dr Wright with a peice of plate ; cost 5*s*. 6*d*. per ounce ; it cost mee 5*l*. 19*s*. 6*d*. as a token of my love to him in giving mee ye schoole.

June. 13. The small pox much in London.

June. 20. Many eyes are on our breach with Holland, [1] and how Lorraine

[1] We were at war with the Dutch.

hath lurcht the princes, which speakes the Kings present successe; God is shaking the earth, and he will doe it.

This day I began to unfold ye assembly catechismes. July. 4.

I received of the Major 15*l.* which he received of Mr Stanbridge in part of my arreares of augmentacon due unto mee.[1] July. 24.

Mr Meredith and his daughter came to Colne with his wife; ye Lord make the young one a blessing unto us all. I p^d^ him 10*s.* and 18*s.* to Mr Heckford of Halsted for a suite of clothes, die 10th. Aug. 8. 10*s.* 18*s.*

I dreamed formerly of our being in France with o^r^ armies and ye time by November next or ye yeare following in 53; now Sept. 4, 1652, o^r^ fleet did ye Spaniards a great curtesy in destroying ye French fleete y^t^ attempted to relieve Dunkirke[2] & for my p^t^ I apprehend wee shall warre with France.

Great feare as if wee should not long imploy o^r^ poore by reason of decay of trade through o^r^ breach with Holland. Sept. 19.

Received of Major Haines 14*l.* p^t^ of 25*l.* he hath received of Mr Stanbridge: the Major hath in hand still 11*l.* Sept. 28.

5. R^d^ of Major Haines, 11*l.* residue of ye 25*l.* which he last received for mee of Mr Stanbridge; I have received in all 65*l.* in p^t^ of 2 yeares & halfe augmentacon due to me on June: 24: 1652, past. I gave to my sister 20*s.* and my wife a good coate & some other things. Oct. 4.

This day I began a Lecture at Wakes Colne. Oct. 7.

This day was set apart for a publike fast to seeke Gods face in regard to ye breach of England and Holland, and that the Lord would direct them, in the things of his w^p^. which I humbly beg the Lord to assist o^r^ state in. Oct. 13.

Heard ye Danish Ambassador was clapt up, till wee heare something concerning o^r^ ships. Oct. 22.

1 In Dr Shaw's "History of the English Church" will be found the following entry "William Stanbridge to the use of W. Clopton minister of Markishall & R. Jocelyn minister of Earles Colne £ 199.0.0." (from the sale of Bishop's lands).

2 "Blake fell upon the relieving fleet whilst it was still on its way from Calais, carried seven of the men of war into Dover and captured, destroyed or dispersed the store ships, with the result that Dunkirk surrendered on the following day. *Commonwealth & Protectorate*, ii, 130.

Oct. 29. 25*l.* Made up to Mr Harlakenden ye Justice 25*l.*, viz. 14*l.* at ye priory and 11*l.* of the Tickett mony, which wee began to repay this day.

Nov. 5. Received from Mr William Harlakenden 1*l.* 10*s.* for to buy a booke, for preaching and printing his wives funerall sermon.

Nov. 25. R^d^ this day the act for propagation of ye Gospel in New England among the heathen; I resolve to give 5*l.* my selfe & wife & children, and to promote it unto ye utmost.

Dec. 2. Heard as if it were ye states intention next yeare to send an army into Holland, and if not ye Hollanders intended ye like against us.

Dec. 5. Heard of a fight in the Downes with the Dutch.[1]

Dec. 26. This weeke God was good to mee and all mine in o^r^ outward mercies; I made a gathring for the Indians. I gave 5*l.* and my family, gathered in mony more, 4*l.* 8*s.* 6*d.* and y^r^ was underwritt more 32*l.*

Dec. 30. Invited to my Lady H. kindly entertained; heard y^r^ that ye Londoners bought up bayes, hull[2] and ivy wonderfully in London, being eagerly sett on y^r^ feasts; oh that my heart were as zealous for God.

Jan. 1. This wee call new yeares day; it was a cleare lightsome day; heard that ye army kept solemne dayes of fasting & prayer, on Jan. 28 & 29, a signe of some great resolucons on foote among them.

Jan. 2. Y^e^ Lord was good to mee in ye sabbath; I renewed the motion for new England; some poore came in, most of ye richer sorte came in; I received in mony 4*l.* 17*s.* 10*d.* & Mr Cressener subscribed 40*s.*; wee have somewhat above 50*l.*; blessed bee our God in what wee shall doe in this worke.

[1] "Off Dungeness the two fleets clashed against one another about three in the afternoon, Blake having still the advantage of the wind. Then followed a scene the like of which has never again been witnessed in the annals of the British Navy. Twenty of Blake's ships—some of them hired merchantmen, some of them men-of-war—held aloof and took no part in the action. The disparity of numbers, great enough before, now became overwhelming. Blake with but twenty-five ships was left to struggle against eighty-five. No heroism could countervail such odds, and, after losing two ships, the Garland and the Bonaventure, Blake was well satisfied to return to Dover, whence on the following day he made his retreat to the Downs." (*Commonwealth and Protectorate*, ii, 150.)

[2] Holly.

The state issued a proclamation against Jesuites to be gone by March 1. next. Jan. 9.

Nan came to us. Jan. 18.

Mr Stebbin with mee to propose a businesse unto mee, wherein he desired my helpe, I promised it as far as I might. Jan. 24.

And now I am sensible this day ends my 36 yeare, in which the Lord hath beene very good to mee and all my family, his provision for mee bountifull, though I have been unworthy; yett I desire in the uprightnes of my heart to owne & serve my God & follow him through any condicon.

The great actions this yeare are ye troubles of France, where ye Princes rather loose than gaine, Orleans fallen of from Condé, Spaine hath gotten much of France this yeare, filled his kingdome with troubles assisting ye Princes, winning Gravelin & afterwards Dunkirke. — Barcellona in Catalonia, and therby even reducing that kingdome, — Casal in Montferrat and reducing that under Mantua, to the great prejudice of the French interest.

The Germans quiet, great noise of y^r diet, but nothing done as yett; the Turkes & the Venetians calmed, and its said now treating a peace.

The English quiet at home and also in all their dominions, favoured by the Spaniard, courted by ye Portugal with whom wee have perfected a peace, he buying it; the French treate us, the Swedes and wee gaze, but each are sending their agents; the Dutch fought us all along this summer at our owne doores, the Dane seizeth o^r shipping and stops us in the Sound. [1]

The Dutch and wee are now making great naval preparations, and so is the Spaniard.

37 yeare of my age, 1652. Jan. 25.

Sensible this day entred me into my 37 yeare; the Lord bee with mee therein to keepe mee from sin & temptacon, and preserve Jan. 25.

[1] "Yet more serious was the news that the King of Denmark, whose good understanding with the Dutch was notorious, had detained in the Sound twenty English merchantmen laden with materials for the construction and repair of shipping." (*Commonwealth & Protectorate*, ii, 140.)

mee spotlesse to his owne kingdome, with thee I leave all my waies.

Feb. 24. Great reports yesterday of our victory over the Dutch.[1]

Feb. 28. This day I brought divers businesse for my estate into order, clearing up divers accounts and evening those reckonings that were on my hand, for which I praise my God; oh that ye Lord alone would cleare the account of my soule.

March. 3. Publiq: fast; few in the contry had notice to keepe it. The enemie begins to appeare both in Ireland & Scotland; its but weakely yet; the issue of thes things God only knoweth.

March. 6. I was afraid of some trouble at London before this[2]: blessed bee God for lengthning out our tranquillity.

March. 19. Pd in unto Mr Crowe for the use of N.E. towards the propagating the Gospell to the Indians, as a freewill offering from divers inhabitants of Earles Colne, 54*l.* 11*s.* 10*d.*

March. 26. 1653. A review of that estate God hath mercifully given mee.

Lands as formerly.

		increase
Mr J. L. as formerly	150*l.*	
Mr Jeff. L. pd in 100 yt is Mr W. H. hands —3—	100.	
Mr P. as formerly	50.	
25. March past improvemt of Mrs Maries land. 4*l.* 5*s.* now in total . .	89. 5.	4*l.* 5*s.* 0*d.*
Stocke as formerly about . . .	32. 0.	
In Young's hands 10*l.* pd. in W. Br.	15. 0. 0.	5. 0. 0.
In Mr W. H. hands	100. 0. 0.	100. 0. 0.
In E. J. hands of W.	25. 0. 0.	25. 0. 0.
My debts were 12*l.* now. 32*l.* so that abate ye 20*l.* out of this.		134. 5. 0.
Their remaineth this yeare a great addicon to my estate, viz.		114. 5. 0.

[1] After a three days fight off Portland, we took eleven ships of war and thirty merchantmen.

[2] *Commonwealth and Protectorate*, ii, 176-181.

This was the roll of my debts, besides divers engagements in those moneyes which I had appointed unto another use. March. 28. *32l.*

P[d] goodman Matthew 21*l*. 10*s*.; my roll of debt is now 29*l*. 10*s*.; April. 3. 29*l*. 10*s*.

Heard the Spaniards had seized o[r] merchants, because of o[r] stop of the Hamburg-plate. April. 7.

Bought some of M[r] Westlyes bookes as amounted to 3*l*. 14*s*. M[r] Tomson had one of mee at 4*s*. 6*d*. I owe unto him the rest viz. 3*l*. 9*s*. 6*d*. April. 8.

This day the army men turned the Parliament [1] out. April. 20.

In regard of y[e] troubles of the times I resolve to buy no more bookes for present then absolutely needfull untill with the mony set a part for bookes and givings, I have paid the 3*l*. 9*s*. 6*d*. I owe M[r] Tompson, & 5*l*. 10*s*. to my sister moneys that I owe for bookes and that I borrowed to give away. May. 4.

Heard but not true Cromwell was made Lord High Protector of England; all apprehend a storme on the ministry. May. 5.

Heard againe of very great pressing at London, both for sea & land.[2] May. 25.

One sett up Cromwells picture [3] at y[e] exchange & over it 3. Crownes, and written tis under it divers verses, beginning.

[1] The remnant of the Long Parliament.

[2] "In the middle of March one thousand men were pressed and it was said—no doubt with considerable exaggeration—that not a serviceable man was left behind.... Merchantmen approaching the coast were boarded and the greater part of their crews carried off. Able-bodied men fled from the sight of the state ships as they would have done from the plague. Orders were sent to secure mariners in Jersey and even in Scotland and Ireland. In London a raid was made on shore, even gentlemen unused to the sea were dragged out of their beds and hurried on board ship. (*Commonwealth & Protectorate*, 192).

[3] "On May 19 a gentleman stepped into the Exchange and hung up a picture of Cromwell with three crowns and the words "It is I" above, and underneath the lines :—

'Ascend three thrones great Captain and Divine
By the will of God, o Lion, for they are thine.
Come priest of God, bring oil, bring robes of gold,
Bring crowns and sceptres, it's now high time; unfold
Your cloistered bags, your state chests, lest the rod
Of steel and iron of the King of God

Ascend three thrones, brave Captaine, and Divine
by the will of God, o Lyon, for they are thine.

heard as if endeavo[rs] were to bring the cheife goverm[t] to one person; divers pretend the visions of God for it; the title of King probably will be waved, and some other pitched on.

June. 1. Rid to London, die. 3° returned safe; I went & bought not one booke: Camdens Britannia is buyable for 25*s.* and Mercato[rs] Maps for 3*l.* 5*s.*

June. 3. Newes of a dreadful fight at sea, brought up by the fishermen of our coasts.[1]

June. 12. O[r] newes of the fight proved not as reported; our victory very great & losses little to speake of; the Dutch cowed before us, and stucke not to their worke like men;[2] this weeke came out the summons for the councell to meete at Whitehall July, 4: next.

June. 13. Told y[e] the Anabaptists, as called, suppose the army agst y[e] protestant religion, and that they will downe with it as now established; Lord thy will be done! I know great things must be done, onely take the care of the glory of thy great name.

June. 14. Reports y[t] wee had landed men at the Texell.

June. 20. Sold my blacke bullocke for 2*l.* 11*s.*

July. 15. Heard y[e] N. Councell,[3] y[t] call themselves a Par. of y[e] commonwealth of England, have as y[r] first businesse taken into considera-

Chastise you all in's wrath; then kneel and pray
To Oliver the torch of Zion, star of day.
Then shout, o merchants, city and gentry sing.
Let all men bare-head cry, God save the King.'

The Lord Mayor, half frightened, took the picture down and carried it to Cromwell, offering either to restore it to its place or to treat it in any other way as he might please to direct. Cromwell did but laugh at the poor man's anxiety to please, telling him that such things were but trifles, not fit to be considered in such serious times." (*Commonwealth and Protectorate*, ii, 228).

[1] The Dutch lost twenty men-of-war of which eleven were brought in as prizes.

[2] "If there was superiority in tactics it was on the Dutch side.... what the Dutch admiral lacked was a fleet equal to his merits." (*Commonwealth and Protectorate*, ii, 239.)

[3] Barebones Parliament.

tion ye matter of tithes [1]; they speake nothing, but God, and godliness; the issue wee will waite.

Delivered to James Linnet for Sr Tho: Honywood 4 quarters and six bushels oates at 20*d.* the bushell, which is 3*l.* 3*s.* 4*d.* July. 26.

Cald up this morning to heare the thumping, thundering canon, [2] which filled into country houses, and or beds with the dreadfull noise; I have not ever heard the like shooting in my life; its no question a terrible sea fight neare our doores between the Hollander and us; the Lord is our hope in all our straites. The roaring cannon sounded till night; ye wind high, hindred or hearing of them very much; God give a good issue to England in this ingagement. July. 31.

Wee shall observe ye effects of this victory by the estate, and whether they attempt any thing at land against Holland. Aug. 7.

Its looked on as certain that Van-Trump is dead of his wounds. Aug. 17.

Wee gatherd for Marlborough, 3*l.* & more.[3] Aug. 28.

MrClopton.

Rd of Mr Clopton 14*l.* 3*s.* 9*d.* & 18*l.* before, my part of 55*l.* 5*s.*; pd in by Mr Man, ye due for 3 yeares out of Dunmow which is 108*l*, ye rest lost; a day wherin God in many perticulars shewed great favor unto mee. Sept. 21.

Mr Nevill buried; at ye funeral I first heard ye Dutch peace was made, [4] and 10 assured of it from Lady Honywood; the messenger found mee praying, and so fitting for death, the fittest duties for ye peace, though carnal hearts are jocund at it, for this will be the hornes rise, and ye ruine of the protestant interest as one 7 yeares will lett us know; and now have at thy skirts, ffrance. Jan. 9.

This yeare brought forth notable revolucons at home, in dissolving parliamts & declaring Cromwell protector who is to rule by a counsell; its said after divers bloudy fights now wee have made peace with the Dutch; ye ffrench have had a good yeare of it, as the Sp: last, tooke much from Condé, reduced Bourdeaux, quieted

[1] The House refused to abolish tithe.

[2] The fight in which Van Tromp was killed.

[3] There had been a disastrous fire here in April.

[4] The Treaty was not signed till April 5.

the protestants, maintained them selves in Italy, and done some feats in Catalonia; Brest yʳ port was like another Dunkirk agst us, & I conceive wee shall remember it in due time; the German diet still continues; they have crowned Ferdinand yᵉ 4ᵗʰ King of Romans; the Cossacks and Polish are in armes, the Turke also agst the Venetian; things are somewhat calmer then formerly, and discourses are of a generall peace. Lord my soule waiteth for thy coming wee intreate thee.

38 yeare now enters, Jan. 25. 1653.

Sensible this was a new yeare to mee, and a yeare of strange transactions at home and preparacons for the like abroad; the Lord keepe mee, in soule and body without spott & without blemish, for in thy grace and strength is my strength & tower; oh lett mee not bee ashamed for in thee I put my trust.

Feb. 31. Heard 2 strange passages of O.C. in his youth, and a strange passage or 2 of other mens thoughts of him.

March. 10. Rumoured yᵗ peace was wᵗʰ Holland, & France included, and that wee were breaking with Spain, who had cosened us of much prize gold, challenging as his, which it was not.

March. 24. Lands as formerly, & mony as formerly: viz. . . . . 440*l.*

Improvemᵗ of Mʳˢ Maries lands: 4*l.* 9*s.* now in the whole . . . . 93*l.* 14*s.*

I have pᵈ of all my debts viz 32*l.* & some odde debts more, and through mercy I doe not owe any person any sum of mony.

My stocke is worth much about wᵗ formerly, & I have in mony more, viz wᵗʰ Mʳ Elliston. 20. 0. 0

Lent to Robt. Potter, 10*l.* to Wᵐ Webb, 5*l.* to Harrington of White Colne, 2*l.* 10*s.* 17. 10. 0

So that my estate is advanced yˢ yeare about 69*l.* one way & other, which is much in thes broken daies, for which I desire to blesse and praise the Lord.

1654.

Heard y^{r} would bee an assembly, and that y^{r} is speech of an high title for the protector viz. Emperor of the South. I am come to a yeare wch is like to bring forth notable counsells, I will mind them; its s^{d} Cromwell was borne in 1600 ye same yeare in which K. Charles was borne. April. 2.

Sold 3 bullocks to Mr Elliston at 3*l.* 15*s.*; he is to pay mee before Christmas next. May. 6.

Offerd my townesmen my tithes at 4*l.* quarter to dischardge mee of all rates and dues w^{t}soever. May. 15.

Y^{e} season very hott at present; the plague is begun at one end of ye land viz. Chester; the Lord prevent the spreading of it, if it bee his good pleasure. May. 21.

Much mutter y^{r} is in ye country y^{t} ye Electors must seale indentures at ye choice [1]; ye cheife Mag. begins to find a burthen on him. June. 22.

This day sett a part for ye choice of parliam^{t} men through the kingdome, & I sett it a part to seeke God, in behalf of my family.

This day knights chosen in o^{r} county;

13; a very small number of choosers appeared, not 500 although it was the sessions time; ye choice as to ye outsides of men indiffer. good; the Lord make them carefull & mindefull of him; its said there were a great number of ministers present, an 100 or more. July. 12.

This day I saw a license under ye hands of the Irish Com^{e} for a souldier to marry, [2] and without such license they may not marry, so that in England y^{r} forbidding ministers to solemnize marriage, and ye souldiers to marry without y^{r} license. July. 24.

Heard of ye rout of ye Spanish army at Arras by ye French under Turenne. Aug. 22.

I heard y^{t} ye protector was proclaimed Emperour, but for my Aug. 31.

[1] "The identure in which under the old system the returning officer joined with the principal electors in certifying that the persons named in it had been duly chosen, was changed so as to include a declaration by them that the new members were debarred from altering the Government 'as now settled in a single person and Parliamont.'" (*Commonwealth & Protectorate*, iii, 8, 9.

[2] Marriages between English soldiers and Irish women had been forbidden by Ireton on May 1, 1651.

part I beleive it not, thinking the time and season is not yett come for the doing of it.

Sept. 1. One cald, and told mee, y[t] this Friday y[e] Pro: was to bee proclaimed Emperour. God good in preserving An in a milke bowle, and Jane from swouning who let her fall in, and, John in falling from y[e] top of y[e] schoole staires; God give his angels charge over us.

Sept. 3. This day y[e] Parl. was to sitt; y[e] Lord in mercy preserve them from acting any dishonourable thing.

Sept. 10. Parliam[t] is now sitting, and great strivings are on foote.

Oct. 13. This day y[e] Parl: appointed a fast at Westminst. & London. I was sensible of y[r] condicon & begd God would shew them y[e] things to our peace, if y[e] decree of ruine were not gone forth, if they had not stumbled in perferring y[r] own things to y[e] Lords, w[ch] I feared; at night M[r] R. H. told me y[t] Tuesday morning 12 they were shutt out of y[e] House,[1] & a guard of souldiers sett on y[e] House; this amazed many men; I see Gods worke going on.

Oct. 28. Wee eate a messe of green selfe sown pease, sent mee by Goodman Bridge, a raritie y[t] I never saw before, but mentioned in the newes as if common in y[e] West.

Nov. 29. I bought Wharton's Almanacke wherin are amazing perticulars.

Dec. 8. I thought by this day, England might heare of y[e] intent of Blakes fleet[2]; I heard, 7, it was before Naples.

Dec. 24. Noisd wee had beat a French fleet,[3] but it was not seconded.

Jan. 25. Rose y[s] morning, and I found my birth day was 26, not y[s] day as I thought hitherto; going down to a fast, my neighbo[r] Burton cald and told mee the parliam[t] was dissolved on Monday, 22, at one of y[e] clocke by y[e] Protector, which proved true; in my night

[1] *Gardiner*, *Commonwealth & Protectorate*, iii, 25.

[2] Blake sailed for the Mediterranean on October 8. "How useful to Spain was the appearance of the English fleet in the Mediterranean may be gathered from the fact that the Duke of Guise was preparing to sail from Toulon at the head of an expedition designed for the conquest of Naples and that Blake was ordered to frustrate that undertaking by attacking and ruining his fleet." (*Commonwealth and Protectorate*, iii, 373.) The expedition was abandoned.

[3] We had taken two French prizes.

vision that night, I thought it was so, and I mett 4 of y^e parliam$\bar{n}^t$ in blacke habits, and gownes, walking in London street, or in a great towne; the Lord take care of us. I am glad I was about such a worke when I heard it.

Jan: 26: 1654: 39 yeare enters

My dayes passe, thine, o Lord, abide for ever; I shall enjoy thee where I shall dwell for ever with thee; sensible it entred mee a new yeare, in wch my heart desired Gods presence with mee, as I desire to praise him, for his abiding presence with mee ye last past. Jan. 26.

Rose more early than formerly; heard just as I rose, a fire on Coln green, quencht and no hurt to mention; blessed bee God: one cald mee down, gave mee a hint of some trouble at London, presently sent for to priory; saw a letter from Major Haines to call divers to Markshall, to communicate a letter from ye protector unto them, to acquaint them with the present state of affaires wch threaten trouble; I was not desired. Its expected the Cavaliers will rise, and Charles Stuart come & head them. The Levellers [1] are up 300 in the west, its thought Grey & Eyres & Wildman head them, [2] also the 5^t monarchy [3] men in London under Harrison and Rich [4]; and w^t if all this bee but in designe? ffeb. 13.

Through mercy the great noise of plots vanish, but whether some mens evill intentions will not take place God knowes; these ffeb. 18.

[1] *Commonwealth & Protectorate*, 116, 117.

[2] "Wildman was seized at a village near Marlborough by a party of horse under Major Butler on February 10 just as he was dictating a declaration inviting the people to take up arms against Oliver Cromwell, and was carried off for security to Chepstow Castle. Grey was apprehended by Hacker and carried to London and ultimately lodged as a prisoner in Windsor Castle." (*Commonwealth & Protectorate*, iii, 118).

[3] "The Fifth Monarchy men, while basing their conduct on religious grounds, directly attacked the existing government on the plea that earthly rule ought exclusively to be in the hands of the saints." (*Commonwealth & Protectorate*, iii, 112.)

[4] Rich was brought before the Protector & Council on the 16th.

things and dayes are very misterious, the Lord bee good to mee y^r in; the weather is wonderfull uncertain, and moist, I wonder, when ye plot is noised to bee so much in ye North, why all forces march to the city, especially from the north; I feare something is to be done in London.

Feb. 25. I find that many men great formerly are now in durance, Harrison by name [1]; y^r is a lex talionis in o^r sufferings and surely ye cup will goe round; let not man trust in man, for he is but a lie; the Levellers & 5^t Monarchy men are for present most shot at; ye Independ^ts in favo^r; the presb: not much medling or medled with.

March. 6. Wett day, rid to Colchester, I find some earnestly oppose Protector; others close with him on grounds that carry a faire face; the Lord keepe my heart closely & wisely to retain ye doves innocency. S^d that Rich is committed. [2]

March. 8. This day was a day I had thought of as ye bound within wch some g^t action would bee [3]; the throning of ye protector really done; he will come up higher in the season of it; I saw a letter from Major Haines, intimating reall apprehensions of the Cavalier attempts; s^d ye prince on ye seas.

March. 13. Heard ye Caval. in arms in Wales, Nottingh: Shropsh: Wiltsh: where they seized ye Judges; dreamd at night, one told mee up in Lincolnshire, and I perswaded, they would be crusht and come to nothing: I saw ye horse march down a long street.

1655. March. 25. I again review my estate. Lands as formerly, and the same personal estate good y^t was last; y^r is added this yeare.

My stocke wch I last yeare valued at 30 I count worth about 20*l*. and I am in debt to 2 persons 5*l*, wch abated, y^r remains cleared 96*l*. 10*s*.

[1] He was arrested with Rich on February 16.

[2] "Rich was allowed to remain at liberty for some time longer to attend on his dying wife." (*Commonwealth and Protectorate*, iii, 117.)

[3] "What really took place on the night of the 8th was the gathering of a few isolated bodies of enthusiasts at their allotted stations, whilst the great bulk of the Royalists, refusing to sacrifice life & property in so harebrained an adventure, remained quietly at home." (*Commonwealth & Protectorate*, iii, 190.)

W: Web:	5*l.*	Mrs Maries land 98*l.* 8*s.* 0*d.*
Mr Elliston. . . .	16: 10.	
M^r W: Harl . . .	25. 0.	
Edw: Brown . . .	20. 0.	
Major Hayns . . .	30. 0.	
In cash:.	15. 0.	
	111. 10.	

Thus, though I am unprofitable, God is mindfull of mee, my heart is to love & serve him.

This day, the Justice and I married Peg. Nevil to Butcher; the first I intermedled with since the late act [1]; the report is of great officers made at London. April. 10.

This day wee went a great p^t of the bounds of Earles Colne, and towards Gaine especially; the season promises hopes of plentie. May. 28.

Heard, w^t formerly I apprehended, y^t Cromwell would bee stiled Emperour. [2] May. 30.

A fast on the occasion of the Savoyards; at the same time imprisonings of men at home on feare of plots [3]; horse raising in all counties of England. June. 14.

I blesse God for some affection stirring in mee towards his truth, his people, the poore afflicted Savoyards [4]; wee gathered this day for Savoy in publique 8*l.* 12*s.* 2*d.*; the hand of God on mee for good; Lord, thy love to mee ingageth my heart to thine, & what I can doe is thine; made this collection, 9*l.* 11*s.* 8*d.* June. 17.

Preacht at Gaines Coln, ye quakers nest, but no disturbance; God hath raised up my heart not to feare, but willing to beare, & to make opposicon to y^r wayes in defence of truth; it is an evill that July. 3.

[1] Passed in 1653, ordering all mariages to be solemnised before a Justice of the Peace.

[2] "There is good reason for believing that the preparation of the first great seal of the Protectorate was delayed because it was still uncertain whether the new title to be inserted was to be that of King or Emperor." (*Commonwealth & Protectorate*, iii, 161.)

[3] *Commonwealth and Protectorate*, 164.

[4] The total amount collected in the country was £38,232.

runs much in all places; some think it will bee dangerous to Cromwells interest, and is so; God knows, I doe not, yett I think he feares them not, & perhaps ye clause in his declaration, not to disturbe ye minister in exercise, was to hint to them they might doe it after, if they would, securely, for y^t^ is y^r^ practice.

July. 7. Major Haines expected at Coln, he came not; ye Protector staid him above; some eminent occasion surely interveneth; the noise of his crowning is not as formerly, though nearer it may be than when most talked of.

July. 8. I gathered this day for Mary Peake whose house was burnt down *3l.* 15*s.* 8*d.*

July. 15. Those called Quakers, whose worke is to revile the ministry [1] made a disturbance at Cogshall, and were sent to goale; oh, many feare ye Quakers to ruine Cromwell; tis not words y^t^ alter governm^ts^, and rout armies; it must forme it selfe into a military posture first, and when that appeares, then enemies of ye state, disturbers of ye peace, seiseth on them.

July. 28. The Quakers set up a paper on the church door at E. Coln.

July. 29. This corner begins to feel ye Quakers; some of y^r^ heads its said are among us, the Lord bee our refuge; an infallible spirit once granted them, what lies may they not utter, and what delusions may not poor men bee given up unto? Lord I see trialls, let me be fitted for them, and saved through them.

Aug. 3. Heard my augmentation was taken from mee on a mistake, but was in good part resetled by Major Haines care. O^r^ mouths ful of a great losse at Hispaniola. Perhaps it will make the good news that is coming more acceptable, and must rouse us up as Joshua at Ai.

Aug. 7. Heard as if o^r^ successe great in the West Indies & yett o^r^ losse

[1] "Not only did the Quakers scandalise the clergy by refusing, as Baxter puts it, to 'have the scriptures called the word of God', but they railed at ministers as hirelings, deceivers, and false prophets, bursting into congregations and directing against the occupant of the pulpit such exclamations as 'Come down, thou deceiver, thou hireling, thou dog.' They defended themselves on the ground of 'the right of all religious persons to contribute to the edification of the assemblage.'" (*Commonwealth and Protectorate*, 197.) Not all who were called Quakers in those days were connected with the Society of Friends.

of San Domingo true; perhaps y^{t} was to ingage us the more earnestly agst Spain, & now if wee can but frame up a religious war of protestants agst papists, wee shall hinder the nacons from looking to y^{r} ballancings each other, & ruining ye papists by ye helpe of protestants, who by y^{r} shipps only can in reason hinder it; wee shall doe our business, & afterwards make y^{m} smart.

The weeke past God good to mee & mine in many outward mercies; God left a young hog of mine to be bitten by Burtons dog; it might have been worse; they cut his eare & taile & threw him into the water. Aug. 19.

I was with Mr Crane; they kept y^{r} day of thanks for y^{r} delivery from Colchester; 3 of the nine dead, and 6 alive, Mr Crane, Smith, Ayloffe, Eden, Barnardiston. Aug. 27.

A hog I had died, bit with Burtons mad dog; blessed bee God it was not a child. Sept. 4.

The W. Indie busines very dismall. Sept. 20.

My good freind Major Haynes, [1] and Mrs H. with us. Nov. 1.

R^{d} of Mrs Haynes, 15*l*.—10*l*. was part of augmentacon that Major Haines procured for mee; blessed bee God that any way provides for so unworthy a person. Nov. 17.

S^{d} H. Cromwell trounces ye Anabaptists in Ireland. Nov. 25.

A fast publiqu, a cold day & thin audience. Dec. 6.

Great rumo^{rs} of the Jewes being admitted into England [2]; hopes y^{r}by to convert them; the Lord hasten y^{r} conversion, and keepe us from turning. Dec. 16.

Jan : 26 : my 40 yeare enters, 1655.

I desire to consider how my dayes passe, some thinke y^{r} very world would end in 56, others the beginning of good dayes to the church, but I expect troubles on ye earth and y^{r} by persons making

[1] He had been appointed Deputy Major General for Norfolk, Suffolk, Essex & Cambridgeshire.

[2] Spanish and Portuguese Jews "had for some years been stealing into England either to escape the terrors of the Inquisition or in pursuit of gain." (*Commonwealth & Protectorate*, iii, 216)

themselves great, who in themselves or successors, will & shall deepely afflict the Lord.

Feb. 10. Great noise of people called Quakers; divers have fits about us. and y[r]by come to bee able to speake; the Lord helpe us to stand fast against every evill and error.

Feb. 16. Heard for certain y[t] one Wade, a Quaker as called, comes to our toune.

Feb. 20. The Protector & his councill having, Aug: 19, 54, passed an ordinance to eject Ministers & schoolem[rs], the Maj. gen. & his deputy required to put it in execucon [1]; on y[s] foote the Commissioners y[r] in named proceeded and began to act, calling on y[s] day all the Ministers, Lecturers, Curates & schoolm[es] through y[e] whole county to attend them at Chelmsford to give in under y[r] hands and churchwardens how they hold y[r] livings, and how long, w[ch] I thought was rigour, Exod. 1. 14. I was y[r], ye wayes wonderful dyrty, close, but it raind not; God good to mee, but my mind was vain. M[r] Sparrow preacht, he commended & encouraged the Com[rs]; for my part I saw no beauty in the day, neither doe I joy to see ministers put under y[e] lay power, and thus on y[r] own head; such is y[e] affection of some y[t] would bee counted the first freinds of God and religion, hoped wee should have been sent from thence to y[e] Barbados; Lord remember us for wee are become a reproach.

Feb. 24. Persons in this corner much withdraw from y[e] word; mens minds unsound; y[r] is feare of Portugal, y[t] he will breake with us, and y[r] by o[r] fleets miscarry for want of his ports; s[d] Cromwell tooke his leave of Mountague [2] in y[e] morning and then spent the day alone in prayer.

Feb. 29. Heard they tooke up many loose wenches at London, to send over to Jamaica. [3]

[1] "In all parts the Major Generals found it necessary to impart vigour to the Boards of Ejectors who had been appointed to carry out the ordinance of 1654 for the ejection of scandalous or inefficient ministers who might have crept into cures during the times of anarchy." (*Commonwealth & Protectorate*, iii, 239).

[2] Edward Montague, who had been appointed to accompany Blake in command of the fleet.

[3] "It was at once rumoured that these women were to be sent to Jamaica, as the Dutch ambassador quaintly put it, to nurse the sick." (*Commonwealth &*

Sd yt ye notion of ye 5t monarchy spreads very much in some parts of Norfolke. March. 7.

Saw Mr Bacon, Mr of requests; he saith or fleet is gone with courage from Plymouth, 43 men of warre, 7 fireships, and victualers.[1] March. 21.

God hath entred mee on that stupendous yeare of 1656, of which men have had strange thoughts and though I am not of their minde yet I expect notable effects, and the desire of my soule is towards the Lord to take an especiall care of mee. March. 24. 1656.

Wn I come to view my estate this yeare I find my receipts lesse by 10*l.* than last yeare, and my expenses about 5*l.* more, and yett God increaseth my lot, above 70*l.* this yeare; I have paid my debts, my stocke is not worth above 10*l.*: I count I am now out upon Mrs Maries land 103*l.* 6*s.* 0*d.* her mother yet living and its not I that will repine at it; God bee my porcon, and dayes to her; I find my personal estate to amount unto 670*l.*; this God hath given mee, and when he pleaseth he may call for it again. View of Estate March. 28.

Heard & true yt Turners daughter was distract in this quaking busines; sad are ye fits at Coxall like the pow wowing among the Indies. April. 9.

Heard this morning that James Parnel the father of the Quakers in these parts, having undertaken to fast 40 dayes & nights, was die. 10, in ye morning found dead; he was by Jury found guilty of his own death, and buried in ye Castle yard. April. 11.

Mr R. H. told mee as seing ye letter sent by Fleetwood to release Parnel, but he was dead first; had he been delivered ye triumph his partie would have made! Its sd in ye contry that his partie went to Colchester to see his resurrection again. April. 14.

About 100 dipt at Colchester by Tillam a papist convert as he saith, if not still a Jesuite; oh how giddy and unconstant people are. June. 6.

Protectorate,) iii, 454.*)* The project appears to have been abandoned.

Jamaica was not at this time an attractive island. "So deplorable did the situation appear about this time on the spot that widows of soldiers preferred to sell themselves into temporary servitude in other islands rather than keep their freedom on the accursed soil of Jamaica." (*Commonwealth and Protectorate*, iii 454.)

[1] *Commonwealth & Protectorate*, iii, 473.

June. 12. S[d] for certain the tax [1] out as formerly; much y[e] thoughts of persons were they would have doubled it; s[d] also y[t] its concluded about to call a parliament, and that its thought one cheife end is to raise more money by them upon y[e] subject.

July. 5. Newes of another parliament to be called togither, Sept. next.

July. 8. Heard how D[r] Owen endeavoured to lay down all y[e] badges of schollers distinction in the universities, hoods, caps, gowns, degrees, lay by all studdie of philosophy; he is become a great scorne, the Lord keepe him from temptacons.

July. 17. Heard y[e] Spaniards routed y[e] ffrench at Valenchienne [2]; see y[e] issue of y[s] event.

July. 25. Major Gen: Haines came well to us, heard by him the French had recovered & routed y[e] Spaniard.

July. 31. M[rs] Church sealed to mee a lease of y[t] land w[ch] should bee mine after her decease at 18*l.* per annum; the Lord make y[e] businesse comfortable to us both.

Aug. 5. Made an end with Shawe; he is to cutt no more wood nor damage the fence, he is to returne the timber to my dispose; Roydon Bridge was witnes to this.

Aug. 14. M[r] Harlakenden sold his hops for 720*l.* to M[r] Montjoy & run a halfe in them; sweet showers, and dewing weather through mercy.

Aug. 17. Constant rumours, as if divers old grandees that were commonwealths men were secured; mens wayes are full of danger, y[e] great ones tumbling down one by another, y[e] sure standing, and safe onely in Gods pathes; this day, Sam Burton, and lame Byat, while I was reading the chapter, were sitting in the maids seate and made a disturbance; the justice commanded the Constable to take them forth to the cage; the mother went out of the church and tooke her son from the Constable, and said her housband paid scott and lott in the towne, and her son should sitt any where.

Aug. 20. This day was appointed a day for y[e] choise of Parliam[t] men in all counties of England [3], I sett it apart by prayer and meditacon

[1] Assessment tax.

[2] *Commonwealth and Protectorate*, iii, 483.

[3] Elections for the second Protectorate Parliament.

to seeke God, Job. 22; latter p[t] much moved mee in perusing it in the feilds.

The Sectaries did not very much appeare at Chelmsford, not a quaker in the feild; noted to bee so; one Loddington was in the head of that partie, which hindred the choice, that it could not be so effected that night, but was adjourned to the next day: between 3 & 4 a remarkable crosse seen in the skie, see in my historical notes. O[r] choise was,

S[r] Harbotle Grimston.	M[r] Wakering.	M[r] H. Mildmay.
S[r] Thomas Honywood.	M[r] Gob: Barrington.	M[r] Carey Mildmay.
S[r] Rich: Evered.	M[r] Ol: Raymond.	M[r] Archer.
S[r] Tho: Bowes.	M[r] Templer.	Maj: Haines.
	M[r] Turner.	

The Independ[ts]. plotted much in y[e] choise but missed two men of y[r] company; the choise to view is not very good nor very bad, a strange mixture of spirits; Lord I cannot trust them with o[r] Gospel concernm[ts] but I will thee, and I trust y[u] wilt looke after them, and not suffer ye nacon to bee wrogt up by thes men into any evill w[t] soever.

Heard togither That ye Venetians have given ye Turkş a mighty overthrow at sea: the Swedes have routed ye Polanders and retaken Warsow; the Spaniards taken Condé town; the Emp. army on ye March for Italy; the English attempt and burning ye Spanish ships at Malaga, the choise of Members for parliam[t]; thes newes arrived to us in one weeke, with a report y[t] at Breme a voice was heard in the aire, Woe, Woe, Woe. Aug. 24.

Gave Sr T. Honywood, the best, & most solemn advice I could; one J. Biford was clamoured on as a witch, and M[r] C. thought his child ill by it; I could no way apprehend it, I tooke y[e] fellow alone into the feild, and dealt with him solemnely, & I conceive y[e] poore wretch is innocent as to that evill. Aug. 30.

Rob: Abot sen: in the street told Tho. Harvy, "there cometh your deluder." Lord, wee are a contempt and scorne, looke upon it, oh Lord, and heale it; he sat on y[e] horse blocke as people came Aug. 31.

to church; Mr H. spoke to him; the Lord help us against thes growing evills.

Sept. 4. I begun ye lecture at Wakes Colne; God good to mee therin; heard of a great plott discovered agst the protector; said on ye K. of Scots interest whom Spain assists.

Sept. 11. Heard Sr H. Vane was sent to ye Ile of Wight to Carisbrooke Castle, the Kings prison, against whom he was a great agent.

Sept. 17. This day appointed for parliamt, I set it apart to seeke God on their behalfe, yt they might be instruments for good if possible, and not circumvented into evill. Mr H. gave mee *3l.* towards the *5l.* he promised mee for his hops.

Sept. 18. 600 foot soldiers yt came out of Scotland marcht through our town to Colchester; great talke of Cavalier attempts again.

Sept. 19. Heard on die. 17. Dr Owen preacht on Isay. 14, 32; the Protector made a long speech before the Parl: men in Painted Chamber; orders were in Westminster hall that none should goe into house till after sermon. They say, above 160 were not allowed by the Councill to sitt, and none might enter without a ticket of allowance.

Oct. 5. Sacrament of baptisme administred this day, in publiqu, which was not of a long time before in Colne.

Oct. 8. This morning much overseen in my carriage to my deere wife; the Lord pardon it to mee, my heart truly sorrowful.

Oct. 22. A few souldiers quartered in or Town.

Oct. 26. Gave notice of ye fast, read the Declaration [1]; the Lord good to mee in the word;

Oct. 30. A. P. fast.

Oct. 31. In ye lane sett upon by one called a quaker, the Lord was with my heart that I was not dismayed; I had some discourse with him, the Lord bee my helpe.

Nov. 5. Kept a thanksgiving day for ye Spanish victory.

Dec. 5. A strange darkenes at London like midnight at noone day; it was a strange fogge.

[1] Probably the Declaration of the previous year, which forbade Royalists whose estates had been sequestrated, or who had taken part in the war under the late King, to keep arms in their houses or to maintain ejected clergy or schoolmasters.

Met upon an order from ye Com^rs of approbation for Ministers at London, about Mr Rogers [1] in wch busines I desired to bee faithful to God & my heart, with tendernes to my brother. Jan. 14.

Heard Tillam, an Anabaptist pastor, had set up the practice of the Satturday Sabbath and indulgeth those of his church that will to use y^r trades; it being y^r Colchester market and observeth the Lord day. Jan. 23.

I heard nothing certain of Dr Wright, by whose death the schoole goeth from mee; Lord how ever y^u deale with mee y^rin, y^u shalt bee my God. Jan. 25.

When I review this yeare past in reference to the affaires of the world I find things much at a stand, no new affaire breaking out but the attempt of the Moscovite against the Swede, which was no great affaire to view, no eminent turne of affaires in the world, except it were the going backe of the affaires of Swede in Poland; the English tooke a prize from Spain; in matters of religion the apostacy proceeds, the pretence of being specially directed by the spirit is drunke in by persons if almost any pretend therunto, and one Nailor [2] in England, was esteemed by some for the Christ, the King of Israel, for which a Parliament then sitting sentenced him, but no great discountenance put on the part by the Court; they rather winke then frown, yea release them; God in mercy thinke on us; some sett up the Satturday Sabbath; in reference to my outward affaires God good to us, and I find I am blessed by him; my heart is open to God and charitable deeds as my estate is enlarged. I find my inward estate mixt of troubles, temptacons, feares and hopes, finding a refuge under Christs wings whither I desire continually to resort, a resolution in my heart to abide by the w^p of God and his people through grace whatsoever cometh theron; the Venetian gave the Turke a great route at sea, and God sadly afflicts Italy with the plague; the protestant troubles in Jan. 26.

[1] Possibly John Rogers, the Fifth Monarchy preacher.

[2] One of Fox early disciples; Sentenced by Parliament "to be branded, pilloried, whipped, and imprisoned at pleasure; all the influence of the Government was required to save Naylor from capital punishment. C. Firth. *Life of Cromwell.*

Savoy, and Switzerland make no noise, they are under some troubles in ffrance, the issue the Lord knoweth.

Jan: 26: 1656, my 41 yeare enters.

The Lords presence bee with mee therin for good, my eye is on him for y[e] same.

Jan. 30. Hints as if things wrought towards an extremity between the Protector & Parliament.

Jan. 31. Heard certainly of D[r] Wrights hopeful recovery.

Feb. 1. God good to mee this weeke in taking care of my livelyhood, in D[r] Wrights life, by whose death y[e] schoole had gone from mee, worth neare 70*l.* yearly to mee, and besides the comfort to teach my children, the feare also of a bad neighbo[r].

Feb. 17. I was straitned for moneys, and this day God ordered it so that two schooleten[ts] brought mee in neare seven pounds, blessed bee God, who hath not dried up y[t] spring.

Feb. 20. A day of thanks for y[e] deliverance of the protector from Sundercombs [1] treason who poisoned himselfe.

Feb. 27. Confident reports that Cromwell was proclaimed King, s[d] also wee shall have an House of Lords; some great alteration is in hand, but what it will bee time will discover ; only he hath outwitted his coactors in former designes, and no duobt his purpose is the like, but none can outwitt the Almighty.

wee & others had damaske rose buds in Februa[ry]

March. 21. Report that wee list and raise men apace under pretence for Flanders.

1657. 1657

March. 25. When I come to view my estate this yeare, I find my expenses far deeper then divers yeares formerly, and my receipts more then ever, God bee blessed. Last year my estate was about 670*l.* I find I have about 590*l.* and I have p[d] for land to M[r] Butcher 150*l.* and to M[r] Weale 85*l.* which is in whole 235*l.* so y[t] I have had a great

[1] He had attempted to kill Cromwell on his way to Hampton Court: failing in this, he attempted to set fire to Whitehall.

increase this yeare of 145*l.* or y[r] abouts, with the life & health of my family, no trouble in my estate; the Lords love in Christ is my life and joy. I have received in to my hand M[rs] Maries land on which I am out 108*l.* 9*s.* This yeare 1657 is like to bee a boisterous yeare in the world.

Talke now of a king, the Lord bee our king and lawgiver. March. 28.

Divers men bustle to make X[t] king; truly Cromwell will carry it from him at present, but surely y[r] is a time when X[t] shall reigne more then inwardly. April. 17.

Heard this weeke the men that are to make Christ King were plotting agst the Protector, and that he seized on divers of them. April. 19.

Heard as if Blake desired landmen to attempt the Canaries. May. 7.

At night M[r] Hubbard of London with mee to teach two boys at 3*l.* per annum if they come. May. 15.

John Eldred a scholler y[t] brought mee in 40*s.* yearly went from mee; the Lord will provide. May. 23.

Protector proclaimed at Halsted by y[e] Sheriffs. July. 17.

This day I publisht the act about the Sabbath, [1] the Lord doe good by it. Aug. 30.

After hopes of a dry Sturbridge faire it rained very much, so that the wayes were exceeding heavy and dirtie, M[r] H. had some hopes to make 500*l.* of his hops; the last yeare he made 790*l.* Sept. 9.

A publiq fast in regard of the general visitacon by sicknes, w[ch] was a feavo[r] & ague very mortal in some places. Sept. 30.

Being up, & riving logs, M[r] Elliston came & told mee D[r] Wright was most certainly dead, I had no warning of his sicknes, I was troubled that such a providence found mee not better imployed, and disposed, but I blesse God though I am like to loose 60*l.* per annum, yet y[t] is not much trouble. Oct. 8.

M[r] Cressener acquainted mee that my Lord of Oxfords Chaplain was come to town and he thought about the schoole. M[r] R.H. made some proffers in it, and I desired to observe God therein, but my owne inclinations rather tend to lay it wholly by, desirous Nov. 3. 4.

[1] An act to punish ale-house keepers for profaning the Sabbath by permitting swearing, drunkenness, gaming, etc., in their houses.

God would open some helpe to mee in carrying on the worke of the ministry.

Nov. 9. Dr Pullein sent mee an offer to procure mee the schoole, if I would helpe him to his living; I had no desire thereto.

Nov. 17. Mrs Marg: Harlakenden having laid out 120*l.* at London, about wedding clothes, her father being exceeding angry, I appeased him, so that though he chid her by letter for her vanitie, yett he paid the scores

Nov. 25. Rd my copies of my two fift parts of ye farme on Colne Green from my Cosin Josselin; yt purchase cost mee about 310*l*; God blesse it to mee & mine.

Nov. 27. Dr Pullein was with mee, shewed mee his grant from my Lord; he lost the living, for which I am sorry, and I the schoole; Gods will be done; I doe not find any trouble on my spirit in it; he desired mee to teach the schoole till spring for halfe the proffits; I consented; Lord I blesse thee for that kindnes and mercy.

Dec. 3. Spent some time in prayer at Mr Cresseners, the Lord good to mee yr in; about yt time at London, Dr Pullein's busines was put to that issue, that if ye Earl of Oxford would stand by his presentacon of Dr Pullein, he might come into his living; the Lords name bee praised for this kindnes, the issue is in thy hand, oh Father.

Dec. 5. Riding over to the Earl of Oxfords to Bently hall, and speaking with Dr Pullein, a full issue was put to that treaty about the schoole; I not having it, in wch disposall of God I desire to bee satisfied, and sitt down contentedly, knowing that he will order and direct every thing for good to mee; I was very sicke at night and vomited, which I judged a mercy to mee.

Dec. 8. Talke as if some uprore in ye kingdom, the militia horse suddenly called togither and the army foot called of again towards the sea.

Dec. 12. Saw a booke esp: of Welsh prophecies, which asserts that Cromwell is the great Conqueror that shall conquer Turke and Pope. I have many yeares on scripture grounds and revolutions judged him or his govermt and successors, but esp. my heart fixt on him, to bee most great; but sad will bee things to Sts and him; this booke of prophecies giveth mee no satisfaction, but perhaps may sett men a gadding to greaten him.

Mrs Margaret Harlakenden married to Mr John Eldred; her father kept the wedding three dayes, with much bounty; it was an action mixed with pietie and mirth; die. 18, the company departed the priory. God gave an emint answer of prayer to him & mee in providing her so good an housband beyond expectation; Mr Bridegroom gave mee 1*l.* & Mr H. 1*l.* God in mercy requite their love and bounty. Dec. 15.

If it bee worth writing this tels yt raisins of ye sun were sold at 12, 14, 16, 18*d.* per pound. Dec. 27.

Received an order to bee an Assistant in Ejecting of Ministers & schoolemrs for insufficiency; had the offer of two schollers, which I undertake to teach; the Lord helpe mee in all my callings. Jan. 8.

This day was the last of my 41 yeare, in which God hath been with mee and blessed mee, and though Dr Wrights death cutt mee short in the schoole, yett I find my heart quiett, rowling it selfe on God, and no way questioning his providence to take care of mee. God hath given mee three children instead of 3 more which I had buried, and thus my dreame of 3 shoots in my parlor cutt down and growing up againe is made good. Jan. 25.

Abroad in the world matters are likely to bee sad, yet I find not the apostacy to increase; this yeare the Emp. of Germany died, and no other yet chosen in his stead; his son the K. of Hungary assisted Poland, wherby the Swedes are driven into Prussia. The P. of Transilvania forced to retreate home, and was deposed for his attempt to please ye Turke. Brandenburg made peace with the Pole and left Swede. The Moscovite was in a manner quiet this summer, yet the Swede brusht him a little in Livonia. Denmarke invaded the Swede in Bremeland, to his losse in Juitland; the Hollander proclaimed warre agst Portugal & tooke pt of the Brasile fleete. The English assisted France agst Spaine & gott footing in Flanders, the Venetians beate ye Turke, but in the winter he regained some Iles as Tenedos; the Turke hath issue male. The Q. of Spain delivered of a sonne, ye King 53 yeares old and no son til now; the affaires in Italy & Catalonia not very boisterous. The Spaniards invaded Portugal by land & tooke some places; thus warre breaks out, but no eminent matter was done in the world;

the English Protector setled by Parliam^{t} and a house of Lords in title erected January 20th.

Jan: 26, 1657, my 42 yeare enters.

Jan. 26. Sensible this days ended my 41 yeare and begun my 42 : the eye of ye Lord bee on mee for good through the same.

Jan. 28. Old Robert Abbott of o^{r} town, being arrested by Mr H. for his tithes, wch come to 3*l.* and which he might have received within 20*s.* went to prison, refusing to appear by an attorney; poore person he accounts to pay or take tith is to deny X^{t} come in the flesh, and is as outwardly bold and confident in his suffering, as if some g^{t} service for X^{t}; Lord leave mee not under ye power of a delusion.

Feb. 2. Reported & afterwards confirmed by letter that the Protector had on Thursday before dissolved the Parliam^{t}. which was true; wee shall see what he intends, and what successe his affaires have abroad.

Feb. 14. Times are sad in regard of the rupture of Parliam^{t}; some great thing likely to bee acted in the goverm^{t}, yet wee are secure; s^{d} the Protector demands great sums of mony of ye City, 1,300,000*l.*

Feb. 22. I bestowed on my daughter Jane a silver tankard cost 4*l.* 16*s.*, on John a porringer cost 36*s* w^{r}of Mrs Eldred gave him 32*s*, & on An a spoone of 10*s.* wch Mrs Abbott gave her, the first plate of value y^{t} ever I bought; this day Dr Pullein here; he hired the Justices house, and intends to come over very speedily; though the schoole bee a great losse unto mee, yet God will provide for mee, and perhaps it may tend very much to my good and my childrens & many others.

March. 2. Wee buried An Williams at o^{r} chardge; it cost us 16*s.*

March. 15. Newes of dangers at home by risings, & from Spain by landing men out of Flanders.

1658. March. 26. For my outward estate, I am out on Mrs Maries Lands as last yeare only I have paid for the land on the Green, and all charges: it amounted in whole unto. } 309. 7. 4.

I have paid all my debts, and owe not 5s. any where that I know of, for wch perticular moneys are not assigned, & laid by; my stocke is about 68; that I desire to preserve as an estate for my children which is more then I had in all last yeare. I have gathered 36*l.* towards Tom's prentiseship, and assigned the arrears of my augmentation due Sept. 29, past, all rents, and moneyes due on bond until this time which I hope will make yt sum up an 100£. This yeare was deepe in expences costing mee about 110*l* and yet I blesse God I received in about an 100*l.* more unto my estate; this is Gods blessing alone: his good will with what I have is better then lands & treasure: God hath added a child to my number; I intend henceforward to bring into one receipt all my arreares of tith, quarters, augmentation, and what ariseth from my ministerial imploiment towards my housekeeping; which if it effect and adde but 10*l.* yearely to my estate I shall have no thoughts of any thing but blessing God in reference to my estate; however I shall endeavor to bee thankfull & contented.

What ariseth out of my own private estate, the tenth deducted as formerly, I desire to lay by intire for the good of my family. I have about 3*l.* in cash for my expence, and good round summes in arreares. I committ my wayes unto thee, I pray thee smile upon mee.

I gathered this day for the Poles, and Bohemians yt were massacred & turned out of all for religion sake, and the hand of God was with mee for good; wee gathered 6*l.* 9*s* 10*d*, ob. April. 18

A day of fasting in regard of a sicknes very generall in London and many places in the contry. May. 19.

This day Dr Pullein came to Towne; he is our schooleMr. July. 9.

Dismist my schollers to Dr Pullein. July. 12.

I preacht at the sessions on Isay. 53. 10. July. 13.

Cromwell died, people not much minding it. Sept. 3.

I was at Sturbridge faire; Mrs Haynes sent my wife 4 paire of gloves for a fayringe. Sept. 8.

Very wett weather; newes scattered of the new Protector's sicknes, which proved not true. Sept. 12

Sept. 19. S[d] Baxter [1] is dead, a great pillar to Cromwell and his way; but not so.

Sept. 25. Heard wheat was in Bedfordshire 11[s]. bushel; with us it is 7*s.*; this scarcity on a suddain, when there never was a more hopeful crop on the ground: but by laying & mildewing the strong corns, a wind that beate out aboundance, and wett in the harvest that spoiled much, this dearth came unexpected.

Oct. 17. Our officers punisht some travellers, a new worke with us.

Oct. 19. D[r] Pullein told mee he would allow me 22*l.* 10*s.* 0*d.* for my pains in teaching the schoole.

Nov. 3. Sent o[r] squirrel to the Countesse of Oxford, who sent for it, and sent us a silver tankard worth about 3*l.* 10*s.* I esteemed it a merciful providence to us.

Dec. 8. Susan Hadley begun her yeare, wee are to give her 40[s], and I promise her 4 paire of shoes, if shee give mee & her M[rs] content.

Dec. 11. M[rs] Harlakenden the younger bestowed a silver candlestand, and porringer cover on my daughter Mary, whom shee named.

Dec. 20. This morning about 6 of the clocke M[rs] Church died.

Dec. 24. M[rs] Churchs busines I suppose may bee 50*l.* advantage unto mee; besides it leadeth mee into her daughters estate; Lord lett mee receive a thankful heart to hono[r] thee with all, for thou art he alone, who carest for me.

Dec. 28. K[ts] chosen at Chelmsford, M[r] Charles Rich, & M[r] Turner, a choice not well rellisht by many honest men, but God knowes what is best.

210 voices carried an election, Turnor that had most had not 240; divers elections were on this day, called Innocents day. Will the Parl: bee harmelesse, or suffer themselves, or make others doe so? secreta tibi deus mi!

Jan. 4. 5. These dayes by a very strange and wonderfull providence of God I agreed for the farme on the Greene with the Nevils, and had an estate in all the coppie hold, very lovingly and quietly.

Jan. 23. Remembered the Parliamen[t]. that most forgett, and very few so much as speake of them; a spirit of slumber and remissnes is wonderfully upon the nation.

[1] Richard Baxter.

Jan : 26 : 1658, my 42 yeare ended and 43 entred.

This day was pleasant, I was working abroad, and visiting freinds; I am ful of busines about my farme, the Lord plant, worke with mee, or all is vain. Jan. 26.

I earnestly sought God to direct mee in my going or staying at Colne ; things seeme to worke out my remove, and my heart is much loosned from y[e] place. Jan. 30.

M[r] Butcher came from Hinningham with an offer of that place unto mee ; M[r] Harlakenden of the Priory entertaind it very heavily, and when I told him I would not leave it for means, he offered mee an 100*l.* to apend in 5 yeares as a further addition ; but Feb: 1, he came up and left against my will 50*l.* with my wife, as mine if he or I died, but if wee lived as an engagem[t] for 2 yeares and halfe until Sept : 29. 61, and then if he did not purchase 20*l.* yearly and adde to my means, if living, he would raise and pay out of his estate 20*l.* yearly,—an act of love not easily matcht, evidencing his zeale to God and love to my ministry ; o Lord might but Colne proffit by my ministry, I should exceedingly rejoyce. Wee mett this day, but no body did mention any thing unto mee ; I shall patiently observe what Colne will say to mee. Jan. 31.

I gathered this day to rebuild a church 11*s.* 1*d*; oh how lamely charity goeth on such errands, though I prest the worke and exampled it. Feb. 20.

Heard of the taking Coppenhagen [1] and the sad slaughter made there ! blessed bee God for Englands peace. March. 13.

A litle past nine a messenger from London brought mee letters acquainting mee with my deare freind Harlakendens dangerous sicknes at Worcester; my heart feared y[e] worst, and indeed then he was new dead. I went down to y[e] priory, and acquainted M[r] H. with it, who was striking at a mole; he was troubled, but hoped; my heart utterly under feares; I resolved for London and Worcester, knowing it my duty to my freinds and Christs serv[t] and committed my selfe to God with a sicke servant & 2 poore horses and rid from one a clocke til past 8, to Burntwood, where I received a letter y[t] poore M[rs] Harlakenden was that day gone from London towards her housband. March. 25.

[1] Frequently besieged but not taken by Charles X. of Sweden.

1659. March. 26. Nic. ye man with mee being very ill and providence thus turning, I returnd towards Colne and mett Mr Eldred & Elliston from Mr Harl. desirous some one should goe on. I went, and came that night weary, and sicke with winde to Beaconsfeild, and mist Mrs H., who hearing on the road the death of her housband, returnd to Uxbridge.

March. 27. Being Lords day I rid to Aynstone in Oxfordshire, the Lord pardon it to mee. It was a worke of mercy; I hoped though I brake the Sabbath, in that I was, as ye preists killing sacrifices, blamelesse; men and horses grew better.

March. 28. Monday towards 4 of ye clocke heard at Stowton just by Woodbridge of Mr H. death which was a sad cutt to my heart; but his gain was death, though my losse.

March. 29. I did w^t I could in his busines to prepare for return, visited Worcester, and stood by the Severne.

March. 30. Ned Mr H. man returned from London with an herse to convey Mr H. body, wch was embalmed and his bowels buried in Kemsey, unto Earles Colne.

March. 31. Wee sett out our jorney, about 30 horse accompanying o^r herse; wee arrived that night late at Aynstone. April: 1, at Beaconsfeild. 2, I turned in to see sad Mrs Harlakenden whose only daughter Mary had newly had the small pox, and came in a dismal tempest, wherin God safely preserved mee and comforted my heart, to Romford where wee rested Ap: 3. the Lords day.

April. 4. Wee came to Colne, not one freind meeting us on the way.

April. 5. I buried my deare freind with teares & sorrow & laid his bones in his bed.

When I come to view outward things I find divers deare freinds dead, especiall my deare and never to bee forgotten Harlakenden, an estate of lands coming into my hands so that I may estimate my lands, viz.

John Crows worth	21*l*.	8*s*.	0.
Toms & my close	5.	10.	0.
Sprigs Marsh	3.	0.	0.
Bollinhatch	7.	16.	0.
Tibbalds	47.	0.	0.
I am much in debt, but I have mony enough	84.	14.	0.

owing unto mee to clear all my debts, and an 100*l.* in my purse; this is the Lord's bounty; teach mee to serve thee with a glad and thankfull heart according to thy great goodnes; I found this yeare I saved some mony, and I hope have gaind acquaintance with and experience of God.

Heard the army had dissolved the Parl: agst the consent of the Protector,[1] seized Thirloe, and some others; it looks sadly. April. 23.

Assured that the Protector had consented to the army to dissolve both houses of Parliam^{t}. April. 27.

Heard a sad account of things at London, Protector deserted, army divided; this selfe seeking, deceitful crew are likely to receive the recompence of their deceits wherin they have disported themselves. April. 30.

The decimated[2] men confined to y^{r} houses & 5 mile for 31 days. Lord, it's mercy I am not an ingaged man in thes hurries. May. 5.

Matters very quiet in England, Cromwells family under much odium for tiranny &c. May. 8.

God good to us in o^{r} outward mercies; men gaze on this change, sectaries rejoyce, others gaze, even all are secure; our society roundly togither at the Lords table, the Lord accept of us, and doe us good. The Lord is calling up my son Tom to London, Lord goe thou with him. May. 22.

I and my sonne being Wednesday in Whitsonweeke sett forwards for London, wee had sweet shoures before & so coole but dry; riding all the way wee came safe to London 26; on Thursday that afternoone Tom at M^{r} Jo. Cresseners putt on his blue apron. I did all Mrs Harlakendens busines. My son is to serve 8 yeares; his time will expire May 1, 1667; in a good time I hope ye Lord sparing his life, Lord make him like Joseph a blessing to his M^{r}. May. 25. Tom. apprentice

Mr R. H. made a bequest of the great tithes to mee & the ministers of Colne. I rejoyce when I draw on any publiq good. June. 4.

[1] Third Protectorate Parliament dissolved by Richard Cromwell, April 22, when he threw in his lot with the army.

[2] An income-tax of 10 per cent. known as the Decimation had been levied from the Royalists.

June. 11. This day Tom returned from London; it was a sad amazing providence to mee but more to my deare wife, God sanctifie all.

June. 12. The small pox came out on Tom, Lord bee mercifull to him, and spare him for his name sake.

June. 15. Toms pox came out after a treacle possett; at night they began to run.

June. 16. Heard so much of Toms foolishnès at London, y^{t} cutt my heart.

June. 26. God good to mee in the preservacon of my family. Tom came down into ye hall this day.

June. 28. Made an end of haying from Sprigs Marsh, whence I had about 20 tons hay this yeare.

July. 9. Bought and brought home 3 cowes one pigge and one wennel from Scots, they cost mee 13*l.* 13*s.* 4*d.*; God blesse them unto mee.

July. 10. God good to mee in many outward mercies. Tom hearing at the church window.

July. 17. In some perplexitie about my son, his M^{r} not being willing to take him.

July. 21. I began to raise my little house in the orchard, I intend it (if God please) for a retiring, meditating place to contemplate and view my God with delight in his word and works and doings in the world; other uses will fall in.

July. 30. Alarmed with the Cavaliers intention to make a rising; the Councill of State gave it; God in mercy secure our peace; this was some disturbance to mee on the Lords day.

Aug. 10. Our county gentlemen are putting the county into a posture of defence.

Aug. 16. Spent this day in prayer at Mr Littells on behalf of the nation, that God would restore our peace, prevent the effusion of bloud; I spake from 1 Sam. 30. 6; at night wee were alarmd; the enemy up in Norfolke, and the prince landed or upon landing.

Aug. 20. The season wett; our parts quiett; the country filled with very strange amazing reports which were invented to disturbe people, & putt on others to action.

Aug. 21. A quaker wench came boisterously into ye church up almost to the deske, I perceived persons expected some disturbance, but shee staid ye end & then went out quietly, blessed bee God.

It was a sad time in Cheshire, and indeed the kingdom full of distractions. Aug. 23.

The land again quiet; the souldiers ordered to their old quarters in our parts. Aug. 28.

This day a publiq fast, Aug. 31.

Heard by Mr R. H. that ye army had on Wednesday, 12, interrupted the Parliament. Or sins threaten our ruine, but in all shakings God is ye same, & he will doe for his name sake; it was done Thursday 13, and Lambert the cheife agent in it; some treaty for accomodation was, but it ended in a dissolucon die. 15°. Oct. 14.

Bat. Hatch begun his yeare Octob: 14: and is to continue until octob: 13, at night, 1660. he is to have 10*d.* per diem every working day,[1] and 2 meales meate in the weeke. Oct. 16.

Rid in ye wett to Hinningham; ye country discontent, but very still, and secure, yett serious men profess to expect sad & strang actings; but ye feare is overly.[2] Oct. 25.

By letter I find a place provided for my son at London; God command his blessing therein for him. Nov. 5.

This day my deare son Thomas rid towards London, to bee an apprentice; the God of heaven bee with him. Nov. 8.

ffrost continued but no violence, a very sweet season, a quiet time in the nacon, yet mens minds exceedingly discontent; the souldiers at present give law unto us, God give a law to us all; my son Tom arrived safe at London. Nov. 20.

Rid towards London, about busines of great import for Mrs Harlakenden wherin God prospered mee; I bound also Tom to Mr Tooky; his time expireth if God lengthen his life, and he doe well, June 24, 1667, the day the new Parliamt was proclaimed; the city very full of tumults. Dec.12.15. being Thursday.

Heard the officers who entred into so high an agreemt. Dec: 22, on the next day, being 23, came & gave up their commissions to the speaker; I hope it is for good; and that ye care of ye army was by him left at present unto Okey and Allured, and London very quiett. Dec. 26.

[1] In 1651 the wages of labourers had been fixed by justices of the peace at 1*s.* 2*d.* a day.

[2] Exaggerated.

Jan. 6. Contry ful of reports, yt ye secluded members arm to enforce yr admission; ye city for a full & free Parliamt; Lambert marching in hast to London; Lord wee are thine save us.

Jan. 8. Things in the nacon quiet, the souldiers submitting to the Parliamt.

Jan. 15. The season very vehement cold; this hard weather hath continued from Novemb: 11 till now. General Monck is coming up to London, wee shall see to what intent.

Jan. 25. When I looke back into ye world I find nothing but confusions, hopes of a peace between Spain & France, but sad warres in the North, the Swedes bustling as a rod tearing the flesh of the nacons, but not advantaging themselves; or poore England unsetled, and her physitians hitherto leading her into deepe waters. Cromwells family cast down with scorne to the ground, none of them in command of imployment; the nacon looking more to Charles Stuart, out of love to themselves not him, the end of thes things God only knoweth; wee have had confusions in England, the issue God only knoweth.

Jan: 26: 59, my 43 yeare complete, & 44. entring.

Jan. 26. This day I reckon my birth day, I preacht at Wakes church, snowy, the way bad, twice I slumpt in & was wett.

Feb. 3. Tibbalds agremt. Tibbalds and I had discourse about ye farme for 6 or 9 yeares. He is to have Crows, Sawyers, Bridgmans, 2 sonnels, Hobstevens & ye meadow: only I am to have ye pightell [1] by Mr Littels, & 2 acres in Hobstevens, and passage; the rent *60l.* per annum, about *3l.* lords rent, pay tithes, ditch 30 rod every yeare, allow 2 load logs, 1 of small wood.

Feb. 12. A sad and troublesome time at London, the Parliamt. much displeased with the city and shewing it.

Feb. 14. Heard that Monke had declared for & with the city for a free parliamt.

Feb. 24. Heard Yorkshire were up and headed by Ld Fairfax, declaring for a free parliamt, and until then pay no taxes, expecting the like through ye nacon; secluded members admitted into the house.

[1] Small meadow.

Worcester jorney.

Mrs Harlakenden & I, with her kinswoman & manservant, sett out in her fathers coach for Wittam wither wee came safe, yett or wayes excessive dirty; our coach from London came into or inn before ye returne of the other; two mercies God afforded us, safety and protection on the road, conveniences and quiett at or inn, whither wee came alwayes in good time; no raine to trouble us but one day which I desire to acknowledge as Gods great goodnes. 16, wee dined at Burntwood; that day afforded a providence not to bee forgotten of mee but especially of Mrs H: wee came early to London, and then to businesse, all which I dispatcht at London not only to our content, but to or delight, but the weather was so stormy, that it was thought or jorny was not to bee performed. 18, I preacht twice, dined with the Ld Major; Lord give a blessing to the word. 20th, a day that lighted my heart in its providence, though I apprehended hazard to mee by cold, and I was in great danger at Stow to have been spoiled by the coach, yett God preserved mee, and none of us tooke any considerable cold in the jorny; or law triall putt of; 21st, wee sett out for or jorny; or coachman encouragd by the stage coach for Worcester, wee arrived at or jorneys end March 24th and found all well. 25, I preacht twice, ye minist. desirous to leave all his worke on mee, and I very readie; God moved and startled people, they said those sermons would not bee forgotten; God grant they bee practised; 26, 27, wee had but one tenant with us; riding out into the meadow by Severn Mrs H. resolved to returne on Friday seing there was no busines. I prayed her patience & submission to Gods will; at night one came to us with whom wee could never agree, yett afterwards divers did to or very great satisfaction. 29, I preacht the Lecture, I hope with some successe as also April 1, twice; on Monday wee kept the Court, very quietly, and 3, dispatcht or busines and returnd to London April. 7th, and so home to Colne April 10th, praise to the name of my gratious God, where I found all well and safe, for which my soule blesseth him.

March. 15.

1660.

When I come to view my outward estate I find my lands as for- April. 14.

merly. I have paid of divers great debts, putt out my son Tom prentice which cost mee in mony & clothes about an 100*l*,; I have done very much in repaire and cost on my farmes, and begun to stocke one; I am now in debt as in my blew booke 150*l*. 4*s*. 6*d*. I guesse not 20*s*. more that I know of in the world, and there is owing unto mee, 314*l*. 15*s*. 0*d*.; my stocke is worth about 25*l*. in cowes, hogs, corne on the ground; so God enlargeth my tedder [1] daily, yearly. Lord enlarge my heart for thee and thy service, and continue to blesse mee and mine indeed, and my soule shall praise thee.

April. 17. O^r choise of K^ts at Chelmsford, where I saw an evidence of Gods providence in ruling the world in the disorders and confusions of publique meetings; the Godly partie lost their choice, but God will not loose his right.

April. 23. Heard Lambert made head in opposicon to the present power, and really appeard in Northamptonshire. 24, heard at dinner that he was taken and it proved true, quicke and short worke.

April. 25. Parliam^t began; if wee judge of the temper of the houses (the Lords house satt) by the ministers they choose to preach unto them, it presents hopes, being Calamy, Gaudon, Baxter.

May. 6. The spring very excellent; the nacon runneth into the King as Israel to bring backe David; Lord make him ye like blessing to our England, and let Gods counsell bee in the worke.

jorney. May. 11. Set forwards for London whither I came safe and thence to Greenwich. 12, at night to my deare Harlakenden. 13, I preacht at Greenwich & prayed by name for K. Charles. 14, I was at Eltham in Kent. 15, God gave us a verdict in trial ags^t o^r adversary at Guildhall barre. 16, I was with deare Harl. again and returnd from her. 17, God counsell and keepe her safe and make her a prosperous person. 18, returned to my dearest wife and found her and all well.

June. 3. Y^e King returned in safety, and with hopes of being a blessing to the nacon.

June. 6. Rid to lay claime to the Kings pardon before ye Maior of Colchester.

[1] Tether.

A great calme in ye contry. The Kings proclamacon agst debaucht courses a cutt to the gentry of England; oh Lord make him a nursing ffather to thy people. June. 10.

A time wherin great armies are on foot, and yett an actuall cessacon of fighting in all Europe, except some thing between ye Moscovite & Pole, the Turke and the Transilvanian; after this calme, perhaps some very sudden storme. June. 13.

This day about a quarter before 3, my wife was delivered of her ninth child, and 5^t daughter Elizabeth; God enter into covenant with it, and make it his own. June. 20.

A day of praise for the Kings returne, I preacht on 2 Chron. 17. 6, putting on people to pray that mercies may lift up o^r hearts in the ways of God; my spirit in a very wretched temper. June. 28.

Ministers pittifully put out of their livings while others advanced. O^r schoolem^r Dr Pullein s^d to bee made B^p of London-Derry. L^d helpe mee to serve and trust in thee for thou art my hope; heard of threatnings against mee, but ye Lord is a sheild to mee who never sought the wrong of others. July. 22.

Heard divers of my freinds and neighbo^rs in trouble, Lord helpe them out by spirit, freinds, providences, and doe them good. July. 24.

O^r Dr Pullein s^d to bee Arch B^p of Tuam, a place in Conaught. July. 29.

The Arch B^p of Tuam with us; people wonderfully neglect ye Sabbath, and yett God holds his hand. Aug. 12.

Rumourd as if some stirs in Ireland agst B^ps and service-booke. Y^e King moulds the English army to his absolute commands, but Gods hand is over & above all. Aug. 17.

Heard of the death of my wives Uncle Shepheard, w^r by a close fell to my wife worth about 50*l*. Aug. 20.

Dr Pullein now an Arch B^p being to remove from us, occasioned great feastings, which are vain tainting things to o^r minds; God in some measure abased my heart. Aug. 26.

Monke, Duke of Albemarle made Lieu^nt of Ireland.

Preacht at Colchester for Mr Stockdale; God good to mee going, and returning; dined with Mr Mayor; s^d the act of indemnity past. Talke as if the honest partie were in hazard of a massacre; I feare Aug. 29.

some jealous hearts are foolishly at worke; I cannot thinke such a wickednes.

This day the King passed the act of pardon; I was glad I was so well imployed on a day when so memorable an act was past.

Sept. 15. Heard of the death of the Duke of Gloucester second brother to ye King, who died of ye smal pox, Sept. 13, and lately before, Esme Stuart the Duke of Lennox, and this day, sister Bridge.

Sept. 27. hedge hogge In the morning the bullock gave bloud, her bag swelled and so continued bloud on that bigge till Oct. 17; wee found ye hedge hog in ye feild oct. 4 & kild it.

Oct. 5. This day Grace Newton begun her yeare, shee is to have 50*s*., God make her a good servant.

Oct. 11. This day I paid 1*l*. 12*s*. 6*d*. for my pole tax. I paid it once formerly in 41, as I remember, this rate unusuall twice in an age; its ground is to disband the army, God in mercy send us peace.

Oct. 17. Heard y^t^ Harrison, and Carew, two of ye Kings Judges were executed but to that day 8 in all were executed, Jo: Cooke, Hugh Peters, Tho. Scot, Gregory Clement, Jo. Jones, Adrian Scroope.

Oct. 27. Said the busines of Hides daughter and the Duke of York was looked on by the King as one of his greatest afflictions; its said a contract, and marriage is pretended; Hides ruine is apprehended. The Queen was sent for to France; said to be come; God preserve the King; all ended faire among them.

Dec. 2. God good to us in many mercies; Gospell liberties and freedom yet continued; feares on many, said lists are taken of the fanatique, and all honest men that are not as formal as others are so accounted.

Dec. 24. This day I preacht a sermon of Christ from Jo: 3. 16; divers not there and some in there antique postures.

Jan. 13. Some stirs at London; Lord doe not give us up to error, it makes men mad; how furious were the fift monarchy men at London a few dayes past, running greedily into ruine; Lord lett not particular mens folly bring a generall trouble on them that desire to feare thy name and bee quiet.

Jan. 20. A restraint put on publiq, private meetings; all forbidden but in some church or parochiall chappell.

Jan : 26 : 1660, my 45 yeare entreth.

Lord bee with mee according to thy wonted mercy and goodnes.

A Fast to lament the Kings death. Jan. 30.

Said on this match profferd by Portugall ye the King is married Feb. 24. to the Princesse de Ligne; oh Lord what is doing in the world.

This day I heard and then saw the youth openly playing at catt March. 10. on the green; I went up, rowted them; y^r fathers sleeping in the chimny corner; Lord heale through grace these disorders.

Children very profane; their parents sitt at home, and they play March. 17. in the streets openly at catt and other sports.

Rid to choose K^ts of the shire; wee lost it, and my heart quiet; 1661. the Lord liveth and reigneth, and, if he putt his own servants and March. 27. things on suffering, his will bee done. Went on to London; returned safe, 30.

When I come to view my expences I find March. 31.

I have laid out.	233*l.*	9*s.*	6*d.* ob.
I have received in all receipts whatsoever only	146.	16.	0.

But my stocke wch I valued last yeare at 25*l.* is worth now about 35*l.* so though I have laid out, 87. 6. 5. ob. more then received, yett on the whole matter I am not abated in my stocke above 50*l.* and in lieu of that I am sure I have laid out above 80*l.* on the house on the green.

My roll of debts as in the blew booke are about.	80*l.*		
Owing unto me	167.	10.	0.

I have in cash towards my building about 50*l.* and my uncle Shepheard being dead, I have a meadow befalls my wife worth about 50*l.* more which when it cometh into my hand I shall value.

This day I sent out a trained armes; its Gods mercy to estate April. 11.

me for such a service, though its hard to presse a minister to the uttermost.

April. 21. Sad discourse in ye nacon, ye Lord prevent o^r^ troublesom feares.

April.22.23. Dry, to serve the pompous shew, and coronacon at London.

May. 3. Rid into London and saw the triumphal arches, stately vanity; no rich cost; in ye front of one, besides Heathnisme, y^r^ is y^t^ troubled mee.

A statue of K. James	In ye midle above promin^t^ a death statue of Charles	Of K. Charles
Divo Jacobo.	Imperium sine fine dedi.	Divo Carolo.

divers sad perticulars on ye face of ye arch. The high motto being Eu quo discordia cives, &c. On ye side of Charles, y^r^ was an effigie of stakes and fagotts to burne people, of ye heads of ye regicides on poles, and warrelike instrumts broken.

Reported ye Portugal princesse will become protestant & goe to Chappell with the King: a Spaniard protestant.

May. 7. Rid to London on wch day the citie force mustred in Hide parke where a remonstrance was gott of the souldiers for restoring B^ps^. 8, the King in great state rode to parliam^t^; between ye coronacon and this day, viz May. 5, the Duke of Yorkes onely son died and was privately buried. 6, some were hurt in ye view by a scaffold breaking and one kild, if not more: in the throng at ye Commons doore to goe out to ye King in ye upper house, Alderman ffouk was s^d^ to loose 50 links of his gold chain. I apprehend this Parliam^t^. The convocation mett in Pauls, I saw 12 bishops there &c.

May. 19. The King and Chancell^r^. moderate in y^r^ speeches, speaking much of good nature; ye Lord divert a storm; it was feard the Act of Indemnity would bee unraveld.

May. 29. A thanksgiving day for K Charles return to the crown. I preacht, very few hearers.

June. 23. S^d^ B^ps^ and their courts are coming in again, Lord helpe us to walke humbly & wisely.

The quakers after a stop and silence, seeme to bee swarming and increased, and why Lord y^{u} onely knowest. June. 30.

My soule mourneth to see how quakers and profanesse increaseth; Gods holy day is most mens vain day. July. 7.

Said a stop put to the eagernes of Episcopall men; men are slippery in y^{r} ways. July. 21.

Y^{e} price of corne riseth much, much sicknes in many places; the quakers busy about us. Sept. 8.

O^{r} Sabbaths yett quiet, and o^{r} liberties continued. Nov. 10.

A deare time for corne, rye 7*s.* and wheat 8*s.* 6*d.* per bushel, but few consider the famine of the word; and yett men loath the ordinances of God. Nov. 17.

Persons wonderfull profane & neglective of Gods w^{p}. Dec. 15.

This day baptized a child in publiq, not done in 12 months before. Jan. 12.

Heard as if Spain, France, & Holland were combining agst England; God can make use of adversaries to doe his good. Jan. 18.

Jan: 26: 1661, my 46 yeare entreth.

This day entred my 46. yeare; God hath been good to mee in the dayes past and will in those are to come, and my saved soule shall praise him. Jan. 26.

A publiq fast for the Kings death; not above 70 persons or y^{r}abouts hearing, surely not an 100. Jan. 30.

In the night it raind, the wind rose and was 18, violent beyond measure, ov^{r}turning a windmill at Colchester, wherin a youth kild, divers barnes, stables, outhouses, trees, rending divers dwellings; few escapd, my losse much, but not like some others; God sanctifie all to us; throwing down stackes of chimneys, part of houses; the Lady Saltonstall kild in her bed, her house falling. Whitehall twice on fire that day, some orchards almost ruind. 27, Trees blown down within priory wall. Timber trees rent up in high standing woods; the winde was generall in England & Holland sea coast, but not in Scotland. Feb. 17.

This day, Corbet, Okey, and Barkstead formerly L^{t}. of the Tower, March.

who were taken in Holland by Sr George Downing formerly scout-master of Cromwells army, were committed to the tower; what changes God maketh in the world.

1662. March. 30. Estate. When I come to view my outward estate, I find my layings out are 192*l.* 19*s.* 11*d.* my whole receipts 117*l.* 15. 9; my debts were 80*l.* now at least 86*l.* 5*s.*; my debts owing mee were more by 27*l.* then now; my charge is 199*l.* 4*s.* 11*d.* wch exceeds my receipts 81*l.* 10*s.* but through mercy my stocke is better then last yeare by some pounds & my building hath cost mee at least an 100*l.* so y^t my estate is not impaired, blessed bee my good God.

April. 27. On 19. ffeb. w^n Corbett Barkstead & Okey were executed at Tirburne, Okey said y^t prophanes was at such an height, that if true, as said, England could not stand 3 yeares; the Court lookt on this with a jear. The Lords day is most sadly prophaned in all places, Lord looke on & helpe.

May. 19. On Monday the Act of Uniformity was past. The King hastened away to his Queen who landed before at Portsmouth, with little joy to the nacon; ye nacon pressed cannot smile; God amend all & keep us upright.

May. 29. A day of thanks for the Kings restoration in 60.

June. 1. I had the Act of Uniformity sent mee.

July. 13. Reports as if the King would respitt the penalties on the Act of Uniformity as to himselfe for a time, God in mercy command it.

July. 15. This night with us being called St Swithins day, at night it raind; the old saying is it raines 40 days after; this 20th its wett and hath bin since.

Aug. 16. The apparitor at Towne with service books; he asked 8*s.* for them, so o^r Churchwarden bought none, and I saw him not; its a sad case that men are likely to bee put in by this Act of Uniformity.

Aug. 17. The last Sabbath of o^r liberty by the Act. God good to mee therein.

Aug. 19. Preacht last lecture at Castle-Hedingham.

Aug. 24. Some hopes given as if there would bee indulgence given to ministers for the present until the return of the parliam^t.

The London Ministers nigh 80, generally declined preaching;

the Bp. tooke care to supply every place, & the like in the country; some of them petitioned this weeke for liberty as reported.

All hopes of suspension of the Act of Uniformity taken away; God good to mee in my freedome to preach, three ministers & multitudes of our christian neighbors. hearing. Aug. 31.

A quiet Sabbath, great droves of people flocke to heare. Sept. 7.

Corn fallen much, a good wheat for 5*s.* 6*d.* mislain 4*s.* 8*d.*; God make us thankfull. Sept. 11.

God good to us in many mercies, the continued liberty of his words & wp, no interrupcon or disturbance. Sept. 28.

Cited this day to the Archdeacons visitation; or professors had rather I should lay down than conforme as J. Day told mee, but I had it onely from him; the Lord direct mee. I appeared not. Oct. 10.

God good to mee in manifold mercies; ye booke of common prayer laid in ye deske for mee. 19, laid again & used in part in the morning, but in the afternoon taken away. 26, brought again, but pitcht & abused. Oct. 12.

A cheerly time, and a quiet Sabbath. Mr Crosman, preaching, actually sent to prison & some others in danger yrof, yett through mercy I am quiett. Searching in London for meeters in private with feare yt they will send such out of the nacon. Nov. 2.

New Ministers this day at Colne Engain, Mr Symonds & at Cogshall Mr Jessop; both of good report; and now I am left alone of the nonconformists, what God will doe with mee I know not. I trust he will bee a hiding place, and help mee that I may worke, and not wound my spirit. Nov. 9.

A snowy bitter rainy windy morning in wch I went to the Court at Colchester, cited for procuracons.[1] Mine are as large as livings of 120*l.* per yeare. I paid & returned well, blessed bee God; none of the nonconformists being cited appeared but onely my selfe; I reckon that day a good day to mee. Nov. 12.

God good to mee & mine in manifold mercies, liberty of his Nov. 23.

[1] Certain sums of money which the parish priest paid yearly to the Bishop or Archdeacon. Formerly the visitor demanded a portion of meat and drink for his refreshment; these were turned into payments of an annual sum "*ad procurandum cibum et potum.*"

Sabbath; I baptized with the Common Prayer publiquly W^m^ ffossets child, the whole congregation in a manner staying; God make us quiet and peaceable.

Dec. 18. Colchester corporation sent to mee to preach there Dec. 25. I declined it; they discourse to choose mee y^r^ weekly Lecturer pro tempore; Lord I am willing to doe thee any service, though allways afraid of that toune as not fitt to deale with y^r^ wrangling spirits.

Jan. 11. Mr Calamy[1] committed to Newgate for preaching at the place where he had been minister.

Jan: 26. 1662, my 47 yeare entreth, 46 ended.

W^n^ I looke backe I find I may set up my Ebenezer; hitherto God hath holpen mee, and w^n^ I looke forward, this promise is mine, "I will never faile thee nor forsake thee." I am now setled in a habitacon of my own on Coln green wch God hath given mee.

Feb. 1. 8. Gods w^p^ is most sadly neglected, and now I feare the use of Common Prayer will cause a rent & separacon of divers asserters of ordinances. God setle & stablish mee.

Hard winter. This winter was the hardest I ever remembred: very wett And cold in Octob. Novemb., on the 24 day w^r^of it began to frize & so continued frost & snow very hard, until Feb. 18th. it began to thaw much, but ye frost scarce full out of the earth. And this 23 Feb. a litle frost again: 27 to y^s^ day frost; so 28; March. 1, snow lying in my guttar; hence goodly weather.

March. 1. S^d^ some in o^r^ town were digging this sabbath morning, Lord whither will this profanes tend? to flat atheism. Lord arise help for thy mercy sake.

March.22. The parliam^t^ viz commons zealous agst papists.

[1] He was one of the ejected ministers. He continued to attend his parish church and on one occasion, in the absence of the appointed minister was prevailed upon to preach. He was committed to Newgate under the Lord Mayor's warrant on Jan. 6. 1663 being the first of the Nonconformists who got into trouble for disobeying the act of Uniformity. He was set free by the King's express orders.

(Dict.: of Nat: Biography.)

Said the newes sad in Ireland, the rebells regaining y^r estates from the English. March.29.

When I review my estate, I find my receipts rather more than my layings out & yett my building and stocke have cost mee about 70*l.* I have sold my wives land at 57*l.* 10*s.* and p^d debts with the mony; the Lords name bee praised, that provides bountifully for mee, oh y^t my soule, and mine might prosper in thy sight. Estate.

Commended Mr Elliston to God who died the 16, a wett day. April. 17.

The lord good to mee in the Sabbath freedom of his w^p. May. 10.

God good to us in our outward mercies, the liberty of Gods w^p is yet afforded mee, and mine in perticular, altough Mr Layfeild tells me (who was judge at this visitacon) that I am suspended; Gods will bee done. May. 17.

This day o^r church wardens brought in ye booke of common prayer, wch I used. May. 30.

Heard of ArchB^p. Juxons death, a quiet man, an advantage to that hot partie, as they thinke; but who knoweth how God may shackle them? June. 7.

News as if ye Portugal neare Lisbon had utterly routed the Spanish army wch was confirmed to bee done neare Evora on May 29, in wch all the English did like themselves valiantly. June. 28.

The wett yet continues, & so almost continually from April 18th past, now a great floud; meadows drownd again & again, very litle hay had in. July. 12.

God good in ye word, a very thin audience, as if daring Magistracy y^t begins to punish absentees from publique w^p. Aug. 23.

At home newes of a trienniall parliam^t. Oct. 9.

S^d strang libels cast about in London agst the King, who is forced to give up house, his table served by a cooke, his Cavaliers very sadly deboist and unruly; a good natured prince but sadly yoked with followers. Oct. 16.

Heard of the Q. death. Oct. 23.

Said die. 23. the Q. died. Oct. 25.

Newes of the Q. reviving, a mercy I hope to ye nacon; now Nov. 1.

discourse of the phanatique plott; Lord hide us from ye snares of men.

Nov. 12. Talks of a Northern plot, yea general; of the phanatiques, divers imprisond, & some nonconformist ministers clapt up.

Nov. 15. Many secured as plotters.

Nov. 26. On Thursday morning about seven of the clocke or before, my deare wife after many sad pains, and sadder feares, in respect of the unkindlines of her labo^r, was yett through Gods mercy, delivered of her 10th child, sixt daughter, and o^r now seventh child and 5^t daughter living, for wch mercy my soule blesseth him.

Nov. 29. O^r English merchants would fain breake with the Dutch; the whole earth is quiet.

Jan. 3. The quakers meetings are in great places disturbed, driven from thence, and other meetings of the nonconformists much omitted.

Jan. 24. W^n I looke abroad thus, in England publiq quiet, and yet nothing but discontents; the state brooks no publiq religious meetings, but legall. Denmarke, Swede, Holland in peace, the Turkish pirats harsh to o^r traders in the midland seas; the great princes young, Turke about 21 o^r 22, France, 25, Emp. 23, Swede a boy, Savoy very young; the Emperor [1] at Ratisbone engaging the Empire to assist agst the Turke, the popish party joyn. France would have ye auxiliaries commanded by a freind of his & then he would assist.

The great difference between the pope & ffrance, wch accused the world y^t ye French designes run high, likely to bee agreed by condescension on ye popes part.

The Polish king carrieth warre to the Moscovites doore with hope of peace, but y^t not likely; great endeavo^rs to declare Duke d'Enguyen, successor in Poland. The Turkes make great preparacons agst Christendom. Apasi [2] gets many places from ye Emperor submitting to him; all Germany & Italy in an amaze, the northern kingdomes quiet; Spain warring to reduce Portugall.

[1] Leopold I.
[2] Ruler of Transylvania.

Jan : 26 : 1663, my 48 entred.

Sensible of this day, ending my former yeare with remembrance of Gods goodnes to mee & mine, hitherto God hath holpen mee, and seeking God my heart filled with hopes, he will never faile nor forsake mee.

A freind robd his freind at London and hangd for it, called Col. Turner ; Lord deliver us from unreasonable men. Jan. 30.

1664.

When I come to review the wayes of God toward mee in the yeare past, I find it mercy & truth, he still smiles on us ; he hath added a litle Rebekah to o^r^ number & the rest grow up ; my publiq libertie strangely continued unto mee & people ; I have purchased this yeare a close cost 28*l.* for my son Thomas ; my receipts more than expences by 8*l.*; receivd 168*l.* 18*s.* 4*d.*, laid out 160*l.* 13*s.* 2*d.*; my stocke as good as last spring, my debts were then due to mee 20*l.* more than now, so that I have saved clearly about 8*l.* and my building wch was at least 40*l.*: now I have about 15*l.* in mony & my tenants owe mee 70*l.*, blessed bee God.

God good in o^r^ peace, reports of smart penal laws, Lord bee o^r^ helpe. May. 1.

Parl. adjourned until Nov. 20, passing a sharpe act agst conventicles. May. 16.

This day, as a caution to forelooke o^r^ ways, and to doe things advisedly, I fell into a great error, bidding to morrow for restauration day of ye king wch was this day. May. 29.

The war with Holland proceeds. Y^e^ king abused by infamous pictures, for which lewd courses give occasion. June. 5.

Discourses aloud of o^r^ breache with the Dutch. Called on again to Court for not administring the sacrament. June. 9.

This day, a day of holy rest, is now the sport and pleasure day of the generall rout of people. June. 12

The King narroely escaped drowning, July, 5. July. 10.

Small pox much in ye country ; such aboundance of cherries, brought by carts ; one in Colne, July 15, sold 3 pound for 2*d.* July. 17.

uttering a load in o^r street, a sickly fruite, and great sicknes feared, but where is the preparation for it?

Aug. 7. Likely that wee quarrel with ye Dutch.

Sept. 11. God good in the word, I had some apprehension it might bee my last sermon.

Sept. 14. Was the B^p of Londons primary visitacon 1664 where I having committed my selfe to God appeared, and through mercy mett with no rubbs, but my path clear so that I hope I may serve my M^r with freedom awhile longer, till I see those wond^rfull revolucons. Mr Smith a nonsubscriber was threatned by the B^p to bee made an example: blesse my God, oh soule.

Oct. 2. S^d wee have great successe agst ye Hollanders in Guinea. [1]

Oct. 9. This weeke, talk o^r fleet gone against the Dutch under Rupert, & peace with Turks.

Oct. 30. This day I gave the sacram^t of the Lords supper: 12 present, some with great devotion & brokennes of heart.

Jan. 8. News stronger of a Dutch warre.

Jan : 26 : 1664, my 48 y. ended and 49 entred.

Sensible y^t this day begun a new yeare with mee, with thankfulnes to God for his continued goodnes to mee & mine, with hopes that ye Lord will never faile mee nor forsake mee.

Feb. 12. The season warme, the times yett wond^rfull hard, no trade by reason of the Dutch troubles.

1665. 26 March, 1665, Easter day. 12 of us r^d ye sacrament of ye Lords supper publiquly for which I blesse God; I believe its 22 or 23 yeares since r^d on y^t day & occasion.

April. 5. A fast kept for good successe in o^r naval forces, God in mercy grant it.

Estate. When I come to view my estate expenses are 141*l.* 4*s.* 9*d.* receipts 139*l.* 4*s.* 8*d.* losse 2*l.* 1*d.* and some debts lesse than last yeare. I cannot say I either loose or gain directly, yett my thoughts

[1] "A little squadron belonging to the African Company, to which also the King added a couple of vessels, led by Robert Holmes, seized Cape Corso." Ranke. *History of England*, iii, 422.

are my outw^d estate will this yeare appeare to better. God prosper my soule.

I began to expound things out of the church catechism for the informacon of youth. May. 7.

At the visitacon, with respect; heard of successe agst Smyrna fleet; the countenances of many ministers sad to eye, Lord heale o^r manners. May. 8.

God good in manifold mercies, the plague certainly in London. 9 dyed last weeke, the drought doth not only continue, but ye heat groweth very much. Lord helpe us to gett into ye gap to turn away thy wrath. May. 14.

My personal illnes abateth blessed bee God; the plague gott into o^r land at Yarmouth, and London, 14 dying this weeke. God good to mee in the word preacht, at which o^r concourse was this day great; its good fishing where many are; catch some, oh Lord, I pray thee. May. 28.

The guns mention a great fight yesterday. June. 4.

The plague increaseth to 43 this weeke, the Lord good in o^r wonderfull successe agst the Dutch, [1] good in his word, the season dry, profanes common, piety very rare. June. 11.

Plague increased to 112. June. 18.

Plague increasd to 168; ye season somewhat shouring. 2063 prisoners Dutch at Colchester; all my 7 children hearing ye word, in whom bee the divine blessing. June. 25.

Plague increased to 267, bill 684; my son had leave to continue in ye country. God in mercy preserve us, & heale the city; medicam^ts used, but no publiq call to repentance; the king goeth to Wilton by Salisbury, the old Queen gone for ffrance: Lawson o^r brave seaman dead of his wound; [2] ye season very moist, Lord send not all in anger. July. 2.

This day a day of praise for o^r victory over the Dutch June 3. July. 4.

God good in o^r preservacon, the plague feares the Londoners; they flie before it & the country feares all trade with London: July. 9.

[1] Off Lowestoft.

[2] A Yorkshireman who had fought his way from the forecastle of a Hull ship to be an admiral of the fleet.

died 1006, of ye plague 470 : the Lord stay his heavy hand : the season ticle[1] for hay time.

July. 16. London sad days increase. 1268 buried. 725 plague. Lord hold thy hand.

July. 23. My farm turnd into my hands ; the plague hott, 1089, burials 1761 : Lord hold thy hand, proceed not in wrath.

July. 28. Plague grows hott ; persons fall down in London streets, 1843 of plague, total 2785 : Lord spare thy people.

Aug. 2. First publiqu monthly fast; wee gathered for distressed London.

Aug. 6. God good in the season, harvest comes in well, a great rain wch ye earth needed to Aug : 1. A small increase of the plague beyond w^t^ feared, viz. 2010, burials 3014.

Aug. 13. To Aug : 9 a great increase of plague, 2817, total 4030. Giles Cripplegate 690. Lord bee not angry with o^r^ prayers ; and now Colchester is infected, and when will Coln lay it to heart ?

Aug. 16. Colchesters infection looketh sadly, by a joyner. Dedham clapt him into a pest house presently ; God spare y^t^ place.

Aug. 20. Londons visitacon sad. 3880 plague, 5319 all diseases ; spread almost over the whole city, and much in ye country ; Lord arise & helpe. Colchester seeke into ye country for dwellings.

Aug. 27. God good in o^r^ preservacon, yet much endangered by Colchester. A lad of o^r^ parish coming thence died in White Colne, feared of ye infection ; another among us of his company ; Lord preserve us : the weather sad, but y^t^ day cooling : died at London plague 4227, all 5568 ; God in mercy stop infection : the increase was small in comparison of what feared.

Sept. 3. God good in o^r^ preservacon. Halsted in danger. ye plague rageth, 6102, total 7496, and twenty some days at Colchester.

Sept. 10. The season cooled and yet the bill Sept. 5 increased, 6978 plague, 8252 died ; they ordered continuall fires in London for 3 days and nights at every doore ; Lord cease thy hand.

Sept. 16. God good in Colnes preservation, yet Colchester increaseth in illnes being spread over ye whole town ; after freq^t^ reports of a most wonderfull increase this weeke it abated through mercy : from

[1] Cf. Ticklish.

Sept. 5 to 12, 562; y^{r} dying in all 7690, of plague 6544, and towards the full of the moon.

Thought y^{r} died at Colchester this weeke 184, from Sept. 12 to Sept. 23
19: the moon at full on ye 14; though the weather cold, and winds stirring yet their was an increase again and esp. within the wals where y^{r} died 1493, of the plague 1189; this bill was 8297, of the plague 7165, and yet Coln preserved.

Deaths at Colnehill, and hazards at Coln, and yet preserved, God Oct. 1.
inheritt o^{r} praises; the small pox with Coln at Potters: a great abatem^{t} of ye plague at London, 5533, totall 6460; and so at Colchester, 59 abated, y^{r} dying 126 or y^{r} abouts.

Wee remembred poore Colchester in o^{r} collection neare 30*s*. & Oct. 4.
sent them formerly 4*l*.

To thy goodnes wee own it with praises y^{t} wee are preserved Oct. 8.
from ye smal pox in o^{r} town & plague in the country, wch is hott at Ipswich, Harwich an 100 dying in 3 weeks: y^{r} graves fill ye churchyard alreadie, and have called for a new burying place; at Colchester it spreads exceedingly; this weeke buried 188; feares of
Cogshall, Halstead, ffeering. Certainly at Kelvedon up land, Brain- 5720
tree, and yett Colne, sinfull Colne, spared; my soule records thy 4929
kindnes with meltings for thy mercy; in ye midst of this sadnes London begins to cleare up, an abatem^{t} of above 700 this weeke; also Spains King dieth; that gives o^{r} merchants a wond^{r}full bays market, so that God finds out ways for o^{r} subsistance.

Wednesday, 11, the plague lookt on certainly at Coln-ford hill, Oct. 15.
and yett Coln preserved; it abates blessed bee God at Colchester above 50, and 652 at London. At Colchester died 145; their charge above 500*l*. per month, wherupon the country within 5 miles round was charged towards there releife.

A wond^{r}full sweet season, dry, cold and frosts; God gave a great Oct. 22.
abatem^{t} to the plague, 3219 in all, plague 2665, decrease 1849 London; praise God: o^{r} tax at ye parl. at Oxford encreasd to 140*l*. per month for 18 months to begin Jan: next; likelyhoods of the ffrench warre also; we assist B^{p} of Munster with mony: without a trade it will be very heavy to the nacon; God good in Colnes preservacon, although at Colnford hill 7 have died & 3 have plague sores as wee

apprehend; at Colchester only 22 abated, died, 106 of y[e] plague, 121 all.

Oct. 27. Saw y[e] London bill: Gods name bee praised for y[e] great abatem[t] of the plague, 1413 decrease, total 1806, of the plague 1421. Cambridge, Royston and many other places much abated, scattered much in the south.

Oct. 29. Over 101 died at Colchester: the plague at Oxford. The visitacon Court suspended one, & I am free, blesse God, oh my soule.

Nov. 5. Abated at London again 408; burials 1388, 1031 of the plague, yet at Colchester it increased; above 20 new houses infected; buried there about 147.

Nov. 12. S[d] y[e] plague mortal to many masters of families; at London it increased 399; in all dying 1787, of the plague 1414; abated at Harwich yet not cleare: at Colchester there died 110. Lord cleare
frost the nacon; the Dutch snapt some of our Tangier fleet, provision
Nov. 18. ships 2, & 1 fregate, and the ffrench tooke 3 of our Levant merchant men; y[r] is a fleet going to the straits.

Nov. 19. The plague abated a litle at Colchester, viz. to 106: at London
1050 plag. abated 428, more then y[e] last increase, the total 1358.

Nov. 26. Frostie weather with wind clearing the aire; the plague abates at London, 905 dying in all, of plague 652: at Colchester also much abated, blessed bee o[r] preserver, 70 dying this weeke, wee heare the like from all parts.

Dec. 3. Plague abates at Colchester to 48: at London 544, plague 333,
544. 333. and wee still preserved blessed bee God.

Dec. 6. Publiqu fast, a very thin audience, yett God good to us in withdrawing his pestilence & o[r] preservation; sent Colchester 7*l*. 10*s*. collected at our severall fasts.

Dec. 9. Weather open & warm, the plague decreasing little at Colchester, there dying 45, but, blessed bee God, abated at London 116, bill being 428, and Colne still preserved, plague 210.

Dec. 17. Y[e] plague increasd, the bill burials 442, plague 243, increase 14; so s[d] at Colchester, 67 of plague, all 71. The weather frosty, begun Dec: 14. Halsted much strucke with the small pox and a fever at Colne in divers poore families.

Frost continues, Londons increase 83, plague 280, bur. 525 : s[d] increasd at Colchester (but not), 60. Dec. 24.

Frost continues, likelyhood of ill times & trade, yet through mercy y[r] was a great abate of the plague at London, when reports contrary ; plague 152, total 330. So at Colchester, total 24. Dec. 31.

God good in manifold mercies; though weather open and warme, plague increasing at Colchester to 29, yet at London it comes low; plague 70, total 253, blessed bee God. Y[e] Dutch & we are preparing to out fleets to sea early, they under Ruyter & wee Monke. Jan. 7.

Plague increasd at London to 158, burials 375, 110 increase. Jan. 21.

Thes perticulars I observed in y[e] generall bill, ending Decemb : 19. 65.

97 Parishes buried	15,209, pl.	9887	Males 48,569	97,306
14 Parishes b.	41,351	28,888	Females 48,737	
12 P.	28,554	21,420	Plague 68,596	
5 P.	12,194	8,403		

Christnings 9,967—increase in burials this yeare 79,009.[1]

The greatest plague in England since y[t] in Edward the thirds time, and yett it continues, as very feirce in many places of England, this Jan. 26. What God may doe, the weather being now cold frostie, I know not, but hope well.

Jan : 26 : 65, my 50 entred.

I was not aware this begun the yeare, the Lord remember mee for good, when my eye is not distinctly on him ; an abatem[t] of plague at Colchester to 36, London 272, plague 79. Jan. 28.

Commonly said y[e] French have proclaimed open warre agst England. Jan. 30.

My son Thomas went up to London having been with us since beginning of June. Jan. 31.

[1] Annual average of deaths in London
1653-1665 including the Plague Year 19,946.
(Creighton, in *Social England*, vol. iv. p. 470).

Feb. 4. This month plague abates, 56, total 227, a low bill: Colchester holds ill still, increasing to 43.

Feb. 11. London reviveth, blessed bee God: plague abated 4 to 52: ye burials increased to 231: hopes of an abatem^t^ at Colchester, died 28.

Feb. 18. A cleare weeke, yet plague increaseth, London 59, total 249, Colchester 30. Wee had plenty of sprats this ffeb. 16. God good to us in his word.

Feb. 25. A very dry season, cold not much, windy; the plague yet increaseth, 69 London, burials 252: so said at Colchester 39. Queen miscarried. My thoughts much about giving over preaching.

March. 4. Plague through mercy abates at London, 42 pl. total 237, but a great increase at Colchester to 55. Yarmouth cleare. Lord heale o^r^ land, and open o^r^ trade, in mercy.

March. 11. Plague decreaseth at London 28, total increase 238; some say it
31 died. abates at Colchester.

March. 18. A cold, dry time at London, plague 29, burials 207, very low, blessed bee God; Colchester 43.

March. 25. Plague somewhat increaseth at London, dying 33, in all 233;
1666. more at Colchester 53, some places cleare.

1666.

April. 1. Wonderfull dry, plague abates at London, viz to 17, total 224, but it sadly increaseth at Colchester to 70.

April. 8. Plague gentle but increaseth at London viz. 26, total 211: feare
73. worse at Colchester, 73; its at Dedham & several villages, Lord in mercy remove thy hand.

April. 15. Plague increasd at London to 28, total 195: sore at Colchester, dying 90 of plague, total 92: administred ye sacram^t^, 16 present.

April. 22. Plague increasd at London to 40, total 215: at Colchester very
72. ill yet abat. 72; it spreads in several places of the country, Lord arise and helpe.

April. 26. Heard B^p^ of Munster had made a peace. and Sabbatai[1] ye Jewes prophet killed.

[1] 1626-1676. Born in Smyrna. When 20 years old he proclaimed himself the Messiah & obtained a great following among the Eastern Jews. He was imprisoned by the Sultan, Mohammed IV. He then embraced Islam, but the movement which he started lasted many years.

Plague, blessed bee God, decreasing at London, viz to 24, bur. April. 29.
215: feares of a great increase at Colchester, 94 died; a large audience.

God good in o[r] preservacon, yet sadly called on for y[e] plague, May. 6.
one dying of spots at night; it increasd at Colchester sadly to 177, at London to 40, total 213: many people resort to y[e] word, Lord doe them good by it.

Plague increased at London to 53, total 234, sad at Colchester, May. 13.
dying 174.

London increased to 58, total 236: its thinly peopled w[t]soev[r] May. 20.
persons speake; most by-places empty & thought y[e] deaths were beyond o[r] counts by far, Lord spare. Feares of Spains quarrelling
us. Sad still with poor Colchester, 161 dying. A trouble coming 161.
up street, where wee found another child stricken, & old Lea not well.

London abates to 31, total 203. Colchester abates also to 110, May. 27.
and not so mortal at Bocking.

Did my last duty to S[r]. Tho: Honywoods dust, laying him up June. 1.
in his earth and long home at Markshal who died at London.

London: pl: 20, tot. 201: Colchester 101. Rumo[rs] of a great June. 3.
fight; wee prayd heartily for successe, & hope it, though some 99.
cry a losse.[1]

The publique fast. June. 6.

Plague increasd at London to 27, total 191: increasd at Colchester June. 10.
at least 20. 120.

God good in London, yet increasd, total 196, pl. 31; increasd at June. 17.
Colchester to 150. 150.

The sicknes decreasd at Colchester 32, being 112: at London June. 24.
to 23, total 179. 112.

God good to admiracon in o[r] towns preservation, when so sad July. 1.
in all other places, Cambridge, Oundle, Needham, Braintree, but above all at Colchester increasing to 180. London, 33, tot. 223.

The land at a low ebbe, o[r] enemies brave it on o[r] coast; God in July. 4.
mercy, helpe & deliver.

[1] vide *Bright's History of England*, Vol. II. p. 370.

July. 8. God good in ye season. I was blamed to neglect a hay day on ye fast; in sad skies my hope was God would make it up and he did. London plague, 35, tot. 222. Colch. 175: the plague in many places in ye country hott, the enemy braves us at sea, o^r fleet unreadie, threatning invasion, o^r counsels divided, and very low in ye esteem of ye nacon.

July. 14. The Dutch continue to brave it on o^r coast, all o^r forces upon the shore east.

July. 15. A very hot season; plague rageth at Braintree, Colchester 169; at London abated to 33, total increasd to 247.

July. 22. The plague sad in many places of England, o^r town well, praisd bee God; London increasd to 51, total 294; Colchester to 178.

July. 24. The guns roard; 26, said a fight began die. 25: God shew us favo^r.

July. 29. Plague sad at Braintree; 40, 50 o^r more dying in a weeke; at London, bill increasd to 326, plague decreasd to 48; Colchester abated to 113.

Aug. 5. Plague abates through mercy in country wherin its much spread; London, 341, plague 38: Colchester, 111, Braintree abated from 57 to 23 this weeke.

Aug. 12. London increasd, total 336, pl. 42. Colchester decreasd to 95.

Aug. 19. Colch. 71. O^r fleet wee have of Holland coast, where they were very successful.[1] Plague much in o^r country, London, 332, plag: 48.

Aug. 23. Day of praise for o^r victory ov^r the Dutch.

Aug. 26. The plague abates, London 290: p: 42. Colch: 51: gott into Cogshall.

Sept. 2. The Dutch again on o^r coasts, forces rais^d, God in mercy send us peace. London abates, 266, pl. 30. Colchester feard to increase, 57.

This day, begun Londons dismal fire, laying the city, the goodliest of ye world in ashes; *quis legens hoc temperet a lachrimis.*

Sept. 9. This weeke dolefull; a fire began in London in Pudding lane at a ffrench bakers about one of the clocke Sept: 2. being Lords day, and on ye 3 & 4 burnt down almost ye whole city but a litle quarter from ye tower to Moregate, and as low as Leadenhall Street; it

[1] One hundred and fifty merchantmen were burnt on the Dutch coast.

burnt up all to Temple barre, few perishing in ye flames ; it ceasd ye 5 at night, on which day being the fast wee prayed heartily, with teares & faith, yt henceforward God would blesse us. Colchester abated to 37, God comand his mercy on or low estate.

Plague abated at Colchester to 25, sad at Cogshall, and other places. Sept. 16.

London bill was 104 of ye plague in 3 weeks. 16 parishes wthin walls, 14 without, by yt compute 81 (sic) wholly burnt down within wals & 2 without besides peices of others. Sept. 23.

Plague abates at Colchester about 10 or 11 dying. Sept. 30.

At Colchester died 9 ; Cogshall under hope. Oct. 6.

A publique fast in regard of Londons burning, with a collection; gathered 6*l*. Oct. 10.

A wettish time ; plague abates at London 14 & Colchester 7 ; litle mention of it. The sacramt of baptism publiquly administred. Oct. 14.

In ye low estate of ye nacon 1,800,000, more voted for ye Kings supplies : God awake for Englands prosperitie in ys low day. Oct. 21.

Plague, Colchester bill 5. Lond: 210. p. 16. Oct. 28.

My son was returnd safe from London : the Lord my God blesse him. Col: 4: London, 220, pl. 14 : many hearing, but few practicing. Nov. 4.

Pd my son 1*s*. for plums, the first he sold. Nov. 5.

London: 213, pl. 10. Colc. 2; plague abates blessed bee God but ye war damps all trade ; the Lord drive his spiritual trade ; feares still in London ; a Frenchman suffered for firing ye house in Pudding lane first, by throwing fire into the bavins. [1] Nov. 11.

Kings stables fired ; feares fill us, and yet careles ; plague abated, London, 3 & Colch: 3. Nov. 18.

I have neglected by reason of wants to lay by of my estate for good uses as I once engaged ; the nature of my estate is very much altered, but I resolve henceforward, to lay by the 10th shilling y. comes in clearly of mony for all ministerial dues, and the 20th shilling of rent, and for every quarter of corn I sell, 1*s*., and to divide this thus—12*s*. of 20, for good uses to freinds, and the 8*s*. to dispose to ease mee in my own perticulars for 10ths, visittacons, Estate.

[1] Wood used for lighting fires.

books, &c. having first out of the whole cleard my debts to town, &c. w[ch] are about 40*s*. and the 10th shilling profitt of fatting catle.

Nov. 25. Col. 1. The country cleares of the plague, London, 235, p. 8, increase after the appointm[t] of thanksgiving for decrease.

Dec. 2. Troubles in Scotland; God continue o[r] peace; plag: London 7, bur. 147.

Dec. 5. Heard great hopes of a Dutch peace. Amen good Lord!

Dec. 9. Scots routed.

Dec. 23. Fears of an invasion from ffrance, one wave after another is y[t] lives porcon.

Jan. 9. John my son went towards London, the Lord Jesus be with him for soule & body; r[d] a letter from him of his safe arrival there.

Jan: 26. 1666, my 51 entred.

Sensible y[t] day entred my 51st yeare, Lord bee with mee therin for good, & to y[e] end of my days, and blesse mee and mine, and let a covent[t] bee between us. I was early on my studdies this morning.

Jan. 27. Heard uncomfortably of my son John. Lord yett in mercy shew mee favo[r] in him, making him a comfort.

Feb. 15. Sadnes in my family, John returnd.

1667. March. Estate. W[n] I come to review my estate, I observe my stocke is fuller than it was last yeare, my debts rather more, but the visible advantage is in Wades house w[ch] I have purchased worth 20*l*. but 8*l*. was paid before, & in setting up my sonne Thomas to whom I gave 50*l*., but 22*l*. or y[r]abouts was gold gathered formerly; I have built nothing this yeare. I have no moneys by mee, not above 4*l*. besides w[t] is in my debt booke and y[t] is in my sons hands, neither had I any sum last yeare; my expenses were 95*l*. 15*s*. 4*d*., yet I reckon it a saving yeare.

April. 7. Hopes of peace, but threats of war, and said the Dutch will presently blocke up the Thames mouth.

April. 28. Going to preach, H. Morly of my parish deliv[d] mee a note of receipt of my procurations, and y[r] in notice I was suspended. I forbore to preach in y[e] afternoone.

June 6, the Dutch on Harwich coast, Thursday, June 12, Wednesday, they attempt Chatham river to destroy o^r great ships with successe & continued y^r their pleasure; June 27, they came up near Gravesend, they put a stop to all trade, and forced us to defend the whole shore, to o^r charge & amazem^t.

A sad face of o^r nacon ; ye French s^d in ye downs. June. 23.

The Dutch landed on ye Suffolke shore, attempting Langerfort, but beat of. July. 2.

One day wee feard the ffrench invasion, then ye papists rising, ye further burning of ye city, the stop of all trade ;[1] then hope good men come in place, delinq^ts called to account, then hopes of peace. July. 7.

Fears of papists, and of the Courts army at home. July.14.21.

The Dutch busy on o^r coasts ; the peace said concluded: the parliam^t high agst a standing army ; hopes of England reviving out of troubles : said the plague in London to 80, increasing from 2 last weeke ; not so. July. 28.

The parliam^t sent home til Oct. 10, by reason of the peace concluded July. 21. at Breda betwixt all ye nacons and us at warre. France prospers in fflanders ; now o^r fears are of a standing army, papists and persecution. Aug. 4.

The attempt on y^a place put a stop to ye French progresse, giving them much losse in y^r baggage by innundacon, and losse of men by storme & sally. The Spaniards also had a good bout upon 500 of y^r horse, & on an inrode by y^r garrisons into Picardie, yett they attempt Lisle. Dendermond.

My daughter Jane went to waite on old Mrs Harlakenden ; her mother wept for it. Nov. 5.

Isaac Hodson 7 Oct. began his yeare, he is to have 3*l*. per annum.

Parliam^t began. The Keepers speech by order of the King good ; Tompkins wth the Commons moved to give the King thanks for disbanding the armie, putting out papists, daming (*sic*) patentees, and laying aside the E. of Clarendon, the late Chancello^r ; agreed too ; a handsome beginning even as I desired. Nov. 10.

1 "It was everywhere said that the Court had sold England to the papists, that a French army was about to land, & the general massacre of Protestants to begin at last." (G. M. Trevelyan. *History of England under the Stuarts*. p. 356.)

Oct. 27. The 23 day the King laid ye first stone of ye exchange, on wch day 26 years before ye flames began to burn in Ireland.

Jan : 26, 67, 52 years enters.

Sensible this day entred my 52, and completed my 51 yeare ; thus my dayes flee away, and good see I not the world.

Feb. 9. Discourst ye Dutch chose o^r^ King y^r^ Protecto^r^. Wee have great plenty of corne, but scarcity of mony to admiracon.

Feb. 16. A cheerful season, but 10, the sitting down of parl. & actings was with great distast ; no moderacon heard of, taxes propounded ; Court careles.

Feb. 20. Preacht Paul Raynhams funeral at Chappel, a great audience : one Mrs Martin s^d^, I being in my coat, if shee should see one preach a sermon in coat or cloake shee would run out of the church : thus ordinances left naked.

March.22. W^n^ I come to view my estate, I find through mercy all my children about mee, my eldest sonne trading in the world, and I hope with Gods blessing, some others able to doe something ; I find no great gain, and its of mercy I doe not goe behind hand ; my stocke I thinke is rather better than last yeare ; I have purchased and paid for an house on the green, cost mee 16*l*., and I have laid out at least 6*l*. on it, and I am not in debt, but have 20*l*. owing mee since last yeare ; the Lord adde to my graces & comforts, for I find a decay in nature ; I observe, since the three comets, though wee had droughts & scarcity of hay, yett plenty & so a great cheapnes of corne.

1668.

April. 26. Noise of ye peace with France & Spain, and y^r^ invading England.

May. 10. Strange newes of attempts to fire London, of feares of French ruine by y^r^ great comings over.

June. 7. Strange suspicions in mens spirits, the Lord bee our hope & help ; man buzzeth nothing but amazing feares.

June. 14. This day my bodies sorenes fully visible on mee.

June. 21. A place at London for An. Lord direct us !

An went y[e] 24 towards London; Lord goe with her, bee the guide of her youth! 25, left her by agrem[t] with M[r] Gresham in y[e] exchange at London, returned weary & sore, but thankfull to God: 27, my son a great greife, Lord reclaim him from disorderlines!

Haveril faire being on the 15 & Satturday, I went this day & bought 7 heifers, 6 runts[1] at 32*s.* only 2*s.* abated, God prosper them: charge 5*s.* June. 17. Haverill

An bound on Aug: 20, her time out June 24, 1674, Lord remember her for good! Aug. 23.

Heard An ill at London. Sept. 26.

Heard An hopefully upwards of the small pox. Oct. 4.

John went towards London, under a sentence of death, having no hopes in him as formerly, the Lord trieth my faith. Oct. 14.

Bound John to M[r] Buggin at y[e] Globe in Barbican: he is to receive 45*l.* Nov. 13.

God good in many providences; I was entred my 53 yeare before I was aware. Feb. 14.

M. Hey with mee; the King, Duke of York, overturned in a coach in Holborn going to y[e] race at Newmarket: March. 8, the K. lost his race: 10, the D. of Yorks closset searcht: March 19, s[d] robd. March.21.

1669.

John sicke of y[e] small pox. April. 18.

Heard hopefully of Johns recovery. April. 25.

S[d] the Q. with child. April. 27.

Rid to Court, whither summoned for not wearing the surplice; dismissed w[th]out fee. July. 9.

Made an end of haying for y[s] yeare, and my hay very good, God bee praised for y[s] mercy: it cost mee the least of any yeare, mowing & making & inning not above 40*s.* besides my own helpe. July. 10.

Drought & heat continues, sickly at London, nigh 700 in this bill: near 300 of the plague in y[e] guts. Heard of y[e] Q. mothers death, y[t] S[t] Albans hath her joynture of 50,000*l.* 2 yeare. Sept. 5.

B[ps] visitacon of London at Kelvedon, where committing my selfe Sept. 8.

[1] An animal below the usual size.

to God without sollicitousness, I appeared with quiet, for which I blesse y[e] L[d] & desire to serve him wth more faithfulnes & care my remaining dayes : visit, fee, 2*s*. 4*d*.

Sept. 12. Drought continues : 707 died at London, mine well.

Sept. 26. I rid to Ladie Veres, 88 years old ; her senses continue, her great grandchild a man, E. of Lincolne : three homely ladies there ; y[e] Lords beauty is best, but bloud gives nothing good.

Sept. 11. Peter hired for another yeare, w[ch] is to end the day after Halsted faire, & to have 4*l*. 10*s*. and paire of shoes.

Nov. 11. Went to preach a funeral ; I r[d] 20*s*. paire of gloves & blesse God.

Nov. 28. State disturbances, fears of insurrection, charges of treason agst Orrery & Ormond.

Dec. 11. In y[e] morning my sons shop broke open, and nigh 50*l*. of good stollen : I providentially heard of them & pursued, but returnd, troubled, yet hoping well.

Dec. 12. Those y[t] robbed us were first found by the man I imployd to pursue ; one escaped with a good part of the goods, the other three committed to Cambridge jayle, Dec. 13 : my son returnd the 14, and most of o[r] goods fetcht home, 16 : God alone have the glory.

Jan. 9. Deaths many ; Monke died. I thinke it was on Wednes. Jan 5, it thundered 3 straks, one very violent with lighting, God preserve us.

Jan. 21. Jonathan Woodthorp of o[r] town, a tanner, askt my consent to come to my daughter Jane and had it, on this ground especially that he was a sober, hopefull man, his estate about 500*l*.

Jan. 26. 69, 54 y. enters.

Sensible of my birth a sinner. Recommended my selfe to Gods care to blesse mee in all my ways ; fears for my children but I leave them on Gods care.

Feb. 2. Monks dutches died, Jan. 23, 20 dayes after housband, persons y[t] by bringing in the King came to a vast estate, but base and sordid.

March. 13. Threats of severity ags[t] nonconformists; God can stop all if pleasd: son returnd : the theives remitted to Chelmsford to bee tried there, burglary.

March. 16. This day my sons 3 theives condemned at Chelmsford to bee hangd; afterwards they confessed the fact: 18, Jonathan Woodthorp, and my daughter Jane, testified y[r] agreem[t]. to marry; God in mercy blesse them.

The L[ds] moderate the act agst meetings, opposing magna charta. March. 20.

1670. 1670.

Cow calved; administred the sacrament, only 14 present. April. 3.

The Kings only sister died suddenly in France, within a few days after her return from Dover, [1] where the King entertaind her with all pleasures might bee; Lord sanctifie this. The ArchB[p] of Canterbury ill, the poore nonconformist hurried; one Hunnicke a disturber in o[r] parts. June. 26.

Begun a jorney into Sussex, returnd Aug. 2, having seen much of Englands glory, Hampton Court, Thames, returnd safe. July. 25.

My daughter Jane married to Jonathan Woodthorp, o[r] first marriage; the Lord blesse them with his grace & favo[r]; for porcon I am to give her 200*l.*; her clothes, and wedding cost mee 10*l.*; shee hath a prettie thing in joynture: blessed bee God who hath thus provided for mee and mine: her plate & worke is worth 40*l.*, and shee hath in mony 20*l.* Aug. 30.

Rid to the visitacon, & found no trouble, God bee praised; preached at Halsted. Oct. 10.

Peters yeare is to come out Octob. 31, 1671; he is to have 5*l.* wages and his mare, going untill Candlemas day. Oct. 27.

Purchased a tan office for my son: setled it on Jane for her life. Jan. 19.

Jan: 26: 1670; my 55 enters.

Lord thou hast been my God, my hope is in thy mercy; looke after mee & mine for soule & body, for on thee I trust.

Johns debauchery in swearing sad, Lord helpe mee; so bad 6, 7, that I resolve to put him to his shifts, for the Lords sake lett it tend to his good. Feb. 4.

[1] By her agency Charles had recently concluded the Secret Treaty of Dover.

1671. 1671.

March. 26. Day warm & calme; death hanseld us at Colne this yeare: the wickednes & iniquity of England increase. Ld Lucas likely to be sent to tower by Lds for speaking somewhat freely agst the taxes, wch are heavy beyond measure, the 20th pt of or yearly state.

Estate. Through Gods blessing I have accomplisht in my estate ye utmost that I desired by June 24, viz. an 120*l.* but my stocke is low.

Sept. 24. Being ye last Sabbath of the yeare, I publiquly declared my submission to yr putting mee away, having for 15 yeares wth held yr contribucon wch was 25*l.* per annum, as also most of there tithes, & now yt wch others allowed, wch I took from God with ye greatest patience, but from them wth great unkindnes, but I trust God will turne it unto good: I am thine Lord, though not theirs.

Oct. 8. This day I went down to preach, & found Mr. Sergeant there: he read Ezech. 2. Lord lett it bee known I have been thy servant & thou acceptest mee: the 12 psalm was sung; not one person spake to mee, coming out of the church: Ld I am dispised, but my confidence is in thee, & with quietnes I roule my selfe on thee.

Jan. 7. A good faire season: 10, at ye Funeral of ye good Lady Vere who lived beloved and blessed of God 90 yeares, died lamented of all.

March. 13. Wednesday rid to London, yt day Sr Robert Holmes yt fired the Fly [1] attempted the Smirna fleet; 16, a declaracon came out for liberty of conscience: 19, the Dutch warre proclaimed and fast appointed, both ordered by the King and Councill on the Lords day.

1672. 1672.

April. 17. A fast on occasion of the Dutch warre, which all are against. [2] 28, or yrabouts, a monster born in or town; the grandfather esteemed religious, but the children wretched.

[1] He captured New Amsterdam in the first Dutch war of the reign of Charles II, & destroyed a large number of Dutch merchant ships at the island of Vlie.

[2] Because the alliance with France was unpopular.

Monday neare 3 a clocke afternoon my daughter Woodthorpe delivered of a son, the first grandchild; God blesse him with his Christ. April. 29

The Dutch bear up gallantly. May. 26.

The Dutch set on o^r^ fleet in Solebay, fight continued. May. 28.

My onely grandchild, John Woodthorp, buried, June 4.

God afflicts the Dutch by French. June. 9.

Sad with Holland, the French prevaile at land. June. 16.

Holland drowns it selfe; oh ye evil of sin, L^d^ drown it in Christs bloud. June. 23.

Sad with Holland, some speake of peace between us. June. 30.

A good season; litle thought of a Dutch peace; o^r^ Councel so for the French, its likely the Dutch come wholly under them. July. 21.

Y^e^ souldiers went from us. Nov. 3.

I heard the report of ye French endeavo^r^ to reforme in religion; if of God it will prosper; God grant it true; it came to nothing at present. Nov. 17.

Being at my daughter Janes at Lexden I was taken in my bed, or coming out of it with ye sciatica pain in my hipbone so y^t^ I could not step, and when I came home not turne my selfe in my bed; wholly deprived of strength on y^t^ side but through mercy God gave mee in ye use of meanes some helpe; y^r^ was a surfett with oysters, wch though they did not nauseat my stomacke, mett with so much phlegme in my stomacke, & being bound, they lay corrupting in my stomacke. I eate at first litle but dranke wine, strong beere pretty freely, & y^t^ carried them of, and my vomit had a tincture of them to Tuesday, Decemb. 3. I sweat, eate well, but gather strength slowly this being 24; but I am under great hopes of a perfect recovery & I hope quickly. I had a servant died; this a mortal time in o^r^ towne, about 15 buried in 7 weeks; to ye praise of my good God I record that on the 25, 26, I began to take many steps without sticke or stay. Nov. 27. Dec. 24.

This day afternoon I went down to church and preacht, Eccl. 9. 5. a great audience. Jan. 5.

Went to Markshall: my L. Honywood sent her coach for me: y^r^ I stayd to March 10, in wch time my Lady was my nurse, & Jan. 27.

phisitian & I hope for much good: on Thursday, Feb. 27, or sooner, some red spots appeard on my lame thigh, wch they conceived ye scurvy. I tooke purge & other things for it; they increased some to a penny breadth, my thigh & leg swelled, but not on ye other side, & so they did before I went from home, & continue so still; God was good to mee in the temper of my heart, though I am sensible I beare my infirmities about mee, but my wife taxes mee for great impatience, when I feare y^r is a carelesnes in her &c. & impatience too much, y^t beares nothing, but expects I must beare all; God inable mee therto, for I have need of patience when I have done my duty.

March. 10. Returned home: a wonderful spirit of zeale agst ye papists.

1673. Mr Eldreds cutting day, feasted.' gave mee 2 ginneys.

March. 27. Thomas Josselin June 15, about one a clocke in ye morning my eldest sonne Thomas & my most deare child ascended early hence to keep his everlasting Sabbath with his heavenly Father, and Savio^r with the church above; his end was comfortable, & his death calme, not much of paine till the Saturday afore.

July. 31. Ann Josselin This morning after 2 of the clocke my deare Ann in her twentieth year died with mee at Colne; a good child, following her brother to London, & from thence hither, to lie in his grave, loving in their lives & in their death they were not divided, lying in the same grave.

Oct. 21. About 5 of the clocke, my daughter Jane deliv^d of a daughter, which wee baptized that day.

Oct. 28. This day my wife & I have been married 33 yeares; this day my son sold Bollinhatch for 123*l.* for wch I have been bid 150*l.* God blesse mee in the dispose of the mony.

Nov. 5. Gods deliverances a hope to us; he will deliver agst ye feares of popery at present in England, the duke marrying Modena's daughter.

Nov. 9. Frost and snow, the Parl. prorogued.

Jan. 26, 1673, 58 enters.

Jan. 26. Sensible this day begins my 58 yeare, in which I desire Gods presence & blessing with mee.

My leg occasions thoughts of the dropsie; the Lord I looke unto to bee my phisitian. Feb. 1.

On y^s day the K. in ye house of Lords declared to them & Commons y^t the peace was made with the Dutch, safe, hon^ble, & he hoped lasting; the D. of Yorks marriage by the French interest with Modena, his inclinacon to the R. religion, the great offers of ye French to ye English to continue ye war, hastned the peace. Fast. 11.

Parliam^t prorogued to Nov. 10; K. speech smooth, a disappointm^t to ye country; no notice of it in the Thursday gazet.[1] They toucht Arlington, succession not in a papist, Ireland, where ye papists are mighty, & popery here & would give no mony; God waited to bee gracious by them to make a peace with ye Dutch. 22.

Reports of a new Parliam^t; all change, only God abides ye same. March. 22.

25. March. 1674. 1674.

Receivd an 100*l.* of the purchase mony for the land at Roxwell & two ginneys for my wife. March. 25.

A cloud brake at Ratlesden in Suffolke & did much mischeife. May. 1.

Gave Ned Harris 1*s.* on condicon to be sober quarter of a year & spend only 2*d.* at a sitting, with a real intent & prayer to God & counsell for his good; Lord second it; he tooke it kindly; s^d never 1*s.* given to any person with so good an intention. May. 12.

Wore a new gown & cassocke, my old one still being in use after 35 years of age; an old freind and a new heart are good. June. 28.

A choice day of civill concourse mixt with religious at ye L. Honywoods, whither came ye Countesse Dowager of Warwicke & her sister ye L. Renula: goodnes & greatnes sweetly mett in them; I writt to ye Countesse who invited mee to Leez. July. 2.

R^d a letter from the Countess of Warwicke writt with her own hand inviting mee to Leez and promising mee a kind welcome as long as she liveth. July. 5.

[1] In the earlier years of the reign of Charles II. *The Intelligencer* was published on Mondays, *The News* on Thursdays. In 1666 *The London Gazette* replaced *The Intelligencer*; the news contained in these papers was meagre, but, such as it was, Charles II.'s subjects had to be content with it.

Sept. 18. I received 11*l.* 8*s.* of Mr Cressener for tithes, ye greatest sum I ever received at once; he paid grumblingly, yett Lord blesse him.

Sept. 27. The Parl. prorogued, & Arlingtons house burnt by fire Sept. 22 at night, to his great losse.

Sept. 30. God good this day in ye kindness of Mrs Harl. & receivd 10*l.* 12*s.* arrears from the priory, a spring opened in a dry place.

Oct. 23. Rid towards London, returnd 29; did ye busines I went for well.

Being L^d. Mayor Viner had his show, ye K. & Court dining at Guildhall; my jorny comfortable.

Offer to John before his mother & foure sisters. John set yor selfe to feare God, & bee industrious in my busines, refrain yor evill courses, & I will passe by all past offences, setle all my estate on you after yor mothers death, and leave you some stocke on ye ground & within doores to the value of an 100*l.* and desire of you, out of your marriage portion but 400*l.* to provide for my daughters or otherwise to charge my land with so much for y^r porcons; but if you continue yor ill courses I shall dispose my land otherwise, and make only a provision for yor life to put bread in yor hand.

Dec. 15. John y^s day ownd his debauchery; God give him a true sight of it & heale him.

Quakers increasd; John Garrod their head in o^r town, building them a meeting place, appointing to meet once a week; I am not ov^r solicitous of the effect, having seen Abbotts meeting house left, expecting God will appear for his truth, and I hope in perticular for mee in this place who truly desire to feare his name. I doe not determine why, but this morning viz 26, y^t Garrods wife died, within 6 weeks of the use of that house; I onely desire to feare and tremble, but doe not question ye downfall of that sect under ye feet of Christ & his servants.

Jan. 1. A new yeare, wherin I lookt up to God for his grace & blessing.

Jan. 3. Warme, dry, calme Christmas, grasse springing, herbes budding, birds singing, plowes going; a litle rain only in two dayes, viz. Dec. 29, 30: fogge Jan. 5, 6, no mention of frost, though some dayes cleare sun shining, moon & starrs appearing by night: most persons said never such a Christmas known in the memory of man;

yet I suppose 37 yeares before ye like & one said 46 o^{r} 47 was such an one.

John declared for his disobedience no son ; I should allow him nothing except he tooke himselfe to bee a serv^{t} ; yet if he would depart and live in service orderly I would allow him 10*l*. yearly ; if he so walkt as to become Gods son, I should yett own him for mine.

Jan. 26. 74. 59.

Sensible this day ended my 58 & begun my 59 yeare; Lord bee good to mee in this & all y^{t} are to come.

Weather cold, windy & drie, God good in o^{r} health, w^{n} the smal pox is in many families & towns about : news of putting the laws in execucon agst papists & nonconformists: I count ye English of y^{t}, the parl. shall sit in April, & bee cajold to give a great taxe ; observe. Feb. 7.

1675.

Wee serve God in peace when others are hurried about by informers. April. 18.

My sweld leg brake, wch at first occasioned thoughts as to sorenes, gangrening by the blacknes of it, & following of the humo^{r}, but I blesse God. April. 25.

My ill leg sweld very much, with some pain, stiffnes and a kind of numnes in ye former part of both my feet as I have had formerly ; it had great influence on my thoughts; God in mercy stood between mee & ye thoughts of death & the feares of it ; my leg issued a litle, I applied a searcloth ;[1] it run but not much, it broke at a blacke spott ; ye like is lower, on my inward knocle ; my wife applied a large roule to my leg of bole arnimake to dry and abate the humo^{r} ; I praise God my mind is composed on his good will.

Applied a poultis of red rose leaves and milke: 18, used Tabors pills, they purgd but twice. May. 17.

The blacknes & swelling of my legg abates. May. 23.

My wife with o^{r} 2 daughters Mary & Elizabeth went for London to Hackney school ; God blesse them in y^{r} educacon both for soule & body. June. 2.

[1] Cloth anointed with some glutinous matter of a healing nature.

Issue. June. 7. On Monday Dr Tabor made an issue on mee in order to ye cure of my leg; Lord blesse it, and restore mee to my perfect health; read Dr Owen on Mortification. I blesse God for some passages therin.

June. 13. The parliamt prorogued, June 9, to Oct. 13; it prevented the Test; [1] it was said by the King the fewd between the houses was from the enemies of the King & Church of England; the Commons voted they knew not of any such thing; it arose about an appeale to the Lds in the case of Sr J. Fagge a member of ye commons. [2]

July. 11. Intend for Tunbridge, God in mercy bee my phisitian; the waters are his prepared phisicke; the small pox next doore to my house, God preserve mee.

July. 12. Set out for Tunbridge wells, whither I came 13; begun to drinke 9 8-ounce glasses: the 14th, I drunke 15 glasses & so continued from 17 to Aug. 1, inclusive: wee came thence Aug: 4, & so home Aug. 12; God merciful to mee in my jorney, the waters passing well with mee, & good to mine in my absence for wch his name bee praised.

Oct. 17. Drought continues; great fears of or poor rising up & down or contry, esp. those yt belong to the wool trade. One Rugles of this parish, a quaker, a rude fellow, disobedient to his mother, sent to ye house of correction.

Nov. 28. Coughs common: parliamt prorogued to Feb. 76.

Dec. 5. News of a parliamt. The smal pox in another house at the mill.

Dec. 12. The smal pox stops at present; God stop it in much mercy.

Dec. 28. Reported the King dead among mean people.

Jan. 18. Reports again of ye Kings death; Lord preserve his life for good.

Jan. 23. My leg runs, sadly painful; healing is thy blessing, yu hast & wilt doe it.

[1] "A Non-Resisting Bill was introduced.... No one was to sit as a legislator until he had sworn to alter nothing in Church or State.... But its passage into law was prevented only by a timely quarrel between the two houses." (G. M. Trevelyan. *England under the Stuarts.* p. 381.)

[2] Fagge had acquired the estate of Wiston which had belonged to the Sherleys. Thomas Sherley brought a suit for the recovery of this estate & carried the case to the House of Lords, but was ordered into the custody of the sergeant-at-arms, Fagge being a member of the House of Commons. *(Dict. of Nat. Biography.)*

Jan. 26, 75, 60.

Sensible this entred my 60 yeare; I grow an old man; my leg Jan. 26.
swels hard on y[e] calfe & so continueth in mornings.

In the morning a litle rubbing my leg, it bled exceedingly above Feb. 5.
y[e] sore place; my leg asswaged y[r]upon; it bled a quart as my wife thought, blackish and coddered.[1]

Leg not so much sweld as formerly; it heals not; sometimes Feb. 20.
painfull, drest but seldome; a wonderfull decay of trade & so of traders, corn cheape, hard with poore for want of worke & rich for want of mony.

Likely to find an hard time agst the nonconformists, upon a Feb. 27.
trouble at Ipswich where was the first stirre at y[e] Scotch troubles.

1676. 1676.

God good in his word, freinds with mee at a good turky. I April. 2.
delighted to eate y[e] good creature with them, blessing my good God.

At visitacon, o[r] mony paid, all peace: Ap. 11, baptized Dol April. 7.
Andrews.

A muster of our County forces. May. 18.

A dismal fire in Southwarke; Lord y[u] cuttest England short; May. 26.
many hundred houses burnt, in y[e] cheife street: there was treachery and firing, God thinke on us.

Mens minds discomposed in the times with fears of French plots. July. 2.

A young man M[r] Smith from London proffered his love to my Sept. 2.
daughter Mary; shee refused him, as shee had formerly done another of good estate: he went away Sept. 5, very sorrowful, most of o[r] affections much to him.

This day wee had a parochial visitacon; somethings complaind Sept. 19.
of, as the want of a surplice, in other things it was well.

At night M[r] Shirly made an offer of his service and love to Sept. 25.
Mary; God direct that affaire.

R[d] a kind present from London from M[r] Smith; some places Oct. 8. 7.
preacht not, it was so wett, I intermitted not.

[1] Clotted.

Oct. 15. My son the seat of drunkennes, oh Lord can thy spirit ever come to delight in him.

Oct. 29. Advised with a surgeon for my leg, but my hope is in God.

Nov. 26. R^d^ from Mr Bowes, Pierson on the Creed, a booke worth 10s.; I accept his love, God return it.

Dec. 3. This weeke John wholly out in his filthy courses; I am resolved to leave him to thee oh God, only I will pray for him.

Dec. 12. Snew again at night; it was ye deepest snow I ever remembred, lying about knee high of a man every where without any great drifts.

Dec. 19. Set apart this day with my familie to humble my soule before God, for our sins, to seeke his direction for and blessing on us & ours: the special occasion, Johns ill housbandry & Eliz. offer of a young man from London who is coming down & shee seems very averse. I read in course in morning Mic: 4, passages y^r^ in comfort, in altering things from bad to good; Lord make them so among mine. I first proposed a duty to looke up to direction from God, Ezra: 8. 21, who hath ye cast in our lott, Is. 34. 17; then I commended all to God in prayer: if God cast yor lot, rest in it, & to know it observe Pro. 3. 6; own God & he will direct you; Psal. 32. 8. was Gods direction, is by o^r^ parents for children. Eph. 6. 1, 2, 3, its right; answer y^t^ in Ezra: rest in a housbands house, Ruth. 1. 9.; y^ts^ done w^n^ both bring Gods feare, mutual love, & industrious prudence; the way is by parents provision, & children following y^r^ counsell, as Abraham tooke a wife for Isaac, whom he tooke & loved, Gen. 24, & thus God comforts in losses in one another. Ruth shee followed Naomis counsell & all well, though ye counsel at ye barnfloure seemd strange. Let mee shew you an instance of a headie marriage in Samson; it turnd to his death; agst his parents advice he would marry, &c. God casts your lot in parents choice, Exod. 2. 19. 21. Numb. 30; vows to God allowd or disallowd by parents, otherwise free; y^r^fore my children receive y^s^ counsel as Gods not mine; tis mine because Gods & so its Gods being mine, a father y^t^ is to counsel, wch wilbee yor crown as theirs, 1 Thes. 2. 13; it will effectually worke obedience, & y^r^fore hear him, Pro. 23, 22, Pro. 8. 8, 9. I am perswaded a blessing will follow y^s^ counsel embraced. Is. 55.

3. Yor soules shall live : & I hope God will give an answer of peace ; I will pray & looke up, & my God shall speake peace. I praid thrice with them ; their mother gave them ye same advice, God in mercy give them his blessing.

Mr Smith came safe. Dec. 23.

Mr Smith returnd towards London satisfied in his jorney with Dec. 29.
hopes of my Elizabeths love : God seen in inclining her heart, wch was very awkward at first. My affections drawn from the hopes his sobrietie & good nature gave, yt grace & industry might meet to make him a good housband, for his estate was small.

1676, Jan. 26, 60, 61 enters.

Sensible this day ends my 60 and enters my 61, wherein I begun with thoughts of God.

The Chancellor Finch was robd of mace & purse. Feb. 10.

A wonderfull wett season, in wch Mr Smith came down to us. Feb. 26.

All my children with mee ; Mr Smith parted with good comfort Feb. 28.
& content.

The Court partie prevaile in Parliamt[1] ; God bee our defence. March. 4

1677.

My Bettie flieth of from Mr Smith ; Lord bee yn my comfort. May. 13.

After some difficulties to mee on both hands, Mr Gilbert Smith & June. 5.
my daughter Elizabeth married by my hand in Lexden privately : 8, shee rod towards London ; the ground and bottom of the match among us was not estate, but good qualities ; lett them shine, Lord, in them both ; let her bee as Elizabeth in scripture.

Sent some houshold towards London for my daughter Smith. June. 16.

Begun to take sirrup of pellitory; God almighty doe mee good by July. 8.
it for on him I trust.

Or booke of common prayer was taken out of the deske. Sept. 2.

At visitacon, where I receivd admonicon to use all the prayers Sept. 5.
alwayes. I found at home a gentleman from London to proffer his love to Mary.

Mr Tims who proffered his love to Mary returnd to London, Sept. 8.

[1] Shaftesbury had been sent to the Tower by the House of Lords in February.

satisfied in us, but not in her : it wrought much as Betties busines; God knoweth the issue ; direct Lord, Betties doth wonderfull well.

Oct. 28. The news of the Ladie Maries marrying the prince of Orange pleasd the kingdome.

Nov. 11. Mr Tims came again, returnd on ye 14, unkindly used by Mary, though kindly by us. Heard to my joy how lovingly Mr Smith & his wife live, wch marriage I urged.

Nov. 16. Heard yt ye city was alarmd yt the papists plotted a massacre there ; was ye marriage a pillow to lull us asleepe ?

Nov. 23. Heard of ye death of James ye eldest son of Mr Shirley, who made great love to my daughter & then fell of ; a mercy shee is not a widdow ; shee never shewd respect to any young man but to him.

Dec. 1. I thought matters were not only uncomfortable, but also unprosperous. I cast up my account & I estimate yt my mony stocke, my debts pd, was about *300l.* I thinke I have been to blame in my charitie moneys : straits make us forgett or selves. Ld I am now old & I have no worke like serving thee and assuring my salvacon through Christ.

Jan. 1. I gave above *20s.* to my tenants & poore in meat.

Jan. 25. I was often thinking of the providence of God that was putting an end to yt familie of Harlakenden, being good men, & thoughtfull of the females ; my heart trembled, and though I was getting up moneys for corn more than ordinary & paying debts, yet this day I reflected on Gods providence in my estate, having of my Welsh heifers three dead calves & but one living ; Lord teach mee humility, & submission, I am the greater sinner.

Jan. 26. 1677.

Sensible it entred my 62 yeare ; read in course Acts 14, of the impotent man in his feete, with faith God would keepe my distemper from hurt, would heale it & doe mee good.

Jan. 30. Heard of ye eagerness of or king for warre with France : ye Parl. voting *70M.* to bury the late King after 29 years being in grave. Strange things. Why is not mony voted to buy[1] . . . . . . & harlots petticoats? God will be seen in ye mount as I preacht. I have no opinion[1] . . . . . . o^r^ medling with France, of o^r^ conduct or sincerity, but y^u^ Lord reignest, & Ile bee quiet.

That day ye Parliam^t^ sat down, the French King began his jorny towards Germany; the King receiving an adresse from them, school^d^ them ; they voted 20 regim^ts^ foote, 4 horse, 2 of dragoons, 90 ships to support the Dutch alliance, Sp. Netherlands & abate ye French; weekely charge per month at 28 days 157*l*.000 & upwards. Feb. 17.

A million granted the King to begin the war with France ; wee are a people peeled & polled. Feb. 24.

The French K. passing on for Germany to Nancy in Lorraine on a suddain came backe to Flanders, his forces seem likely to attempt Namur ; the Dutch forces marcht to Hasselt. March. 1.

S^d^ Gaunt was taken after defence of severall dayes. March. 10.

1678.

Parl: adjourned until April. 11. March. 28.

A publique fast, which I endeavoured to keepe with all solemnes, and I had a considerable audience of my people & some strangers; it was called by the King, no mention of his Council o^r^ parliam^t^ advising, though both in sitting. Y^e^ proclamation past March 30: no mention of it in the Gazet of Monday Ap. 8, til the Thursday Gazet : no mention of war o^r^ peace, nor blessings desired on ye counsells on foote. The King & city kept it Ap. 10, while ye Parl. was adjourned, so y^t^ neither House kept it by themselves and called preachers to them. I thought it shewd that the King had no great esteem for his good & blessed parliam^t^ ; no notice in the Gazets of the keeping this fast. April. 24. Fast.

Things in a cloud at London, the King saith the Dutch bafled and ruind, a separate peace with the French. The Dutch jealous of the English least they have a designe to greaten Orange. Lord secure England in religion from popery & in liberty and from an army. May. 5.

Went not to Court ; I came of well for present as to surplice. Gods name bee praised. May. 14.

The King asking his parl: counsell, and they denying to raise a million of mony & reflecting too plainly on the evill counsello^rs^, May. 19.

[1] The MS. is mutilated.

the King prorogued them from 13 to 23: 23. the Kings speech imports displeasure agst the Parl.

May. 26. The King seems to chide the Parl. to a doing what he would have.

June. 2. In or publiqu affaires hopes yt ye crisis we apprehended to or religion & liberty may admitt a longer putting of.

Parl. voted to disband the army presently.

June. 23. News that Spain ffrance & Holland have made peace. England is to bee the securitie for it. The King demanded thereon 300*ml.* yearly for his life therupon, but ye house voted negative.

Aug. 18. Peace between France & Holland; but before known in ye Holland camp, in order to releiving Mons, they fell on ye French with great fury & slaughter [1]; ye French retired, so ye honor of ye feild was to ye Dutch & English who fought valiantly.

Sept. 12. Mett the Bp at Wittam. I was much complained of to him by Mr Lampkin, preist of Hatfeild, & Mr Paul preist of Easthorp, & but coursely used by ye Bp. I thanke God for my patience & his goodnes to mee going & returning.

Sept. 15. I urged for Pauls, wee gathered 3*l.*

Nov. 17. A good day: the plotters [2] seem to make opposicon in or councels.

Nov. 24. The House committed Secretary Williamson to the tower, [3] the King releasd him, a passage that looks not well, God amend all.

Dec. 1. Heard good news from London; sd the Queen is accused in this plott.

Dec. 8. The King and House of Commons are a litle off one another; God prevent a breach to sever the parliamt: the army is to bee disbanded: some threat as the greatest revolucon wee ever saw were at the doore.

Dec. 22. Jesuits tried & condemned.

Dec. 29. The Treasurer [4] impeacht by the Commons. The Jesuites, Groves, Pickering and Ireland that were condemned, [5] repreived

[1] William of Orange knew that peace was almost certainly signed.

[2] In the Popish plot.

[3] For issuing commissions to Popish recusants.

[4] Danby.

[5] "By Jeffreys, in a speech which wavered between pure abuse or a sermon which would have done credit to the most strenuous divine." (Pollock. *The Popish plot*, p. 332). They were all eventually executed.

by the King during his pleasure; the Houses addrest to know the reasons.

New yeare entred with the news of ye prorogacon of the Parliam^t till ffeb. 4th; people lookt on it as much troubled, so am I. Jan. 1.

The souldiers under the best officers disbanding. Jan. 12.

Heard y^t the Parliam^t was prorogued for 3 weeks longer until Feb. 25. The King declared in Councill on Satturday he would doe it. Lord publish thou thy decree. Jan. 21.

1678.

I awaked toward morning & was sensible this day ended my 62 & begun my 63 yeare; glad a Sabbath. Jan. 26.

In the morning before I rose about 6 of ye clocke, I awakned & had just dreamed, that one told mee that ye parliam^t was to meet but for a morning & y^t there were 11 men intended to make speeches: about 10 of the clocke I heard it was to bee dissolved & a new one chosen. God is still where he was: it cannot bee chosen till March: this was according to the counsell in Colemans letter: God is where he was. Honest men formerly desired y^e dissolucon $y^r$of but now its continuance was desired in reference to y^e discovery of y^e plott. I supposed the Cabal doth it to gaine time & to bring on the French assistance. Many thought this parliam^t had so corrupted themselves & done so ill in the matters of the nacon & were formerly so odious y^t God would doe his worke by some other & never hono^r them; on the 26 at night a great fire at London, wch amazed us in ye country pittying ye city under the treachery agst them; my legge sore with cat bites. Jan. 27.

A cold snowy day, news of the kings illnes continues: busy in chosing parliam^t: the first choice I heard of was at Harwich, two royall officers to ye fleet. Feb. 9.

The nacon busy about the choice of parliam^t, God direct them, y^t they bee not outwitted, as the former were to raise an army; s^d good choices in many places [1] & y^t the K. saith the contry Feb. 16.

[1] The Whigs swept the country.

would choose a dog if he stood agst a courtier : the peace goeth on beyond the seas, & the fears of France are on this side.

Feb. 21. Heard the Duke of York had taken the Test & oaths & that he was made Admiral & Generall ; things worke, but God is awake and yr I rest my selfe.

Feb. 23. Sd good choice made of Parl. men.

Feb. 25. This day all or Town in a manner went with Mr Andrews & my son for the choice of Kts of the shire. I endeavored for my contreys good ; wee chose Mildmay, and Harvy, without the opposicon of any one person in the feild appearing agst them. [1]

March. 6. I desired to send or choice men into the Parl. house with a blessing ; the country shewed themselves in ye choice, though much divided in sects.

March.7.8. The old Scotch regimt of Douglas marcht for Harwich, & so for Ireland or sea to have an eye on the French : sd the Duke of Yorke gone out of the kingdom to Holland.

1679. March. 30. The parl. seemeth wonderfull couragious not fearing prorogacons or dissolucons. Court are surely plotters or knowing of it.

April. 18. Wee shall see whether ye K. will comply with Parl. advice, or the Cabal. God incline his heart to his go & publique good.

April. 19. Heard the treasurer Danby yeilded himselfe ; ye lords sent him to ye tower, and the King prorogued the parliament ; sd he was going to Windsor ; not true.

April. 24. Perfected the purchase of Robert Carters land & setled it on my daughter Mary.

May. 4. Affaires darke, yett the K. & Parl. seeme to bee on good termes.

May. 28. Heard of the prorogacon of the Parl [2] ; not amazed.

June. 29. Heard of the Scots route, [3] Lord thou wilt maintain thy interest.

leg. 10. 11. 12. The weather being very hot, & after the day I preacht I found a great humor in my legge, hot, pimpling, sore as catbites, running, hard, as tending to an inflamacon ; I was as quiet & litle urging of

[1] It will be remembered that at the elections in 1661 " we lost it. " " The principal reason of the whig success was the panic of the country. " (Trevelyan. p. 403.)

[2] To prevent the passage of the Exclusion Bill.

[3] At Bothwell Brigg.

it ; God in mercy preserve my health, & remove the troublesome pains.

I heard the p. was dissolved. July. 16.

News amasing. s^{d} Sr G. Wakeman [1] & divers Jesuites all cleard by a vast shout of the papists. Lord I understand not the secret strings of this busines ; bring things to light, & let wickednesse punish the wicked whence it comes. July. 20.

Nel Guins mother died by one sudden & violent *(sic)*, drunke with brandie as s^{d}. [2] Aug. 3.

The choice of Parliament men at hand ; I publiquly stird up people to choose. Aug. 10.

Begun to picke hops. Aug. 26.

Great reports of the Kings dangerous illnes [3] ; Lord spare him if thy pleasure. Aug. 3.

S^{d} Monmouth banisht. Sept. 14.

I cannot but thinke ye Courts designe is to make parliam^{t} useles, or rid ye crowne of them. Oct. 12.

The parliam^{t} is prorogued to Jan: 26. next ; [4] tis my birthday as I reckon & I hope a good day. Oct. 19.

Good winter weather, God good in o^{r} health ; a strang fog formerly at London wch caused colds y^{t} the Bills were above 700 in beginning Decemb; it decreased 307, God preserve us. Dec. 14.

A wett day. My Cosin Gatton brought Mr Williams to mee on Maries account, whom I entertaind kindly & dismist well satisfied ; God blesse them. Dec. 28.

Allen the quakers speaker buried, the men & women following severally in some order. Jan. 25.

Jan. 26: 79, my 64 enters.

I was sensible of it & affected with Gods goodnes, not troubled in 63 as a critical & dangerous year though I often thought of

[1] The Queen's physician, charged with conspiracy to poison the king. These were the first prisoners, accused by Oates, who were acquitted.

[2] She was drowned : ill natured persons said she was drunk at the time.

[3] He was expected to die.

[4] There was again a Whig majority.

it. The Parl. should have satt this day; its petitiond for, but if they may not sitt for Gods interest, he will stand up for it. Parl. broke Monarchy, perhaps God will have Parl. broken by Monarchicall; time was, no addresses to the King by subjects; now the K. will admitt no addresses to him; we will to God, who will heare.

Feb. 8. Dry & windie, great apprehensions of danger to the city & kingdom from the papists on the Dukes [1] return from Scotland; God send peace.

Feb. 22. Maries busines at an end; God I hope did it in mercy to us all.

1680.

May. 16. An offer to Mary; God direct. I wore ye surplice.

May. 17. Rid to court, I avoided receiving articles, through Gods goodnes. I cast my care on him, he cared; the matter is the surplice, which I see no sin to use, & shall endeav^r^ to live as quietly as may bee to the end of my race; s^d^ the King much better.

June. 27. legg. Legg much swelled; we laid burdock leaves to leg & foot; God preserve mee.

July. 25. Legge something asswaged by the use of clote [2] leaves.

Sept. 19. Leg rund much; use green tobacco leaves, much asswaged: God cure.

Oct. 10. My wife very ill, litle hopes of life; my faith held God would spare her & I hope it shal bee so: my body emptied by vomitt & purge, that my leg is very small.

Oct. 24. Parl. satt. Kings speech good; the Lord blesse the assembly.

Jan. 10. Parliam^t^ prorogued to Jan: 20. City petitioned 13, they might sitt again.

1680.

Jan. 26. Sensible this day entred my 65 yeare, I mourning it with God that he would bee with mee, subduing my corruptions, & keeping my heart close to him through the grace of Christ.

Feb. 6. Wee were gathering for the captives of Algiers.

[1] Duke of York.

[2] Water-lily.

My wife very ill again, God restore her; one of o[r] town in jayle for the highway trade, [1] to my great losse I fear. March. 20.

Parliam[t] sits. [2] March. 27.

Parl. dissolved. [3] Duke expected at London. March. 28.

Grasse backward, hearts naught, my wife afflicts mee & her self; God learns mee patient submission. May. 1.

On June 3, Mary quitted M[r] Rhea; her exceptions were his age being 14 yeares older, shee might bee left a wid. with children; shee checkt at his estate being not suitable to her porcon, w[ch] estate of his I suppose not above 350 at most, besides his living of an 100*l.* considering his debts; he seemed to her not loving; it was no small greif to mee, but I could not desire it, w[n] shee said it would make both y[r] lives miserable. I shall observe the issue on both parts. M[r] Rhea's estate was not as I thought. June. 4.

My leg indifferent; I take the golden spirit scurvy grasse. [4] July. 3.

All quiet in city & contry, und[r] noise of imprisonm[ts]. July. 10.

John married unknown to mee; God pardon his errors. Oct. 16.

The good Lady Honywood died early. I went to see her & found shee was dead; I prayed with her y[e] 17: she was in a good frame, she was my good freind, & I hers; wee lived in love about 40 years acquaintance; I was serviceable every way to her for soule & body, and in her estate more then ordinary; shee left mee no legacy in her will; shee s[d] shee would adde a codicile to remember mee & some others, but not done. Oct. 19.

The good old Lady Honywood buried; not a glove, ribband, scutcheon, wine, beare, bisquett given at her burial but a litle mourning to servants. The serv[ts] carried her, six persons with scarfs & gloves bare up the pall. Oct. 26.

[1] Does this mean that the man arrested had, for a price, protected Josselin's goods from other thieves? "It was related of William Nevison, the great robber of Yorkshire, that he levied a quarterly tribute on all the northen drovers, and in return not only spared them himself, but protected them against all other thieves." (Macaulay's *History of England*, i, 301.)

[2] The Third, at Oxford.

[3] The king had received a promise from Louis xiv. of three years supply of money.

[4] The leaves of an anti-scorbutic.

Nov. 27. Nothing yet of winter, heard of E. of Shaftesbury acquitall by
leg: ye grand jury [1]; ye country & city wrung of it with joy. [2] My legg swelled much in the calf & upwards, Lord bee my salvacon.

Dec. 4. Ys morning the first meat given catle abroad. Gathered for ye French protestants.

Jan. 1. Things very quiet in ye land, notwthstanding threats agst dissenters.

Jan. 8. Quietnes in or borders & in ye city, on which by a quo waranto [3] they endeavr to gain mercy.

Jan. 26. 1681.

Sensible this day entred mee into my 66 yeare; read this day in course Deut. 30, 20. God is my life & obedience ye way of life.

March. 12. Sd Duke of York come to Yarmouth to meete the King at Newmarket; God send all well.

1682.
April. 9. Things calm, but surely the papists have some great thing in doing.

May. 7. Wett; flouds this weeke; I could not stirre a plow; much soft corn spoild; I had a bad markett for corn; my family troubles continue, esp. a froward wife.

May. 26. The citie much hated by ye Court; the Judges much pervert justice.

Aug. 13. The popish partie seem to overdrive & flag, yet publique peace.

Oct. 29. Mr Day writt about Mary & his son; God shew us mercy therin.

Nov. 12. Yet quiet, though alarmd with a great tumult, 6, about ye bonfires.

Coal. 14. Began to burn coal.

Nov. 19. Quiet in or streets; persons forcd to church about us.

Dec. 24. On the 25 at one of the clocke my freinds came from London; the greatest chrismas I kept, yr being 2 young men Mr Day & Mr Spicer, wellwillers to my virgin daughters; wee had good society; 3 of them went away, the 29th, well satisfied.

[1] They were zealous Whigs and threw out the bill.

[2] "The last Whig demonstration of this period." (Trevelyan. p. 419.)

[3] A writ of Quo Warranto (Edward I.'s) was issued and the city accused of breaking the terms of its charter: the charter was confiscated.

Jan: 26: 67 y. begun.

Sensible this entred my 67 y. I blest God for his presence thus far with mee. I heartily repent me of my sins & hope in his mercy.

A bitter morning from my wife, twice I mett with it already, God give mee patience : poore dissenters hatterd (*sic*), yet wee are in publique peace, praisd bee God. Jan. 28.

Kept the Kings day. Mr Day with us ; poor dissenters hatterd at London. Jan. 30.

This weeke my breath was much stopt, wch in such a body of humors was very dangerous ; my leg sweld much : ors well at London, but freinds hattered. Feb. 18.

This morning being cold windy & wett I preacht not ; God pardon mee, it was not out of neglect, it was a force on mee ; some days past, my breath so short as if I should have died ; if I stird but a litle, my leg sweld wonderfully, & issue run out litle ; when I sat still I felt no pain nor trouble : the thoughts of ye dropsie returnd on mee . . . . God remove the fear of death from mee : my two daughters on yr marriage, wch I was desirous to perfect. Feb. 25.

At night wonderful ill, I tooke pils, wch did much open & lighten my body. 27, I slept ill, & find pains in my right side. Feb. 26.

I walkt before ye house, my children alarmd at London. Mr Day came hastily down & found mee at ye gate. God gave mee liberty for his holy word : my breath returns. 6, my children came down. 7, Jonathan came with his bullocks : 12, Mr Day, Mary, Bettie & my litle Jane rid up to London. 15, 16, I took a draught of Daffy Elixir ; it wrought much with mee : 17, I was taken ill at ye priory, sneezing ; all things presented themselves duoble to mee ; I was lead home ; none preacht. 20, my children returned from London ; my great & dangerous cough ceasd. March. 3

This day I had an indifferent good day ; Mr Ludgater supplied my place. 1683. April. 1.

My freinds being here from London, Mr Spicer & son Smith came in before 8 of the clock. I went down & read prayers & preacht a litle more than an houre from ps. 8. 6. " I will dwell April. 8.

in the house of God for ever ;" goodnes should stirre up to more obedience . . . in Gods outward w^p^.

April. 10. Mary Josselin my 3^d^ daughter being somew^t^ above 25 y. old married to Mr Edward Day . . . . license under Bets hand ; he was a tallow chandler of St Martins. He is his fathers only child, a man of a good estate, & godly conv^r^sacon. I gave her for porcon my house I dwell in & land belonging y^r^ to worth 400*l*. and an 100*l*.

April. 15. I was very short winded & with much difficulty went up & down to church. . . . I was very ill, and concluded by ye swelling of my thighs & belly it was the dropsy . . . . London to Dr Cox about it ; God blesse the means I shall use.

May. 2. My children went to London ; y^r^ sister Jane tooke on at mee & them for y^r^ great porcons ; God give mee patience for I have more than ordinary need of it.

May. 4. Heard of ye health of my children : Cox sent me his old receits ; the apothecary made mee pay deare.

May. 6. Mr Spicer married my youngest daughter Mrs Rebekah: I rid down in her coach & performed it for them ; my son Smith came down with them ; they returnd die the 12 : my wife . . . first much troubled ; I was joyd God had so well provided for her. I gave her 500*l*. down & with my blessing sent her away.

May. 14. Taking ye harts horne drops, I found my phlegm gathered much & thicke in my chest . . . Still my hope is in God to bring mee out of all thes troubles, though I am much sweld in my leg that I can scarce goe, & much strained in the nights in my chest ; my stomacke was indifferent well this 19 day & I rellisht my beare, & my bakt meate.

May. 20. Mr Livermore preacht. I began Mr Spicers ale, I thought it did mee good . . . My drinke works well with mee.

May. 25. Drunk my broome beere in my bed ; I endeavourd to sleepe after it ; I sweat indifferently.

May. 31. A wonderfull wett May ; I was as sweld, and short breathd as if I should not have lived through the night, but God had mercy on mee.

June. 1. I saw my countenance much changed ; it was 3 days y^t^ my left leg ran much: 3. I did not perceive I gathered strength nor lost any, but in ye use of means continued in ye same way ; however I stay myself on my good God, yt ye sicknes doth not issue in death, but in a trial to doe mee much good.

The weeke past, I slept well, my hands dry, my swelling much in my thighs ; above I seem pretty well ; I find not my breath so troublesom as some nights formerly. Mr Livermore preacht for mee ; heard of a new plot ; sd L. Russel & Grey sent to the tower ; wee shall heare more afterwards ; . . . My wife & all the children well at London. July. 1.

My wife returnd safe from London, my six sons & daughters came to the coach with her in health. About ye 10th day I took my scurvy grass drops, 12 at a time; I thought once it purgd mee . . . . . Laying a plaister to my backe, it was better. July. 7.

God good in my preservacon. I . . . . went to Colchester. July. 15.

Saw a breif account of my Ld Russels trial & others, who were all condemned. July. 22.

Wee begun harvest July 27 reaping and mowing. God send us[1]. . . . . . Heard all well at London, the German nearly . . . . . by . . . . . . July. 29.

[1] This is the last entry in the MS. It is written in a feeble hand. The rest of the entry is mutilated.

INDEX

D

E

F

I

J

K

L

P

Q

R

S